REMEMBER NOW...

Daily Devotionals for Young People

WALTER DUDLEY CAVERT

ABINGDON
Nashville

REMEMBER NOW . . .

A Festival Book
Copyright 1944 by Whitmore & Stone
All rights reserved.

Festival edition published May 1979

ISBN 0-687-36127-3

To My Wife
HARRIET HARRER CAVERT

FOREWORD

DURING THE PAST YEAR THE AUTHOR HAS BEEN IN SEVERAL GROUPS of young people who expressed a desire for daily devotional material adapted to their needs. Many excellent devotional books and magazines are already available, but most of them have been written primarily for adults. This book is intended for youth and for older persons who seek to look at life from youth's viewpoint.

The illustrations and quotations have been taken from many different sources. Their authorship has been given, where known, and permission has been secured to use all copyrighted material. Gratitude is expressed to publishers and individuals for their courtesy and co-operation. A list of the acknowledgments will be found on the final pages of the book. If any omissions or oversights have been made, sincere apology is hereby offered.

The writer is deeply indebted to his daughter, Elizabeth Harrer Cavert, for her assistance in reading the manuscript and for many valuable suggestions and criticisms.

WALTER DUDLEY CAVERT
1943

CONTENTS

REMEMBER NOW...

REMEMBER THY CREATOR

SUNDAY—Week 1

DON'T FORGET THE BEST   Read Eccles. 12

A legend tells of a shepherd boy who picked a strange flower on the mountainside and suddenly found a cave opening before his feet. Entering, he saw a heap of sparkling diamonds. He placed the flower on a stone and filled his hands with the shining gems. As he started to leave a voice said, "Don't forget the best." Surely nothing could be better than diamonds, thought the boy, and hurried out. The cave immediately closed behind him, and the jewels crumbled to dust in his hands. He had forgotten the best—the magic flower without which nothing taken from the cave had lasting value.

What is the best thing in human life? The author of Ecclesiastes, after a successful search for education, riches, and power, and indulgence in many pleasures, summed up his conclusions about what is most worthwhile in life by giving this advice to his young friends: *"Remember now thy Creator in the days of thy youth."*

Make me grateful for the gift of life, O God my Creator, and give me a vision of what life can mean when it is lived for thee. Forgive me that so often I am satisfied with the second best. Help me to remember thee and to find my joy in doing thy will. Amen.

MONDAY—Week 1

KNOWING EVERYONE EXCEPT GOD   Read Acts 17:22-30

When Mark Twain made a trip to Europe with his wife and eleven-year-old daughter, they were the guests of many famous people. Kings and nobles vied with each other for the privilege of having Mark Twain at their dinner parties. European universities conferred honorary degrees upon him.

At the end of the trip, while they were on the train which was taking them to the port where they would set sail for America, Twain read his family a list of the celebrities who had entertained them. At the end of it his daughter looked up and said, "Daddy, you must know almost everyone worth knowing except God."

Mark Twain was not the only person to leave God out of his list of acquaintances. TV and radio make us familiar with the faces

13

and voices of the noted people of our day, but God is often ignored. We all need to cultivate the friendship of the Eternal.

Father, I thank thee for the many friends and acquaintances who have enriched my life. Help me now to have a deeper knowledge of thee and to make thee the dearest friend of all. Amen.

TUESDAY—Week 1

EVER PRESENT BUT UNRECOGNIZED   Read Ps. 139:1-12

One summer a man who had a cottage on the coast of Maine decided to start a Sunday school class for the children living on a small island not far from the shore. He went over in his motorboat and met the boys and girls who had gathered together. Like a good teacher, he tried to establish a point of contact by starting to talk about something with which his scholars were already familiar.

"How many of you have seen the Atlantic Ocean?" he asked.

The children stared at him with blank faces. No one answered or raised his hand.

All their lives these boys and girls had been within sight and sound of the Atlantic Ocean. It was a major fact of their existence. But none of them had ever heard it called by any name.

Is not this an illustration of what happens in many lives today? God is round about us. In him we live and move and have our being. But God is unrecognized.

Heavenly Father, grant that I may have the ability to see the things of the spirit. Take the dimness of my soul away and enable me to recognize thy presence in all of life. Amen.

WEDNESDAY—Week 1

IN THE BEGINNING GOD   Read Gen. 1:1-25

Napoleon with many of his leaders was on the ship "L'Orient" headed for Egypt. One evening, as the men sat on the deck, they engaged in a discussion of religion. The opinion was generally expressed that belief in God was an ancient idea which had once served a valuable purpose but was no longer needed by intelligent people. Napoleon was silent as he listened to the conversation. As he rose to go to his room, he pointed to the stars shining brilliantly in the darkness and said, "Messieurs, who made all that?"

It is a reasonable question. If we do not believe that the universe has a divine origin, then we must accept the theory that it is merely a chance collection of atoms with no purpose or meaning. No simpler or more sublime interpretation of the world's origin has ever been given than the opening words of the Bible, "In the beginning God . . ."

O God, there are many mysteries that I can never fully understand, but give me the faith to believe that a universe in which there is order and beauty is created and guided by a supreme Intelligence. Amen.

THURSDAY—Week 1

BEHIND THE UNIVERSE, A MIND OF LOVE
Read Isa. 40:25-31

Kepler, a famous German astronomer of three centuries ago, was once called to the supper table by his wife after he had spent the day studying the nature of the universe. A salad was served which he especially liked. He looked at it for a time and said: "It seems, then, that if pewter dishes, leaves of lettuce, grains of salt, drops of vinegar and oil, and slices of eggs had been floating about in the air from all eternity, it might at last happen by chance that there would come a salad."

His wife retorted, "Not a salad so nice as mine."

This suggests a logical answer to the one who says the universe could have come together by accident. A world as "nice" as ours, which contains goodness and love, and which has produced a person like Jesus, must have not only intelligence but love behind it. A soulless universe could not produce a Christ.

Eternal God, I know there is evil as well as good in my universe, but in my Master I see one who rose triumphant over all evil. May I believe that a universe which can produce a Christ is controlled by a Soul as loving as his. Amen.

FRIDAY—Week 1

REMEMBER WHO YOU ARE
Read Gen. 1:26-31

In *The Birds' Christmas Carol*, Mrs. Ruggles gives her children instructions on how to behave at the party to which they have all been invited. Her most important advice is this: "Whatever you do, all of yer, never forgit for one second that yer mother was a McGrill."

Remembering the family tree of your mother might be a poor guide to the accepted rules of etiquette at the dinner table, but as a general help to wholesome living few things are more important than to remember who you are. You have been created in the divine image and are a child of God. If you have faith in God as the heavenly Father of us all, you will have faith in the dignity and sacredness of your own and every other human life.

Dear Father, after whom the whole family of heaven and earth is named, make me grateful for the privilege of being called thy child. Help me to be a worthy member of thy family. May I never give thee cause to be ashamed of me. Amen.

SATURDAY—Week 1

A GREAT MAN'S GREATEST THOUGHT   Read Mic. 6:1-8

At a dinner party Daniel Webster was once seated next to a woman who took the opportunity to ask him what he considered to be the greatest thought that had ever come to his mind. She expected the famous statesman to begin expounding on some theory of government or to suggest some new law that he would like to see passed by Congress.

But Webster answered very simply—"That of my individual responsibility to God."

No more important question ever comes to anyone than that of one's relationship to one's Creator. If you believe that God has a plan for the universe he has made, and for each person whom he has placed upon the earth, then you have a sacred obligation to discover that plan and carry it out. That is your individual responsibility to God.

Dear God, help me to remember each day that thou art my Father and that I owe my life and all I own to thee. Reveal to me thy will, and give me the courage to follow it in a spirit of glad obedience. Amen.

WE NEED GOD NOW

SUNDAY—Week 2

THE HOUR OF NEED SENDS US TO GOD   Read Deut. 8

On the walls of the barracks at a British army post in Delhi, India, someone wrote the words:

> When war is on and strife is nigh
> God and the soldier are all the cry.
> But when war is over and peace is sighted
> God and the soldier are quickly slighted.

The soldier's complaint was undoubtedly justified, for nations which have called their young men to arms in time of war have often forgotten them in time of peace.

The other part of the poem is even more true. In the day of danger people call upon God and pray for his help. In periods of ease and security they often fall back into spiritual indifference. We need God's help in the midst of a crisis, but we ought to give him our steadfast devotion which will continue throughout our lives.

O God, give me the strength to endure hardship as a good soldier of Jesus Christ. Grant that I may still remember thee when difficult days are past.
Lord God of Hosts, be with us yet,
Lest we forget, lest we forget! Amen.

MONDAY—Week 2

A PRESENT CHRIST   Read Matt. 28:16-20

Leonardo da Vinci in his painting of the Last Supper depicts the Savior as a present Christ. The landscape which can be seen through the window in the background of the picture is like that near Milan rather than Palestine. The table and chairs, the cloth and dishes are not like those used in Jerusalem in the first century but the kind that were to be found in Italy when the picture was painted. The men sit around the table in European rather than Oriental style. Probably the artist copied the objects that were actually being used in the monastery where the picture was painted. He wanted people to know Jesus as a contemporary, one who was actually in their midst, blessing them with his comradeship, and calling them to unselfish loyalty.

The artist's view is one that we all ought to have. Jesus is not

17

merely a figure of the first century. He said, "Lo, I am with you alway," and he is still seeking to be the present companion of those who make their lives a fit dwelling place for his spirit.

Thou Christ who once worked in the carpenter shop at Nazareth, walked along the streets of Jerusalem, and rowed across the Sea of Galilee, I seek thy companionship in all the experiences of the present day. I need the inspiration of thy presence and pray that wherever I am, I may feel myself to be with thee. Amen.

TUESDAY—Week 2

KEEPING CALM IN THE MIDST OF STORM
Read Luke 8:16-25

Scientists tell us that even the most violent storms, when they sweep over the ocean, only disturb the water a few hundred feet below the surface. The hurricane which lashes the sea into a foaming fury, causing shipwreck and disaster, is unable to affect the depths. Below the turbulent waves there is peace and calmness. In a similar way, the one who gets beneath the surface of life and lives in its spiritual depths can find the peace of God that passes the understanding of man. On the last night of his life, under the shadow of the cross, Jesus told his disciples that he would give them his peace. His peace was not that which comes from being undisturbed; it was a tranquillity of spirit which resulted from Jesus committing himself to the keeping of God.

And I smiled to think God's greatness flowed around
  our incompleteness,—
Round our restlessness, his rest.

Almighty God, thy power and goodness are ever round about me. Help me to feel that thy everlasting arms are underneath me, and to trust myself to thy care. May nothing have the power to disturb my confidence in thy love. Amen.

WEDNESDAY—Week 2

FAITH IN GOD GIVES COURAGE
Read Acts 5:17-29

Hugh Latimer, one of the leaders of the Protestant Reformation in England, was appointed a royal chaplain to King Henry VIII. His bold and uncompromising preaching finally brought him into disfavor, and he was executed during the reign of Henry VIII's successor. At the beginning of his sermon before the royal court one day, he exclaimed:

"Latimer, Latimer, thou art going to speak before the high and mighty king, Henry VIII, who is able, if he think fit, to take thy life

18

away. Be careful what thou sayest. But Latimer, Latimer, remember also thou art about to speak before the King of Kings and Lord of Lords. Take heed thou dost not displease him."

Remembering God gives moral courage. If you will keep in mind that you are living and speaking in the presence of the Most High, you will be more anxious to please him than to receive the flattery of friends.

Grant O God, that my first aim may ever be to make my life acceptable in thy sight. Keep me from being too much concerned about the praise and criticism of man. May my chief ambition be to win thy approval. Amen.

THURSDAY—Week 2

ABIDING VALUES IN A CHANGING WORLD Read Ps. 125

As a young man, Abraham Lincoln lived for a brief time with a devout but ignorant deacon. One night he was aroused from his sleep by a loud rapping at the door. The deacon's voice cried out, "Arise, Abraham! The day of judgment has come!" Lincoln jumped from his bed and looked out the window. He saw indeed a great display of shooting stars. But looking beyond them, he was reassured when he saw the familiar constellations fixed and true in their places.

In a world which is rapidly changing and which sometimes seems to be falling to pieces, we need to center our attention on the eternal things which abide unchanged. Truth, righteousness, justice, love—these are like fixed stars. They are the same throughout all generations. They endure unchanged because they are a part of the nature of God. Faith in the Eternal gives a sense of security amid the fluctuations of time.

Change and decay in all around I see;
O Thou who changest not, abide with me. Amen.

FRIDAY—Week 2

GOD HELPS US TO FORGIVE   Read Matt. 5:21-24

During the first World War, an Armenian nurse saw her brother murdered by a Turkish soldier. Afterward she was compelled by the Turkish government to take care of the wounded in an army hospital. One day the soldier who had murdered her brother was brought into the hospital unconscious and so badly wounded that he would die if he did not receive careful attention. The girl recognized him instantly, because his face was indelibly stamped in her memory. The desire for revenge was strong within her, and his life was in her hands, but as a Christian she felt it her duty to care for him.

As the soldier regained his strength, he recognized his nurse and asked why she had not allowed him to die. "Because I am a Christian and must love my enemies," she replied. "If Christ can make you act like that, he is stronger than my Mohammed," said the Turk. "Your Christ shall be my Christ too."

In a day when we are in danger of being engulfed by a wave of hatred, we are desperately in need of a God who can help us maintain a spirit of goodwill.

Thou God of Love, save me from hatred and from the bitter desire for revenge. May I have the spirit of Lincoln, who was able to say, "With malice toward none; with charity for all." And so may I show myself to be a true follower of a forgiving Christ. Amen.

SATURDAY—Week 2

FORGETTING GOD IS A SPIRITUAL TRAGEDY
Read Ps. 119:33-40

A play which was given on the New York stage some years ago centered around a man's forgetting to mail a letter. A peasant farmer in Ireland was about to have the mortgage foreclosed on his little homestead. His only hope was that his prosperous brother who lived in Canada would send him the money which he needed. The Canadian truly intended to help but did not put the letter in the post office in time. The family in Ireland was broken up, and tragic consequences followed in the lives of the daughter and son.

What spiritual tragedies often result from our careless forgetfulness of God! We have good intentions, but we don't always carry them out. We are cowardly when we need to be brave, distracted when we ought to be calm, vindictive when we should be forgiving, and weak when we might be strong.

Thou dost never forget thy children, O God. Grant that I may not forget thee, but may ever have a sense of thy continuing presence. May I stay near thee in times of my prosperity. May I find thee nearest me in my hours of deepest need. Amen.

REMEMBER GOD IN DAYS OF YOUTH

SUNDAY—Week 3

WILL THE NATION BE SAVED BY ITS YOUTH?
Read I Kings 20:13-21

When a great battle was to be fought by Israel against mighty Ben-hadad, king of Syria, the outlook seemed hopeless, but the prophet of God boldly proclaimed to Ahab that the enemy would be delivered into his hands and a great victory won. "By whom?" asked Ahab. "By the young man," replied the prophet. "Who shall order the battle?" inquired Ahab. Back came the answer, "Thou."

In a crisis of civilization great demands are always made upon youth, but no generation has ever had heavier responsibilities than the present. "It is a glorious thing to see a state saved by its youth," said Disraeli. Youth are winning the war. Can they save the nation? Only if they seek from God the moral courage to purify its politics, remove its racial pride and class competition, purge it of injustice, strengthen its moral foundations, and deepen its religious faith.

Save us who are young from self-pity, O God. May we not lament that we live in evil days, but rather rejoice that our age needs the service of youth. Make us adequate to the tasks that are placed upon us. Trusting thee for guidance and strength, may we go bravely forward in the adventure of building a new world of righteousness and goodwill. Amen.

MONDAY—Week 3

MAKING THE WORLD MORE BEAUTIFUL
Read Matt. 20:20-28

As a young lawyer, Edward Bok's grandfather was appointed by the king of the Netherlands to be the mayor of a pirate-infested island five miles from the Dutch coast. He carried out his orders to clean out the criminals and then decided to live there permanently. It was a barren place, but he saw possibilities of making it beautiful. Every year he set out trees and shrubs, which grew and flourished, although the older residents said they would be killed by the storms. Nightingales in great numbers were attracted to the leafy shelters, until the island became famous for the music of its songsters and the beauty of its scenery. One determined man changed a desolate part of the earth into a place of loveliness.

Does the world seem to be ugly and lawless? If youth have vision and courage, they will not only drive out the bandits but see the possibility of making the earth a beautiful place on which to live.

Dear God, grant that the world may become more orderly and attractive because of my life and what I succeed in doing. Keep me from being discouraged by the pessimism of others, and give me strength and perseverance. Amen.

TUESDAY—Week 3

A NEW WORLD DEMANDS NEW MEN   Read Rom. 8:1-17

A new world can be created only by new men. Those who would cleanse society must first purify their own lives. Until one is strong enough to overcome one's own temptations, one can never be a source of strength and new life to others.

After King Louis XVI and Queen Marie Antoinette had been executed, during the French Revolution, their son was placed in the custody of a brutal shoemaker named Simon, who tried to corrupt the boy's morals. But again and again, in the face of temptation, the boy is said to have replied, "I cannot do that, for I am the son of a king." Conscious of his royal lineage, he would not stoop to anything he considered wrong.

Keep alive in your mind the consciousness that you are the son of a King! You may well say to yourself in the face of temptation, "This is unworthy of me. I must be true to the high standards set for me by my Father, the King."

My Father and my King, help me to become strong against every tendency to do wrong. May I be able to resist the tempter by my desire to be worthy of being called thy son. Amen.

WEDNESDAY—Week 3

"MASTERS OF THEIR OWN SOULS"   Read Heb. 11:32-40

A Christian of the third century, in a letter to his friend Donatus, gives a remarkable testimony to the influence which the gospel of Christ exerted upon the lives of men in that day. Here are his words:

If I should ascend some high mountain, you know what I would see—armies fighting, brigands on the highways, pirates on the seas, men murdered in the amphitheater to please the applauding multitudes. But in the midst of this I have found a quiet and holy people. They are persecuted, but they care not. They have found a joy a thousand times greater than any pleasure. These people are the masters of their own souls. They are the Christians, and I am one of them.

The writer was finally put to death, but the letter shows the power of Christian faith to make a man the master of his own soul in the face of a hostile environment. Only the weak excuse themselves for being moral failures because of the difficulties which surround them.

Thou God of courageous souls, I remember with gratitude those who have made their lives an adventure for thee, who have lived in thy love and died in thy service. May their example stir me to follow in their train. Amen.

THURSDAY—Week 3

GUARDING OUR HERITAGE   Read I Kings 21:1-3

A family had a beautiful and valuable vase which had been handed down by past generations. Although it was carefully treasured, it was kept on the living-room mantel as an object which all might enjoy. One day when the mother came home after making an afternoon call, her high-school daughter said to her:

"Mamma, you know that vase which you told us had been passed down from generation to generation?"

"Yes, my dear," replied the mother.

"This generation just dropped it!" said the daughter.

It is easy for us to become so familiar with treasured possessions that we handle them carelessly and fail to appreciate their value. Our Christian faith has been preserved through the ages at a great price, but it must be lived and cherished anew by each generation. Only so can it be kept alive and passed on to those who come after us.

I thank thee, Father, for the blessings which come to me from the past. I rejoice in my Christian heritage. Grant that the faith of our fathers may be my faith too, and that I may find in it a living source of light and strength. Amen.

FRIDAY—Week 3

THE POWER OF REMEMBERING CHRIST
Read Luke 22:7-20

Jesus knew that his cause would be victorious only if his disciples remembered him and found him a living power in their lives. So he had made careful plans for the meeting during the last

23

night of his life where he gave his friends the simple ceremony which we call the Lord's Supper. "This do in remembrance of me," he said.

The disciples never forgot that evening in the upper room. They went on to defy death and to laugh at danger. Nothing could stop them from witnessing for their Lord. In less than three centuries Christianity became the official religion of the empire, and the cross was carried above the eagle of Rome. The fact that eleven young men remembered Jesus changed the course of history. The future of civilization today is in the hands of those who remember Christ and live in a spirit of courageous devotion to the Kingdom for which he died.

Lord, I would belong to the company of those who can never forget thee because thou art a living presence within their hearts. With quiet trust and steadfast devotion, may I live by thy truth and become one of those who shall be the pioneers of a new and more Christian civilization. Amen.

SATURDAY—Week 3

RELIGION MUST BE USED OR LOST Read Matt. 25:24-30

Charles Darwin during the early part of his life was fond of both poetry and music. But as the years went by he became absorbed in the study of evolution. Scientific pursuits crowded out other interests. He admitted in later years that he had gradually lost the ability to appreciate the beauty of verse and melody which had moved him in his youth, and added that if he were to live his life over, he would make it his habit to read some good poetry and listen to some good music every day that he might not lose his capacity for such enjoyment.

The experience of Darwin shows how easily we may lose our sensitiveness to many of the finer things of life. If the sense of God's presence is not cultivated continually by prayer and worship, even the dim spiritual vision we already possess will quickly be lost. We must use our religion or we will lose it.

Heavenly Father, grant that I may daily grow in grace and in the knowledge of thee. Forgive me when I forget thee, and forbid that by neglect I should allow my ideals to lose their glow and my faith to disappear. Amen.

HEARING THE VOICE OF GOD

SUNDAY—Week 4

GOD SPEAKS THROUGH NATURE   Read Matt. 6:28-33

A Frenchman incurred the displeasure of Napoleon and was put into a dungeon. He seemed to be forsaken by his friends and forgotten by everyone in the outside world. In loneliness and despair he took a stone and scratched on the wall of his cell, "Nobody cares."

One day a green shoot came through the cracks in the stones on the floor of the dungeon and began to reach up toward the light from the tiny window at the top of the cell. The prisoner kept part of the water brought to him each day by the jailer and poured it on the blade of green. It grew until at last it became a plant with a beautiful blue flower. As the petals opened in full blossom, the solitary captive crossed out the words previously written on the wall and above them scratched, "God cares." God had spoken to him through a flower.

> God, who touches earth with beauty,
>   Make me lovely too,
> With thy spirit re-create me,
>   Make my heart anew. Amen.

MONDAY—Week 4

THE VOICE OF GOD IN CONSCIENCE
Read I Kings 19:9-18

Theodore Parker, famous New England clergyman, was walking through the fields one day in his childhood and stopped to play around a pond. He saw a turtle sunning itself on a rock and started to hit it with a stick. Suddenly a voice called out "Stop!" No one was in sight, and the frightened youngster ran home to tell his mother what had happened. She took the boy in her arms and told him that the word he had heard spoken so plainly had come from his inner voice. She explained to him that God was speaking through his conscience and that he must form the habit of obeying the inner voice whenever he heard it, for if he ignored it, he would be left without a guide and unable to tell the difference between right and wrong. His obedience to his conscience was afterward one of the secrets of Dr. Parker's courage and greatness as a preacher.

Thou who art my Judge as well as my Father, keep me from ignoring the voice of my conscience. Whenever I hear thy still small voice speaking within my soul, may I be willing to say, "Lo, I come to do thy will, O God." Amen.

TUESDAY—Week 4

A MAN SENT FROM GOD   Read John 1:1-8

Red Elk was a Nez Percé Indian who lived in the northwestern part of our country. Missionaries had been sent to his tribe, but he made fun of their religion. Trouble came with the white men, and the Indians went on the warpath. The Nez Percés made a valiant fight, but were finally captured by the United States Army. The Indians were then sent down to Indian Territory, where many of them became ill and died. Red Elk was desperately ill and for many days lay unconscious. When he began to recover, he found that he owed his life to a missionary who had been caring for him and serving as his nurse. Later the Nez Percés were allowed to return to their own country in the mountains. The missionary went to visit their church and found that Red Elk was a church leader. The Indian said to him, "I am a Christian, because I saw Christ in you."

There is no way in which God speaks to us more convincingly than through the lives of Christlike people.

Dear Lord, help me to know what Paul meant when he said, "Not I, but Christ liveth in me." May my religion be so simple and earnest and sincere that others will see something of Christ in me, and will desire to become his followers. Amen.

WEDNESDAY—Week 4

THE BIBLE IS THE WORD OF GOD   Read II Tim. 3:14-17

There is no more accurate phrase with which to describe the Bible than "The Word of God." A word is the expression of a thought. The Bible brings us the thoughts of God as he revealed himself in past centuries through truth-seeking people and especially through Jesus Christ. As an illustration of the way the Bible can speak to a man about God, consider the way in which a Japanese general, Murata, became a Christian.

A New Testament dropped from an English warship in a Japanese harbor back in 1854 was picked up by the general, who was keeping a watch on foreign ships. He was unable to read English,

26

but succeeded in securing a Chinese translation. Impressed by the story of Jesus, he went to Guido Verbeck, one of the earliest missionaries to Japan, and asked for further instruction. Soon afterward General Murata and his brother were baptized by Verbeck at the risk of their lives, since the Christian religion was then strictly prohibited in Japan.

I confess before thee, Father, that I often fail to appreciate the Bible, through which so many people have come to a knowledge of thee. Create within me a new desire to know the great scriptural truths which have guided so many great and good men in the past and can be my guide today. Amen.

THURSDAY—Week 4

GOD REVEALS HIMSELF TO THOSE WHO PRAY
Read Ps. 143

Voltaire once stood on a Paris street corner as a religious procession, headed by a man carrying a crucifix, passed by. Voltaire, usually considered an atheist, saluted. "Have you finally become reconciled to the church?" asked a friend. Voltaire replied, "We bow, but we do not speak."

Could not the same words be used to describe the religious attitude of many people today? They have a certain amount of reverence and occasionally go to church, but they never really pray. They have no direct, intimate relationship with God, and do not give him a chance to come into their lives.

Prayer is one of the means by which God reveals himself to the individual soul. Spend much time with him in secret if you wish to receive important messages.

O thou divine Spirit that, in all events of life, art knocking at the door of my heart, help me to respond to thee. Whether thou comest to me in sunshine or in rain, I would take thee into my heart joyfully. Thou art thyself more than the sunshine; thou art thyself compensation for the rain; it is thee and not thy gifts I crave; knock, and I shall open unto thee. Amen.—George Matheson.

FRIDAY—Week 4

GOD IN HISTORY
Read Ps. 46

Said the historian Froude, "History is a voice forever sounding across the centuries the laws of right and wrong." Thomas Arnold reviewed the great world empires of the past and summed up their downfall by saying, "Down they come, one after another, and all for lack of righteousness."

If one looks back over the centuries with reverent mind, one will see evidence that God controls the universe by moral as well as physical laws. Greed, selfishness, injustice, exploitation of the weak, and ruthless use of military force may bring success and power for a time to those who rely upon them, but in the end they bring destruction.

If the nations today could hear the voice of God above the thunder and confusion of the battlefields, they would hear him say: "Whatsoever a nation sows, that shall it also reap. No nation can permanently endure that defies the laws of righteousness and brotherhood."

Have mercy upon me, O God, for I live in a sinful world that has refused to listen to thy voice and obey thy laws. Help men to learn that righteousness exalteth a nation while sin is a reproach to any people. Give me thy guidance that I may become a leader for truth and justice. Amen.

SATURDAY—Week 4

GOD SPEAKS—DO YOU LISTEN?   Read I Sam. 3:1-10

Joan of Arc was the most spectacular military leader of all history. A simple peasant girl, she had the courage to lead what seemed a forlorn cause and to free her country of its enemies. She depended entirely upon the guidance of what she called her voices from God. She started her career by getting a French army commander to arrange an interview for her with King Charles VII. When she told him her voices were bidding her to become the leader of her nation's armies, the king impatiently replied that if God had any word for France it should come to him as the ruler.

"The voices do come to you, but you do not hear them," said Joan. "If you prayed from your heart and listened, you would hear them as well as I."

God is continually sending you his messages. He speaks to you in many ways, but you cannot hear him unless you open your heart and listen.

> O let me hear thee speaking,
> In accents clear and still,
> Above the storms of passion,
> The murmurs of self-will;
> O speak to reassure me,
> To hasten or control;
> O speak, and make me listen,
> Thou Guardian of my soul. Amen.

GOD IN NATURE

SUNDAY—Week 5

A REVELATION OF GOD'S BEAUTY   Read Ps. 147

No artist can put colors on a canvas to compare with the natural loveliness of a sunset or a rainbow or autumn foliage. Professor J. Arthur Thomson points out that the beauty which seems so striking in visible objects of the greatest grandeur is typical of what the scientist sees in all nature. Even the minute organisms gathered from the hidden depths of the sea, too small to be seen by the naked eye, are shown by the microscope to be beautiful.

Is not this beauty a revelation of something at the very heart of the universe? The Creator is a lover of beauty, and the loveliness we see about us is the expression of his own nature.

> Heaven and earth are full of thee,
> Heaven and earth are praising thee,
>   O Lord Most High!

Creator of all beauty, I see thee in the sunset radiance, the sparkling lake, the majestic mountains, the stars overhead, and the flowers at my feet. Thou who dost reveal thyself in all nature, make my life as beautiful as thine. Amen.

MONDAY—Week 5

NATURE TELLS OF GOD'S LAWS   Read Ps. 19

A few years ago when an eclipse of the sun was visible in the South Pacific, astronomers from all over the earth went to study it. Months were spent in preparation, and large sums of money were invested in scientific equipment. The eclipse arrived on time, to the fraction of a second. How typical this is of the orderliness which governs everything in God's universe, from the tiniest snowflake to the planets that whirl through endless space!

What is the meaning of these universal laws which are both physical and moral? Simply that God, in his love, is making the universe an intelligible place where we can discover its secrets and live together in plenty and happiness if we obey his will. The laws of God are a revelation of both his sovereignty and his love.

> I have gone the whole round of creation: . . .
> All's love, yet all's law.

Thou who art Law as well as Love, give me an obedient heart that I may observe thy commandments. Let me not wander from the paths of thy righteousness; then shall I know the joy of those who faithfully do thy will. Amen.

TUESDAY—Week 5

THE IMPARTIALITY OF GOD'S LOVE   Read Matt. 5:43-48

God clothes his world with beauty for the enjoyment of all and establishes his laws for the common welfare. He makes his sun rise on the evil and the good, and sends rain on the just and the unjust. By so doing he tries to bring to us a sense of our social oneness and of our equality in his sight. The divine revelation in nature seeks to make us more impatient of the artificial barriers by which we are divided, and more sensitive to the call of human need.

Thackeray once stood on the heights above Edinburgh as the setting sun was casting a mystic splendor over the city and surrounding hills. Looking down at the slums of the city, where thousands of people were herded together in dark and crowded tenements, he murmured to his friend, "Calvary." The great novelist could not feast his soul on the beauty designed by the Creator for the enjoyment of all without feeling that God was suffering a new Calvary through men's denial of human brotherhood.

O God who dost love all mankind, give me a heart that throbs with sympathy for my fellowmen. Whenever I see thee in thy beauty, may I remember thou dost also live in the hearts of men, and that whatever I do for those in need is done unto thee. Amen.

WEDNESDAY—Week 5

SEEING GOD IN EVERYTHING   Read Ps. 148

A boy was taken by his father on a camping trip in the Adirondacks. They hired a guide, left the beaten trail, and spent a week in the heart of the woods. The boy was greatly impressed by the ability of the guide to see all sorts of things invisible to the ordinary eye. One day, after the guide had been pointing out some of the hidden secrets of nature, the lad asked with an awed voice, "Mister, can you see God?" The old man replied: "My boy, it's getting so I can hardly see anything else when I'm out in the woods."

This was the experience of Jesus. The flowers and grass reminded him of the Father's love. Birds flying through the air suggested the personal interest of God in every creature. Nature to him was not merely birds and flowers and grass and trees, but objects vibrant with a message from God. You too can have such an outlook if you approach nature with a reverent heart and cultivate seeing eyes and listening ears.

Heavenly Father, remove the veil from my eyes that I may behold the spiritual nature of thy universe. Help me to see that thou art never far from every one of us, and that in thee we live and move and have our being. Amen.

THURSDAY—Week 5

QUIETNESS HELPS US TO KNOW GOD
Read Mark 6:29-32; 45-46

Nature makes it easy for us to find God because of its quietness. God is seldom noisy; he does his greatest work in silence, and he speaks in whispers. We must be still if we would know him. "Come ye yourselves apart . . . and rest awhile," said Jesus to his disciples, and he rowed with them across the lake to a secluded spot. Again and again he sought some solitary place of natural loveliness where it was easy for him to commune with God.

Buried beneath the ancient city of Shechem is said to be a river of running water which makes a soft murmur. During the day, because of the noise of the traffic and the cries of hucksters in the bazaars, it cannot be heard. But when the sound of tramping feet and bargaining voices dies away at evening, the rippling of the concealed stream is easily audible. Like the music of the hidden water is the voice of the eternal Spirit. It comes and goes unnoticed amid the shouts of the market place and the clang of whirring machines, but it is readily heard by those who seek the quiet seclusion provided by nature.

> Drop thy still dews of quietness,
> Till all our strivings cease;
> Take from our souls the strain and stress,
> And let our ordered lives confess
> The beauty of thy peace. Amen.

FRIDAY—Week 5

MOUNTAINS MAKE MEN
Read Ps. 121

Solitude amid surroundings of natural beauty has often produced men of spiritual vision and stalwart character. America has had no finer souls than Henry David Thoreau and John Burroughs, who led a simple life in close communion with nature. The great spiritual leaders of Israel were men who lived long amid the hills. Moses tended sheep for forty years around Mount Sinai. David was a shepherd on the hillsides of Bethlehem. John the

Baptist was a product of the desert. Jesus spent forty days in the wilderness before beginning his public ministry. What Bayard Taylor said about David is true of them all:

Remote from courts, corruption, crime, in that high shepherd land,
With God alone his soul had grown to stature bold and grand;
For many a wild, in many a land, and many a peak sublime,
Can tell how solitude with God breeds souls that conquer time.

Dear Lord, grant that here in America we may have men whose rugged manhood will match our mountains. By abiding in thy presence may we learn not to fear what others do to us and to care only for thy approval. So may we make thee our all-in-all. Amen.

SATURDAY—Week 5

WE NEED MORE THAN NATURE'S REVELATION
Read Gal. 1:11-24

The fact that you can find God in nature should not deceive you into thinking you do not need the worship of the church. Those who habitually excuse themselves from church on the plea that "the groves were God's first temples" are not the ones with whom nature has her true spiritual ministry. Bryant says nature "speaks a various language." To the completely dull of heart she says nothing at all. To the one who speeds along at sixty miles an hour she whispers goodby. To the one who tramps the road for exercise she speaks of physical health. To the man who goes into the forest to fell trees for timber she talks of money.

Only if you go to nature with spiritual aspirations will you be sure to discover a spiritual presence. You will be certain of finding God through his revelation in nature if you first see the revelation in Jesus Christ.

O Father God, keep me from being satisfied with the lesser revelations of thyself. May all I see of thee in the physical universe create in me a deeper longing for the fullness of knowledge which thou dost give in Jesus Christ. Amen.

THE REVELATION OF GOD IN JESUS CHRIST

SUNDAY—Week 6

IT TAKES PERSONALITY TO REVEAL GOD
Read John 1:1-18

God reveals himself in nature, but his highest revelation must be in human personality, which is made in the image of the divine. The law and order and beauty of the physical world, with its evidence of a divine purpose, give us knowledge of God as the Creator and Controller, but they cannot show forth the most important part of his character—his goodness and love.

If you wish to see God most clearly, then seek him not in the beauty of the sunset nor the power of a roaring Niagara, but in a being who can think and love. There is more of God in a child than in the mightiest earthquake or the most beautiful landscape. However, even the best men and women are so sinful that they can show only a tiny part of God's goodness. We need the Christ before whom we can bow and say: Here is one who completely sets forth what the universe and mankind have been imperfectly trying to show—the fullness of God's love.

O Father God, I see thy glory in the physical universe and catch a glimpse of thy guiding hand in history, but I long for a clearer revelation of thyself. So I praise thee for Jesus Christ, in whom thy love and goodness are fully manifested. Amen.

MONDAY—Week 6

TWO OPINIONS ABOUT CHRIST
Read Matt. 16:13-20

"Who say ye that I am?" is the question Jesus asks of every person. All sorts of answers have been given, but they sift down to the two which Jesus received from his disciples when he first asked the question. They replied: "People are divided in their opinions. Some say you are John the Baptist, others Elijah, or Jeremiah returned to earth, but all agree that you are worthy to be ranked as a prophet." Jesus then insisted on knowing their own opinions, and Peter responded, "Thou art the Christ, the Son of the living God."

Ever since, there have been these two replies. One says Jesus is a great and good man, the other that he is the divine son of God. It is this latter idea which is the rock on which the Christian church is

33

founded, and which has given courage and strength to countless people for nearly twenty centuries.

Dear Father, as the disciples came to recognize Jesus as their Lord because they had been living in companionship with him, so may I have the personal experience of conviction that he alone is worthy to be the Lord and Master of my life. Amen.

TUESDAY—Week 6

THE PERFECTION OF JESUS' CHARACTER
Read Matt. 4:1-11

Jesus is unique among men in his moral perfection. He represents the divine ideal for human existence. While the Gospels contain a record of only a brief portion of his life, they give a clear picture of the impression he made on his contemporaries. He defied the Pharisees by asking, "Which of you convinceth me of sin?" And neither his enemies nor his friends could point to any flaw in his character.

It is significant that the very idea of a man's being sinless had never occurred to anyone until the Jewish people saw it realized in Jesus. There had been many idealized leaders in Israel, but the Bible depicts them all as feeling themselves sinners in the sight of God. Jesus was so free from the consciousness of wrongdoing that in the hour of death he prayed for the forgiveness of his executioners but felt no need of praying for himself. The author of Hebrews sums up his character by saying that he "was in all points tempted like as we are, yet without sin."

Dear God, I would set my standards high. May I seek to be perfect even as thou art. Though I fail continually in my high endeavor, may I still cling to my ideal and press forward toward the goal which thou hast set for me in Christ Jesus. Amen.

WEDNESDAY—Week 6

GOD IS LIKE JESUS
Read John 1:26-34

A Jewish soldier who had attended Protestant services a few times went to a rabbi and asked him the difference between the Messiah of the Jews and the Jesus of the Christians. The rabbi explained, "The difference is that we Jews believe the Messiah is still to come, whereas Christians believe he has already come in Jesus." After a momentary hesitation the soldier replied, "But Rabbi, when our Messiah does come, what will he have on Jesus?"

It is a fair question. Who can suggest a change that should be made in Jesus' character to make it more what the life of God ought to be? He was such a complete incarnation of goodness and purity and truth, of long-suffering, forgiving, and sacrificial love, that he could truly say, "He that hath seen me hath seen the Father."

O God, in the matchless life of thy Son I see what thou art and what I ought to be. Make me dissatisfied with myself—with my littleness, my fickleness, my sinfulness. Help me to find in thee strength to become more like Christ. Amen.

THURSDAY—Week 6

THE UNIVERSE IS INCOMPLETE WITHOUT CHRIST
Read I John 4:7-16

The gospel is the good news that God has made himself known in Christ. Because it is such a familiar story to us, we do not realize what it means to those who hear it for the first time.

Helen Keller never went to church during her early childhood. Deaf and dumb and blind, she did not learn the story of the love of God as revealed in the life of Christ until she was taken to Phillips Brooks for religious instruction. The great preacher told her, in the simplest possible language, how God had sent Jesus to teach us his will, show us his love, and make himself known to humanity. The face of Miss Keller lighted up as she spelled into the hands of her interpreter, "I knew all the time there must be one like that, but I didn't know his name."

We need a person like Christ. Our knowledge about the universe and about life is sadly incomplete until we become acquainted with him.

Father, grant that the story of Jesus and his love may never grow old to me. May it always make life glow with new meaning. Knowing that thou art seeking to be my Companion, may I walk through life without fear or loneliness. Amen.

FRIDAY—Week 6

JESUS REVEALS A GOD WHO SUFFERS
Read John 3:14-21

A boy disobeyed his father and was sent to sleep in the attic. Angry and impenitent, he remained wide awake. The father, grieving over his boy, was also unable to sleep. At last he arose, went to the attic, and climbed into bed with his son. "My boy," he said, "I punished you because you did wrong, but I love you and have come to spend the night with you." The defiant boy could no

35

longer stand out against a love that followed him and shared the consequences of his wrongdoing.

So God has established his moral and physical laws, and those who violate them suffer the penalty of their sins. But because God is a Father, he also suffers and in his love seeks to bring his children back to obedience to himself. This is the message of the cross. The Christian church has always thought of Jesus' death not as the mere martyrdom of a good man by the Romans, but as a revelation of something eternally true of the suffering heart of God.

O God, I bow in awe before the cross, unable to fathom all its mystery, but seeing there something that shows me the fullness of thy love. My heart is melted by thy suffering, and I cry out to thee to forgive my sins and make me more worthy of thy goodness. Amen.

SATURDAY—Week 6

JESUS OUTLASTS THE CHANGES OF TIME
Read I Cor. 3:11-23

One of the evidences that Jesus is a revelation of eternal truth is his ability to outlast all the changes of time, for only the truth has enduring power. Empires have come and gone; systems of thought have succeeded one another; science has changed the manner of living for a large part of mankind; yet Jesus is still the ideal of what every man's character ought to be, and thoughtful people in increasing numbers are saying that the only hope for civilization is to live by his teachings.

It was Jesus' power to retain a permanent hold on the hearts and minds of men that made Napoleon say: Alexander, Caesar, Charlemagne, and I have founded great empires, but upon what did these creations of our genius depend? Upon force! Jesus alone founded his empire on love, and to this very day millions would die for him. I think I understand something of human nature, and I tell you that all these were men and I am a man. None else was like him. Jesus Christ was more than a man.

Thou changeless Christ, when old things are passing away and the whole world seems to be in chaos, I turn toward thee to find the one solid rock on which I can stand and look toward the future with faith and hope. Amen.

GOD IN HISTORY

SUNDAY—Week 7

WHERE IS GOD GOING?   Read Mic. 6:1-8

"The task of statesmanship is to discover where Almighty God is going in the next fifty years," said William E. Gladstone to his English friends over half a century ago. It ought not to be difficult for Christian people to tell the direction in which God is going. Let them open the Bible and they will find that twenty-five hundred years ago the Old Testament prophets knew God was headed toward justice and righteousness. Listen to Micah as he cries out: "What doth the Lord require of thee, but to do justly, and to love mercy, and to walk humbly with thy God?"

God has never changed his course, but people have lost sight of him. Blinded by selfishness and greed they have wandered from the King's highway and have been caught in the quicksands of war. Order can come out of international chaos only when chastened nations are willing to walk in the same direction with God.

God of the prophets, raise up among us a generation of men who will share thy vision of eternal values and walk steadfastly in the direction of thy truth. Lead us out of the night of confusion into the day of the Lord. Amen.

MONDAY—Week 7

THE HOUSE ON THE SAND   Read Luke 6:43-49

Shortly before the outbreak of World War II, a newspaper cartoonist drew a picture of a terrific storm. Jagged streaks of lightning are flashing across the sky, while wind and rain are relentlessly beating upon the prostrate form of a woman who symbolizes civilization. Lying upon the rocks with nothing to protect her from the downpour, she is covering her face and crying out in despair, "Has God forgotten us?" In another part of the picture old Father Time is hard at work keeping his records. Pausing to look up, he replies, "No, he has not forgotten you, but you have been neglecting him."

The cartoonist was expressing his conviction that the universe is governed by moral laws whose violation or neglect bring tragic consequences, that he who builds his house on sand need not be surprised if it finally collapses over his head.

Most high God, I plead forgiveness for my bungling neglect of thy laws. Too often I have done the things I ought not to have done and have left undone the things I ought to have done. Incline my heart now to do thy will. Amen.

TUESDAY—Week 7

FRANKLIN'S FAITH   Read Isa. 40:1-17

That the ultimate outcome of history is within God's control has always been a part of Christian faith. One of the finest expressions of this idea comes from Benjamin Franklin, who was the oldest member of the convention which framed our Constitution. When the delegates were worried because they were not making more progress, Franklin called for a greater reliance upon the guidance of God. He said:

I have lived, sir, a long time, and the longer I live, the more convincing proofs I see of this truth: That *God governs in the affairs of men.* And if a sparrow cannot fall to the ground without His notice, is it probable that an empire can rise without His aid? We have been assured, sir, in the sacred writings, that "except the Lord build the House, they labor in vain that build it." I firmly believe this; and I also believe that without His concurring aid we shall succeed in this political building no better than the builders of Babel."

With thankful heart, O God, I acknowledge thy blessings to the people of this nation. Grant that we may show our gratitude by willingly sharing our privileges and seeking a larger life for all mankind. Amen.

WEDNESDAY—Week 7

THE SHOUT OF THE CENTURIES   Read Dan. 5

Mussolini, presiding at a celebration in Rome while at the height of his power, cried out: "Since prehistoric times, one shout has come down on the waves of the centuries, 'Woe to the weak!' "

Evidently Mussolini had not listened very attentively to the shouts of the past. Had he done so, from the spot where he stood he could have heard the dying groans of the Roman Empire. All about him were the relics of a civilization that was unable to perpetuate itself by force. Perhaps Mussolini had never studied the history of Egypt, Assyria, and Babylon. Evidently he had never meditated on the downfall of Napoleon. In his ignorance of the past, he was blind to the fact that his own house was built on sand.

No nation has ever maintained itself permanently by force alone. If it does not go down before the joined forces of other powers, it suffers inner disintegration because it loses the loyalty of its own people. Only when force is the expression of righteousness does it permanently endure.

I thank thee, dear God, that throughout history evil has shown itself to be self-defeating, while right, if overthrown, has had the power to rise again. Teach me to see that in serving thee I become strong, and that forsaking thee I become weak. Amen.

THURSDAY—Week 7

GOD CANNOT BE STOPPED   Read Isa. 42:1-16

During Woodrow Wilson's last illness, his friend Ray Stannard Baker went to the hospital to call on him. They talked about the future of the League of Nations. Baker expressed doubt about its future, but Wilson said, "Don't worry, Baker, they can't stop God!" All that has happened in later years confirms the belief that the League, with its recognition of the need for some kind of international organization, was the expression of a great ideal in the mind of God, and that those who opposed it were standing in the way of God.

The nations of the world have been brought so close together by airplane that they must learn to cooperate or be destroyed.

> Keep heart, O comrade! God may be delayed
> By evil, but he suffers no defeat.
> God is not foiled; the drift of the world will
> Is stronger than all wrong.

Give me a confident faith in thee, our Father, that I may go forward into the future without discouragement or fear. If cherished plans fail, may I entrust them to thy keeping, believing they can yet be realized if they represent the purpose of thy will. Amen.

FRIDAY—Week 7

ARE WE ON GOD'S SIDE?   Read Ps. 124

During the Civil War a pious citizen said to the President, "Mr. Lincoln, the Lord is with us. God is surely on our side in this great conflict." The great leader replied, "I am less anxious, my friend, to know that the Lord is on our side, than I am to make sure that *we are on the Lord's side*." This must always be the chief concern of the Christian.

We may be sure that any temporary victory which is won by sheer force of arms will not long endure unless the victor nation reverently seeks to make itself an agency for carrying out divine purposes. God's moral laws are as inescapable as the law of gravitation. The nation that persistently disobeys them will finally fall.

God is the Father of all mankind, and love and righteousness are his basic laws. Let every nation follow these principles as its guiding star if it would be worthy of divine favor.

O God, help me to maintain the spirit of unconquerable goodwill toward all men, honestly seeking their welfare as my own. Then shall I be confident that I am on thy side and am becoming a co-worker with thee in building a better world. Amen.

SATURDAY—Week 7

GOD'S PURPOSE FOR AMERICA   Read Gen. 12:1-9

"And I will make of thee a great nation, and I will bless thee, and make thy name great; and thou shalt be a blessing." These words were read by the Rev. John Robinson to the Pilgrims shortly before they embarked to seek a home in the new world.

They set sail not only to find a place where they could worship God as they pleased, but to lead a movement that would bless mankind. During the hardships of their early years in New England the Pilgrims were sustained by a faith in the high destiny which sent them forth.

All through the finest chapters in our history runs this underlying theme of becoming a great nation not for our own glory but that a nobler life may be achieved for mankind. If this note is now being lost in our American outlook, we must return to the vision of our ancestors. If we adopt a program of national selfishness, we betray the purpose for which God established us as a nation.

Almighty God, who dost determine the destiny of men and of nations, incline my heart to do thy will as thou hast revealed it in Jesus Christ. Keep me true to the spirit of those who endured danger and sacrifice that the generations of the future might be blessed by their efforts. Amen.

GIVING PRIORITY TO GOD

SUNDAY—Week 8

GIVING GOD THE REMNANTS   Read Isa. 44:1-20

The prophet has a striking description of the ignorant pagan who gives his leftovers to God. The man cuts down a tree, keeps himself warm, and roasts his meat. Comfortable and well fed, he takes what remains of the wood and carves it into an idol. "And the residue thereof he maketh a god."

Is not this still an accurate picture of the religion of many people? They arrange their homes as comfortably as they can, provide for all the necessities and most of the luxuries of life, and give to God the money, time, and interest which they can easily spare. They go to church on Sunday if there is nothing else they particularly desire to do; they contribute to the church and its world-wide enterprise the little that remains after they have spent generously on themselves. God is not given priority; he is allowed only the remnants of their lives.

Forgive me, O God, for keeping so much for myself and giving so little to thee. I pray for the life that asks nothing for itself but in complete trust in thy will is wholly dedicated to thy service. Amen.

MONDAY—Week 8

CROWDED OUT OF THE INN   Read Luke 2:1-7

It was a busy time of year when Joseph and Mary went to Bethlehem to pay their taxes. The town was crowded with strangers, and the only hotel was already full. The only available shelter was the stable. The innkeeper had nothing against the carpenter and his wife; he was willing to let them do anything just so it did not interfere with the comfort of his other guests.

In these events surrounding the birth of Jesus was a significant foreshadowing of the future—Jesus' gospel has also had difficulty finding a place in our overcrowded world. In our own country the gospel is not opposed or fought against; it is simply pushed aside.

If the innkeeper had known the importance of the person who was crowded out, he would have evicted the other guests and prepared his best room for the Savior's birth. And we today would find room for Christ in our crowded lives if we fully realized his importance to us and our world.

Heavenly Father, I pray that my soul may not become such a busy inn that it has no room for thy Son. May it be a place of humility and reverence, ready to welcome him as its honored Guest. Amen.

TUESDAY—Week 8

LET GLASGOW FLOURISH   Read Luke 12:21-31

The city of Glasgow in Scotland was settled by religious people who adopted a motto that reflected their spiritual devotion, "Let Glasgow flourish by the preaching of the gospel." As one generation succeeded another, the city grew into an important commercial and industrial center. Business loomed larger than religion in the minds of its civic leaders, and the Chamber of Commerce shortened the motto to make it read, "Let Glasgow flourish."

Is not this a symbol of what has taken place in our own country? When our ancestors settled a community, the church was the first building to be erected after their own homes. It was the center of the community life; everything else was secondary. Now the average city or village pays far more attention to business than to religion. The basic difficulty with our nation today is that we are seeking the kind of success which is not based on spiritual ideals.

We must confess before thee, O God, that in our desire for gain we have forgotten that only righteousness can exalt a nation. Help us now to cast out of our hearts the throne of mammon and to set up the throne of thy Son, who came to give fullness of life to all thy children. Amen.

WEDNESDAY—Week 8

THINGS ARE IN THE SADDLE   Read Heb. 2:1-9

Before the war someone figured out that fifty years ago the average American wanted 72 different things and considered 18 of them important, while today he has 496 wants and considers 96 of them essential to happiness. Many people are becoming slaves to the effort to secure the vast number of things they consider desirable, or else are getting soured on life because they feel cheated out of things they think indispensable to their happiness. What Emerson said of his age is even more true of ours:

> Things are in the saddle,
> And ride mankind.

We need a clearer insight into the values of life. The author of the Epistle to the Hebrews describes the high position given to man by his Creator: "Thou hast put all things in subjection under his feet." If you can keep things in subjection and not let them become your master, you have gone a long way toward solving one of life's most difficult problems.

Dear Father, my life is in danger of spiritual defeat because of the many interests, not bad in themselves but simply unimportant, which demand my attention. Help me to put them under my feet and to set my heart on things above. Amen.

THURSDAY—Week 8

A GREAT CORPORATION'S MISTAKEN IDEA
Read Isa. 2:1-5

In the New York World's Fair, General Motors had an exhibit called the Futurama which depicted what the world of tomorrow would look like to the motorist. There were great trunkline highways, beautiful schools and public buildings, model homes and factories, attractive parks and amusement centers; but the only building which had anything to do with religion was a monastery on a secluded mountainside, a quiet and lovely place far removed from the main currents of life.

Isaiah had a different idea. In his vision of the ideal civilization he saw all people going to the temple, which was at the heart of the nation's life in Jerusalem. General Motors had an inadequate conception of the place of Christianity in modern life. Religion must be on the main highway so that the voice of Christ can be heard "where cross the crowded ways of life." Scientific power, with its machinery, must be brought under the control of Christ, unless the world of tomorrow is to be an endless chamber of horrors caused by recurring war.

Grant, O God, that my religion may mean more to me than going apart to worship thee in some place of loveliness. May it enable me to see the Son of Man in the midst of human need, and to hear his voice of love and brotherhood above the cries of race and clan. Amen.

FRIDAY—Week 8

OUR SUPREME LOYALTY
Read Isa. 40:1-17

The arrangement of the flags in the majority of churches is an evidence that people give their chief loyalty to their country instead of to their God. The place of honor is most often allotted to the national emblem while the Christian flag is put in a secondary position. Even in the sanctuary, which is dedicated to the worship of the Father of all mankind, God is made to take a back seat for Uncle Sam.

Strangely enough, from this standpoint the United States Navy is more reverent than the church. When the time comes on a battleship for the chaplain to hold a formal religious service, the flag which symbolizes allegiance to Christ is hoisted above the stars and stripes.

No question is more vital than that of our highest loyalty. Down through the ages Christian people have held that allegiance to Christ is above every other, and they have endured persecution and death for the sake of complete obedience to their Lord.

Father of all nations, teach me to acknowledge thee as a great God above all gods. Forbid that I should place love of nation before devotion to thee. Make my beloved country worthy of thy favor and a fit instrument for the achievement of thy plans for mankind. Amen.

SATURDAY—Week 8

IS YOUR RELIGION A PASTIME OR A PASSION?
Read Matt. 10:23-31

When David Livingstone was a medical student, he decided that since he had but one life to live, he ought to make the most of it. He secured a map of the world and studied it to find the neediest spot. He concluded that it was China and planned to go there as a medical missionary. But soon after, he heard Dr. Robert Moffat of Africa say: "From the hill where I live I can see the smoke of a thousand villages where no Christian has ever gone." Livingstone then decided there could be no place more in need of Christ than Africa; and he went out to live with savages, be bitten by tropical insects, suffer with fever, live in separation from his family, and finally die in a hut in the wilderness.

To the service of Christ, Livingstone gave his all—his youth, his medical skill, his pioneering spirit, his money, his family, his life. He left the world a living example of what it means to have a religion which is not a pastime but a passion for service.

O God, cleanse my heart of its love of ease and comfort. May I hear the call of thy Son to leave all and follow him. Help me, like Livingstone, to set no value on anything I possess except in its relation to thy kingdom. Amen.

SEARCH THE SCRIPTURES

SUNDAY—Week 9

TAKE UP AND READ   Read Rom. 13

When the Roman Empire was breaking up in the fourth century, a young college professor by the name of Augustine was worried over the national outlook and unhappy because of the sinfulness of his personal life. One day in Milan he heard a group of children, who were playing in a garden near his home, singing, *"Tolle lege, tolle lege,"* which means, "Take up and read, take up and read." The words reminded him of his Bible, probably given to him by his mother, who was already a Christian. It was in his room. He went in and opened it at the verse, "Put ye on the Lord Jesus Christ." He gave his life to Christ and became a new man. Later he was made a bishop, and largely because of his leadership Christianity was kept alive after Rome went to pieces.

Are you worried and unhappy? Take the Bible and read it. You will find a new source of joy, and the power that can make you a leader for righteousness.

Almighty God, enter thou our hearts, and so fill us with thy love, that, forsaking all evil desires, we may embrace thee, our only God. Show unto us, for thy mercies' sake, O Lord our God, what thou art unto us. Say unto our souls, I am thy salvation. Amen.—Augustine.

MONDAY—Week 9

NEW LAMPS FOR OLD   Read Gal. 1

The Arabian Nights contains the tale of Aladdin, who found a magic lamp in a cave, but was later robbed of it by a man disguised as a peddler, who went through the streets crying out: "New lamps for old, new lamps for old! Who will exchange old lamps for new?" The princess, in whose keeping the magic lamp had been left, did not appreciate its value and foolishly made the exchange.

We have outgrown the days of our childhood with their stories of genii and enchanted palaces, but we are not unlike the princess in our willingness to cast aside the book that for hundreds of years has been a lamp to those who have followed it, spending our time instead on literature of far less value. Books and newspapers clamor for our attention. All sorts of magazines, good and bad, are spread before us on the bookstands. The danger is that the Bible be pushed into a corner.

Why not put it first on your reading list and give it some time each day?

Eternal God, I thank thee for the lamp of thy Holy Word and pray that it may ever shine upon my pathway. Keep my mind open to every fresh revelation of thy truth, but save me from forsaking the source of wisdom which has refreshed and strengthened so many generations of mankind. Amen.

TUESDAY—Week 9

USE THE BIBLE INTELLIGENTLY   Read Acts 8:26-40

Too many people have superstitious ideas about the way the Bible can guide and help them. A soldier's wife recently told an army chaplain how she decided to travel twenty-five hundred miles to an army camp to see her husband. She went to a "wise man" who told fortunes by the Bible and asked him if it would be advisable to make the journey. She was afraid that her husband might suddenly be ordered overseas and that she would be making the trip in vain. The man pretended to go into a trance, then opened the Bible at the last chapter of Matthew which contained the words "Go ye" and told her she should go at once. The woman was greatly impressed by the guidance she had received in this manner. She seemed not to realize that such use of the Bible is sacrilegious.

The Scriptures were never intended to be a charm. They give us moral and spiritual guidance, but must be read intelligently. We must use our minds in studying the Bible as much as in reading any other book.

> Holy Spirit, Truth divine,
> Dawn upon this soul of mine;
> Word of God, and inward Light,
> Wake my spirit, clear my sight. Amen.

WEDNESDAY—Week 9

THE INFLUENCE OF THE BIBLE ON LINCOLN
Read Ps. 119:1-16

The Bible was one of the few books which were available to Abraham Lincoln during his boyhood, and it exerted a profound influence upon his life. Listen to what two writers have said about Lincoln's debt to the Bible.

Said Theodore Roosevelt: "He built up his entire reading upon his early study of the Bible. He mastered it; mastered it as, later, he mastered only one or two other books; mastered it so that he became almost a man of one book, who knew that book and instinctively put into practice what he had been taught therein."

Hamilton Wright Mabie has written of Lincoln and the Scriptures: "These sixty-six books emancipated him at once from the harsh and narrow conditions in which he was born; they set him in the great currents of human life; they brought before him the highest ideals of human character; and above all, for the purposes of education, they presented to his imagination the loftiest examples of human speech."

I thank thee, O God, for the wisdom and courage that have come to so many people by reading the Bible. Truly it is a way in which thy voice still speaks to men today! Grant that it may speak to me. Amen.

THURSDAY—Week 9

MUTINY ON THE BOUNTY   Read Ps. 119:89-104

Truth is often stranger than fiction. One of the strange tales of history is that of the mutiny on the British ship "Bounty" in 1787. The rebellious crew put the captain and his eighteen loyal men in a rowboat with limited water and rations and left them to their fate. After incredible hardships these men succeeded in returning to England.

The other members of the crew went to Pitcairn Island, taking with them some of the native women of Tahiti. All the men died except John Adams, who found a copy of the Bible in a sailor's chest and became converted. He started to teach the truths of the Book to the women and children. Twenty years later, when a United States ship called at the island, a community was found there which was entirely free from crime and disease, and all of whose members were able to read and write. People were living together in peace and health and happiness because they were basing their lives on the Bible.

We pray for our land. Let us not be left unrich in manhood. Raise up nobler men—men that shall not be devoured by selfishness; men that shall fear God and love man. And so we beseech of thee that our peace may stand firm upon integrity, and that righteousness may everywhere prevail. Amen.— Henry Ward Beecher.

FRIDAY—Week 9

A SPIRITUAL GOLD MINE   Read Ps. 119:129-152

A man died not many years ago after having made a comfortable fortune in an unusual way. In his youth he started out as a gold miner and hoped to strike it rich by finding a new mine. Years went by and he failed to make his discovery, so he began to go through abandoned mines, exploring the veins that were supposed to have been entirely exhausted. He learned that by following the veins further, or by digging deeper, he could often find paying dirt that other miners had overlooked.

The Bible is a kind of spiritual gold mine that can be explored again and again with rich results. We read a chapter, or a book, and suppose we have received all the value to be derived from it. But when we go back and read it again, digging deeper and searching more carefully, we find new treasures of meaning that we had previously overlooked.

I thank thee, Father, for the enrichment of my life through the knowledge of the Scriptures. Make me more diligent in their study and give me grace to expect fresh light to break forth from thy Word each time I read it. Amen.

SATURDAY—Week 9

THE BIBLE AND DEMOCRACY   Read Luke 15:1-10

In Colonial America there were three different types of schools —public schools in New England, church schools in the Middle Colonies, and private schools among the plantation owners of the South. In all of them the Bible, or else the *New England Primer,* which was based on the Bible, was the book from which everyone learned to read for nearly a century. All intelligent people became familiar with the great scriptural truth about the sacredness of the individual in the sight of God. Instilled in the minds of those who framed our Constitution was the idea that no one had a right to become a dictator, because liberty was one of the "inalienable rights" which came from the Creator.

Back of our democracy is the Bible. If you today are concerned about the future of our nation, you can do nothing more practical than to study and teach the great liberating ideas which are embedded in its foundation.

God of our fathers, I thank thee for all those whose stern devotion to the truth achieved the freedom which Americans now enjoy. Make us obedient to thy will and grant that we may remain strong and great because we love and serve thee. Amen.

STRENGTHENING THE CHURCH

SUNDAY—Week 10

THE BODY OF CHRIST   Read I Cor. 12

Paul wrote to the church in Corinth, "Ye are the body of Christ." No better name could be given to the church. It is the agency through which our Savior does his work in the world. Without a body, Jesus is only a vague spiritual influence and not a vital force in the life of mankind.

The great works that have been done by Christ have been accomplished through the church. The church kept Christianity alive through the dark ages and preserved the manuscripts of the Bible. It sent missionaries throughout Europe, from Europe to the United States and around the world. The church has pioneered in education, built hospitals, established homes for the homeless, and championed the cause of human rights.

When the church is strong, Christ becomes strong; if the church is weak, he is almost powerless. Christ has worked through the church in the past; he is doing so today; he will continue to do so in the future. If we would have a victorious Christ, we must have a strong and conquering church.

I thank thee, dear God, for the promise of thy Son that our achievements may be greater than his if we follow the guidance of his Spirit. May we who make up his church today be willing to let him work through us, with hands and hearts quickly responding to the service of thy will. Amen.

MONDAY—Week 10

AN ENDURING INSTITUTION   Read Ps. 90

Back in the eighteenth century Voltaire said the church was a dying institution. He predicted it would not last over fifty years, but fifty years later the house in Paris where he had made that prediction was being used as a center for distribution of the Bible.

Skeptics frequently foretell the funeral of organized religion, but the cynics die and are buried while the church goes marching on. The church is far older than any existing nation or organization; and if one may forecast the future from the past, it will outlast every institution of our day. If you wish to give your life to something that will endure through all the changes of time, invest it in the church.

O where are kings and empires now,
Of old that went and came?
But, Lord, thy church is praying yet,
A thousand years the same.

O God, who hast been our help in ages past and art our hope for years to come, I thank thee for the church, which has stood unshaken during the centuries—a reminder that there are still eternal values in our changing world. May I seek first the things that last longest. Amen.

TUESDAY—Week 10

VOTING TO CLOSE THE CHURCH   Read Luke 4:14-19

One way everyone can help to strengthen the body of Christ is regular attendance at church worship. If you stay away on a Sunday when by a little effort or inconvenience you could go, you are voting to close the church. If all should follow your example that day, there would be no voices singing in praise of their Creator, no heads bowed in a common prayer for strength and guidance, no public reading of the Scriptures, no preaching of Christian truth.

The Sunday attendance of the average Protestant church is much less than half of its membership. Too many people belong to what someone has called the new C. E. society—those who go to church on Christmas and Easter. If you wish to increase the influence of Christ in your community and in the world, you can start by being a faithful attendant at public worship on the Lord's Day.

Dear Father, may I always be glad to go to thy house of prayer and praise. Lead me to a deeper understanding of what it means truly to worship thee, either alone or in the sanctuary. May I become conscious of thy presence and find peace and joy through my faith. Amen.

WEDNESDAY—Week 10

GOING TO CHURCH MAKES A DIFFERENCE Read Ps. 73

What happens as the result of going to church may change the whole course of one's life. Mainly out of curiosity, a student in England attended a religious service to hear Dwight L. Moody. The words of the American evangelist started a chain of events that took Wilfred T. Grenfell to Labrador and made him a doctor to the needy fisherfolk. A boy named David Livingstone went to a village church in Scotland and heard a missionary speak about the work being done for Christ in Africa. The story gripped the lad's heart and stirred his imagination. His own dedication to serve Christ in the mission field was the result.

Countless people, by the influence of public worship, make decisions which strengthen their characters, overcome their hate, transform their homes, and start ripples of influence which are felt on faraway shores. You know not what adventure may await you in God's sanctuary.

Whenever I bow before thee, O God, my thoughts turn away from myself toward the needs of the world. Through the windows of spiritual vision I see my fellowmen whose lives have been blighted by war and hate and ignorance. Show me some way by which I may be to them thy messenger of mercy and love. Amen.

THURSDAY—Week 10

THE RIGHT DIRECTION   Read Ps. 122

A little girl who had recently moved to a new city became lost in a holiday crowd. A policeman found her crying on the street corner. She told him her name but did not know where she lived. Since her father had been in the city such a short time, his name was not in the telephone book or the city directory. The policeman was baffled; but as he talked with the child, she said, "If I could find the church, I would know my way home." He inquired about the appearance of the church, knew at once which one she meant, and took her there. She stood on the steps, pointed down the street, and said, "This is the way." Soon she was home. Her parents had taken her to Sunday school their first week in the community, and she was not lost when she was at the church.

Is not this what the church does for us all? It points us in the right direction. It enables us to find the true home of our souls.

Keep me, O God, from losing my way in the journey of life. May I find guidance in the Bible and the teachings of the church. Direct my steps into ways of righteousness, and suffer me not to turn aside into bypaths of error or evil. Amen.

FRIDAY—Week 10

THE MISTAKE OF A GOOD KING   Read II Chron. 27

The scripture reading about Jotham tells the story of a good and successful man who paid no attention to the church. How modern it all sounds! He was an energetic leader and a builder. He erected cities, strengthened the national defense, and subdued his nation's ancient enemies. He was a model king except that he had no use for religion. What was his net result in the life of Israel? "The people did yet corruptly." Jotham, because of the influence of his God-fearing father, Uzziah, was an upright person without going to church; but the influence of his example had disastrous results in the life of the nation.

George Washington was wiser than Jotham. He knew that the stability of a nation rests on religion. He said: "Let us with caution indulge the supposition that morality can be maintained without religion. . . . Reason and experience both forbid us to expect that national morality can prevail in exclusion of religious principle."

I thank thee, our Father, for those who laid the foundations of our American life in the knowledge and fear of God. Help us of a new generation to establish and complete their work. Amen.

SATURDAY—Week 10

THE ROCK ON WHICH THE CHURCH IS BUILT
Read Matt. 16:13-23

What did Jesus mean when he said to Peter, "Upon this rock I will build my church"? Like many other passages of scripture, this verse cannot be understood without studying its context. Jesus had just asked his disciples who they thought he was, and Peter had made the reply, "Thou art the Christ, the Son of the living God." Peter was the first of the disciples to make the statement that Jesus was no ordinary man, not merely a great prophet like Elijah or Jeremiah, but a revelation of the Eternal. Peter was setting him above all others as a person to be believed and followed and obeyed. He was giving Jesus the primary allegiance of his life.

This confession of faith and this spirit of loyalty to Christ—not Peter as a man—is the rock on which the church is founded. So long as there are people who will be steadfast in such a conviction and put Christ first in their lives, nothing can overthrow his church.

Be thou my Lord and Master, O Christ. Grant that I may put my devotion in thee above every other allegiance. Make me a faithful member of thy church, and help me to become, like Peter, a rock in my loyalty to thy cause. In thy name. Amen.

LEARNING TO PRAY

SUNDAY—Week 11

A LOST ART   Read Acts 2:41-47

Wendell Phillips had a famous lecture called "The Lost Arts of Civilization." He described the many achievements of the ancients which people of his own day were unable to duplicate. Since the death of Phillips men have regained a knowledge of some of the arts which he listed as lost. But there is one art, well known in the days of early Christianity, which is lost to many twentieth-century church members and which needs to be recovered.

People call themselves Christians, but do not know how to pray and have no custom of frequent communion with God. They overlook the place which prayer held in the life of Jesus and in the history of the Early Church. The disciples were so impressed by what prayer meant in the life of their Master that they asked him to teach them to pray. The Book of Acts describes the Christians as meeting for prayer each day and as praying for each other. We will never succeed in our quest for Christ-like lives until we begin adventuring in prayer.

O Lord our God, grant us grace to desire thee with our whole heart, that so desiring, we may seek and find thee; and so finding thee we may love thee; and loving thee we may hate those sins from which thou hast redeemed us. Amen.—St. Anselm.

MONDAY—Week 11

WHAT IS THE USE OF PRAYING?   Read Luke 18:9-14

Andrew Carnegie, the wealthy steel magnate of a past generation, once remarked to a group of men that he did not feel the need of prayer. "What is the use of praying?" he asked. "I already have everything I want. What more could I ask for?" One of his hearers remarked, "Perhaps, sir, you might pray for the grace of humility."

The person who thinks he does not need to pray does not understand the meaning of communion with God. The purpose of prayer is not to get something from God, but to allow God to make us into the kind of men he would have us become. We are prodigal sons if our only words to our Father are "Give me." We begin to

53

be true sons if we kneel before him and humbly say, "Make me."
One thing prayer can most certainly do is change the spirit of the
man who prays in sincerity and in truth.

Heavenly Father, through the gate of prayer may I enter into a quiet
place of communion with thee where I can enlarge my vision and renew my
hold on the secret sources of spiritual strength. Send me back to the crowded
ways of life with increased sympathy for the needs of my fellow men. Amen.

TUESDAY—Week 11

PRAYER CHANGES US   Read Ps. 91

The following poem by Archbishop Trench is a beautiful description of what can happen in the life of one who prays:

> Lord, what a change within us one short hour
> Spent in Thy presence will prevail to make—
> What heavy burdens from our bosoms take,
> What parchèd grounds refresh as with a shower!
> We kneel, and all around us seems to lower;
> We rise, and all, the distant and the near,
> Stands forth in sunny outline, brave and clear;
> We kneel how weak, we rise how full of power!
> Why, therefore, should we do ourselves this wrong,
> Or others—that we are not always strong;
> That we are ever overborne with care;
> That we should ever weak or heartless be,
> Anxious or troubled, when with us is prayer,
> And joy, and strength, and courage, are with Thee?

O merciful God, fill our hearts, we pray thee, with the graces of thy Holy
Spirit, with love, joy, peace, long-suffering, gentleness, goodness, faith,
meekness, temperance. Amen.—St. Anselm.

WEDNESDAY—Week 11

PRAYER CAN CHANGE HISTORY   Read Acts 2:1-21

If prayer can change the quality of men's lives, it can change
history. Let prayer change one timid, hesitant leader into a man of
physical and moral courage, and a decisive victory may be won on
the battlefield or in the halls of Congress.

Consider what happened in 1824 when there was no electoral
majority for president and the election was thrown into Congress,
which voted by states. Andrew Jackson and John Quincy Adams
were the leading candidates. New York State had the deciding
vote, and its representatives were evenly divided between Adams

and Jackson. The decisive vote for New York was held by Major General Van Rensselaer, who was opposed to Adams. Clay and Webster both talked to Van Rensselaer about the importance of his vote, and the old general made it a matter of prayer, with the result that he reversed his first intention and voted for Adams, whom he did not personally like.

There is no limit to the power of prayer as long as ideas from the mind of God can pass into the receptive minds of men.

Dear Father, help me to prove in my own experience that prayer can strengthen and purify my character. May I have the faith to see that prayer is one of the ways in which thou dost work in the lives of men and in the world. Amen.

THURSDAY—Week 11

THE VALUE OF LOOKING AT THE HEAVENS
Read Ps. 34

"Prayer seems to me a good deal like stargazing," said a young man. "I can't seem to link it to the practical things of life." Did you ever feel that way about it? Then remember that the people who spend their time looking at the heavens are the ones who control many vital aspects of our daily lives. We get our time from the heavenly bodies. Every time you look at your watch you are indebted to the stargazer. Whenever you write a date on a letter, keep an appointment, or get to your class or your work on time, you ought to thank the astronomer for what he has accomplished by gazing at the stellar regions.

Much of the knowledge that controls our practical affairs has come from those who were looking far away and were once considered mere dreamers. The most important part of our day may be the time we spend in seeking the face of the Eternal.

O Lord our God, keep me from being earthbound in my outlook. May the light of thy truth and love shine upon me and illumine my pathway. Help me to walk in the right direction and to make right decisions because I am seeking thy guidance. Amen.

FRIDAY—Week 11

PRAYER REQUIRES PRACTICE
Read Ps. 63

Paderewski said that if he stopped practicing on the piano for a single day he could notice the difference in his playing; if he stopped for two days his family knew it; if he stopped for three days his friends knew it; and if he did not practice for a week his public knew it.

Discipline and perseverance are essential to success in acquiring any kind of skill. Why should we think that we can learn the greatest art of life by giving to our praying only a few hurried minutes at irregular times? When a young man said to his minister that he wished prayer meant as much to him as to his mother, the pastor asked: "How long has she been praying?"

"Every day for forty years," replied the youth.

"Keep on praying daily for the same number of years," said the minister, "and prayer will produce the same results in your own life."

O God, help me to understand that there is no easy way to secure any of the great blessings of life. With earnest spirit and persistent mind may I ask and seek and knock, so that the door of spiritual truth may be opened unto me. Amen.

SATURDAY—Week 11

JESUS TELLS HOW TO PRAY   Read Matt. 6:1-8

In the Sermon on the Mount, Jesus gave his disciples simple instructions on how to pray. "Enter into thy closet," he said. We would do well to have a special place regularly used for prayer that reminds us of God. "Shut the door," Jesus added. One needs quiet and seclusion. A person can pray to God anywhere, but he will be better able to pray amid distracting influences if he regularly has his own quiet place. A worship corner, or a picture of Christ on the wall, will help us to center our thoughts upon God.

By his example Jesus taught the disciples to pray early in the morning. If we are wise we will direct our thoughts toward God when we first awaken, for what we think of in the morning helps to give tone to the day. We will pray also at night, for, knowing the power of the subconscious, we will not wish to go to sleep without thinking of God. Knowing that the mind is active while we sleep, should we not seek to make it active on the highest level?

Dear Father, lead me closer to thyself through prayer. May I remember thee in the morning, knowing that those who seek thee early will find thee. May I be conscious of thy presence throughout the day, and may I meditate upon thee in the night watches, that thy Spirit may be round about me as I sleep. Amen.

THE LORD'S PRAYER

SUNDAY—Week 12

OUR FATHER WHO ART IN HEAVEN   Read Matt. 6:9-15

In Dickens' *Bleak House* the chimney sweep, who is called "Little Joe," became ill with tuberculosis. Allan Woodcourt went to visit him and inquired if he knew how to pray. The boy, whose life had been entirely lacking in religious background, answered that he didn't know any prayer. The visitor asked him to repeat the Lord's Prayer after him. Allan began with the words, "Our Father which art in heaven."

Little Joe repeated the words and stopped. Then he said again, "Our Father," and added, "That's very good, Sir."

There are no better or greater words in the whole language of religion. They remind us that God is not a judge or a policeman, but a being of love; that he is the Father not only of the individual, but of all mankind. Every true prayer must begin by keeping in mind the great ideas for which these two words stand.

Thou Father of all, renew my faith that above all earthly changes thy love standeth sure. Teach me how to treat my fellow men as brothers, that we may live happily together in this great universe which thou hast created as our home. Amen.

MONDAY—Week 12

HALLOWED BE THY NAME   Read Exod. 3:1-6

The first petition in the Lord's Prayer is a rebuke to the irreverence of our age. We use the name of God carelessly and say, "I didn't mean anything by it." But if we remember that God is our Creator and the sustaining love of the universe, such profane words will die upon our lips and turn into a prayer.

We need to recall the story of the spider whose web was supported by a long thread on which she slid down from the rafters of the barn. The spider laid its eggs and hatched a family. The little spiders were playing tag when one of them spied the filament which ran up to the roof above. Not realizing its importance, the young spider snapped the thread, and the web fell in ruins.

Our civilization needs the thread of reverence which connects us with the higher values of life. Without it, our lives and our society are in danger of moral collapse.

Father above, give me such a sense of thy gracious majesty that I may ever hallow thy name. "Let the words of my mouth, and the meditation of my heart, be acceptable in thy sight, O Lord, my strength, and my redeemer." Amen.

TUESDAY—Week 12

THY KINGDOM COME   Read Matt. 13:1-23

The phrase "The kingdom of God," or its equivalent "The kingdom of heaven," was used by Jesus more than one hundred times. The great concern of his life was to establish upon earth a civilization in which people would live together as brothers because they recognized God as their Father and King.

To advance this cause has since been the earnest ambition of every sincere Christian.

A woman in the southern mountains went a long distance to attend a church conference which spent its time discussing problems of the world-wide kingdom of God. Much of what she heard was new to her, and when she arose to leave, she said: "I can't do much about some of these matters, but I will go back and bring the kingdom as far as my own home." That is the way to start. Do what you can where you are.

I thank thee, O God, for the blessed hope of a better world which has haunted the minds of the noblest souls of every age, and for Jesus' vision of a kingdom where men would be ruled by thy love. Help me always to keep the vision bright and glowing and to do my part for its achievement. Amen.

WEDNESDAY—Week 12

THY WILL BE DONE   Read Matt. 26:36-47

"I suppose it is God's will, because I hate it so," said a young man who was sincerely religious, but had little understanding of what it means to do God's will.

Some people think that the will of God is something unpleasant, a bitter medicine, good for one's health but not to be taken without a wry face.

Many times when people express resignation to God's will in a time of disappointment or sorrow, what has happened is not the working out of God's purpose, but a denial of it.

God desires that men should live the abundant life and have health, food, education, friendship, and freedom from oppression. My surrender to God's will means that I give him the opportunity to work out his purposes of love for me and to make my life a channel through which he can achieve his high goals for mankind.

Eternal Goodness, keep me from being resigned to the evils that ought to be banished from thy world. Help me to do thy will with gladness, remembering that I am not thy slave but thy child, who has the privilege of sharing with thee in the work of thy kingdom. Amen.

THURSDAY—Week 12

GIVE US THIS DAY OUR DAILY BREAD
Read Matt. 14:13-21

Jesus was not a pious dreamer who ignored the practical needs of men. He healed their bodies as well as their souls, fed the multitude in the wilderness, and taught his disciples to ask God for daily bread. "Needful," rather than "daily," is perhaps closer to his thought. Jesus was suggesting that men pray, not for strawberry shortcake and quail on toast, but for the food necessary to keep their bodies fit for work.

Notice that Jesus says "Give us." God's children sit around a common table. No person has a right to grab more than he needs while others starve. If we use our imagination to look out over a needy world, we shall see countless people stretching out their hands and crying, "Give us our daily bread."

Whether the prayer is answered depends in part on our generosity and on what we do to help establish principles of justice among all people.

O God, we find thee in the hearts of common folk striving for bread, for justice and freedom, and for human brotherhood. As we share their struggle and bear our part in the danger and the suffering, we meet thee face to face, for thou art in the midst of them. Amen.—James Myers.

FRIDAY—Week 12

FORGIVE US OUR TRESPASSES
Read Matt. 18:21-35

How much is involved in the petition "Forgive us our trespasses as we forgive those who trespass against us"! We are asking God to forgive us to the extent that we forgive other people. Do we really mean what we say? Do we want God to forgive us in the same way that we forgive Germans and Japanese? That is what we are praying for.

During these days of bitterness we may think that forgiveness is too difficult a virtue for the average person to practice, yet it has been a distinctive characteristic of great Christians throughout all centuries. Abraham Lincoln was able to stand on a battlefield of the Civil War and say, "With malice toward none." Like a refreshing breeze in a stifling atmosphere is the plea of Madame Chiang Kai-shek that people in the Allied nations keep themselves free from hatred and resentment.

Father of love, give me the grace to put resentment and malice out of my heart and to forgive others as I desire to be forgiven by thee. Help me to practice the new commandment given by Jesus, that men should love one another. Amen.

SATURDAY—Week 12

LEAD US NOT INTO TEMPTATION   Read Phil. 4:1-9

Ulysses, returning from the siege of Troy, wanted to hear the famous sirens whose singing had lured so many hapless sailors to their doom. After pouring wax into the ears of his seamen, he had himself bound to the mast.

The dangerous island drew near, and Ulysses could hear the sirens; but since his men were temporarily deaf and Ulysses himself could not reach the rudder, the ship passed safely by instead of striking the rocks.

Orpheus, the divine musician, later, sailed over the same course. His crewmen needed no wax in their ears to insure the safety of the ship, for Orpheus played his harp and sang so beautifully that his sailors never heard the sirens.

A positive, not negative, act is the Christian ideal. Far better, is it not, to live a life so filled with interesting activities and an awareness of the finer things that the notes of the harp drown out the siren voices?

Heavenly Father, help me to create for myself an environment of beauty and goodness, that the evil things, which have power to wreck my life, will have no charm for me. So may I overcome evil with good, and show myself to be a true follower of thy son. Amen.

THE BLESSED ATTITUDES

SUNDAY—Week 13

THE POOR IN SPIRIT AND THE MEEK   Read Matt. 5:1-12

The Sermon on the Mount, found in the fifth, sixth, and seventh chapters of Matthew, is a brief summary of Jesus' teachings. It begins with the beatitudes—the "blessed attitudes"—which give Jesus' formula for happiness. The first and third, dealing with the poor in spirit and the meek, have a similar meaning. Do not confuse meekness with weakness, or think that to be poor in spirit means to be poor spirited. The main idea back of both beatitudes is that one should be open-minded and receptive to new ideas, willing to be guided and molded by the spirit of God rather than conceitedly thinking one has a corner on the truth.

To be meek and poor in spirit means to have the attitude of the scientist Huxley, who said one should be willing to sit down before facts like a little child and follow where they lead. The teachable person is the one whom Jesus calls blessed.

> Take thou our minds, dear Lord, we humbly pray;
> Give us the mind of Christ each passing day;
> Teach us to know the truth that sets us free;
> Grant us in all our thoughts to honor thee. Amen.

MONDAY—Week 13

BLESSED ARE THEY THAT MOURN   Read Ps. 84

Jesus did not mean that every person becomes blessed because of his mourning, but only that there is a way to endure disappointment so that it becomes a minister of good. His thought is like that of the Psalmist who spoke of passing through the valley of Baca a barren place and making it a well.

Inner peace for one's self and joy for others may be the outcome of suffering rightly borne. Instead of brooding in self-pity, a man can make adversity a servant of his higher life. Henry F. Durant, Boston lawyer, was plunged into grief by the death of his only son. What was the result? Transforming his love for his child into a desire to help other young people secure an education, he established Wellesley College. He found comfort in the joy of giving opportunity to others.

Father, when adversity becomes my lot, keep me from being bitter. Place thy everlasting arms around me and support me by thy love. May my sorrow give me greater sympathy with all suffering humanity and lead me to find my comfort in helping to ease the load of those whose burden is heavier than my own. Amen.

TUESDAY—Week 13

HUNGER AND THIRST AFTER RIGHTEOUSNESS
Read Phil. 3:7-21

When Nathaniel Shaler was dean of the Harvard Scientific School, young men used to come to him to talk about their life plans. "What do you want to be?" he would ask. When the youth had expressed his greatest desire, the dean would say, "Be that." He was sure that anyone who had a controlling purpose could achieve it.

Whatever may be the case from the standpoint of one's occupation, it is true that the one who has a consuming passion for a good life can attain his ambition. Jesus does not say that one can acquire goodness by dreaming about it, or by praying, as Augustine did, "O Lord, make me pure," and then adding, "but not now!" The Master's teaching is that one must want moral strength as a starving man hungers for food, as a thirsty sailor in a lifeboat wants fresh water. In the moral and spiritual realm, such passionate desires are always granted.

> Take thou our wills, Most High! Hold thou full sway;
> Have in our inmost souls thy perfect way;
> Guard thou each sacred hour from selfish ease;
> Guide thou our ordered lives as thou dost please. Amen.

WEDNESDAY—Week 13

BLESSED ARE THE MERCIFUL
Read John 8:1-11

When William E. Gladstone was Chancellor of the Exchequer, he made a speech on government finances before the House of Commons in which he quoted some figures that had been prepared for him by a treasury clerk. It happened that a glaring mistake had been made in the statistics, and the newspapers were quick to call it to public attention.

It was a humiliating experience for Gladstone, who always prided himself on his accuracy. He personally assumed the responsibility for the error and then congratulated the clerk on never having before made a serious error in handling difficult figures.

The clerk had expected to lose his job and was overwhelmed by the greateartedness of his chief. One does not need to be told that throughout the rest of the man's life he was a devoted follower of Gladstone.

Thy goodness and love are ever round about me, O God, and I thank thee that I am the recipient of divine blessings which I have done nothing to deserve. Give me thy spirit of mercy that I may have compassion upon my fellow men. Amen.

THURSDAY—Week 13

BLESSED ARE THE PURE IN HEART   Read Ps. 51

Do you sometimes wonder why it is so difficult to make God a real presence in your life? Jesus says one reason is that our spiritual vision is clouded by the veil which is created between our lives and God when we fail to keep our hearts pure.

An old man who was living by himself complained to a neighbor woman that he was losing his eyesight. He said he could no longer look out of the window and see the beauty of the outside world. The woman took some soap and water and cleaned the windows, which were covered with dust and dirt. To the old man's delight, he could see as clearly as ever. "It was not your eyesight," said the woman. "You allowed your windows to get dirty."

If your vision of God has grown dim, you need to clean the windows of your soul. The pure in heart will find it easy to see God.

Deliver me, O God, from the bondage of unwholesome thoughts. Give me a clean mind and a pure heart. Renew a right spirit within me and grant that nothing may be able to veil my eyes from a clear view of thyself. Amen.

FRIDAY—Week 13

BLESSED ARE THE PEACEMAKERS   Read Mic. 4:1-7

The Chinese have three words meaning "peace." One of them—"Ping"—is formed by two signs. One of the signs means a heart. The other sign, which consists of two horizontal lines, stands for "two." The idea underlying the word is this: When two hearts are level with each other, we have the conditions necessary for peace.

If one person is cherishing resentment and hoping to get even, the hearts are not level. If one nation is trying to keep the other nation down, the hearts are far from level. So those who would be peacemakers must put the hearts of men in the right relationship to each other.

Peace is not simply the cessation of fighting and the laying down of arms; it is the disarming of the nation's mind through the practice of goodwill. Millions of people are needed as peace-makers, and God's blessing will be upon them all.

Hasten the day, O God of all nations, when the angel's song of peace on earth, goodwill to men, may once more be heard throughout the world. Cleanse my heart of hate. Teach me to forgive my enemies and guide me in establishing righteous relationships with all men. Amen.

SATURDAY—Week 13

PERSECUTED FOR RIGHTEOUSNESS' SAKE Read Acts 12

Whittier believed that the movement to free the slaves repre-sented the greatest cause of righteousness in his generation, and he became one of the ardent leaders of the Abolitionists. Naturally timid and bashful, he knew what it meant to be denounced by the newspapers and criticized by public leaders.

He was threatened with physical violence and on one occasion escaped from a mob only by fleeing in disguise. But listen to the advice which he gave in his old age when he was talking to a young man about the worthwhile things of life: "My son, if thou wouldst win success, join thyself to some unpopular but noble cause."

If you have the courage to speak out against injustice and wrong, you may not have an easy time, but you will have the bless-ing which comes from being true to your conscience and from helping to advance the cause of righteousness.

O Lord, thou dost present to every man the choice between being a hero and a coward. Make me brave to speak the truth and to be a ready defender of the right. May I not be afraid of what others may say or do so long as I have the consciousness of thy approval. Amen.

OTHER HIGHLIGHTS FROM THE SERMON ON THE MOUNT

SUNDAY—Week 14

THE SALT OF THE EARTH   Read Gen. 18:16-33

Salt was an important article in the ancient world. Its scarcity made it valuable, and soldiers were sometimes paid in salt instead of money. Our word "salary" has its origin in this fact. Salt was used as a flavoring and as an antiseptic, but its main function was to preserve things. It prevented decay. When Jesus called his disciples the salt of the earth, he meant that their influence would keep society from rotting and going to pieces.

Moral character is the chief safeguard of any community. God told Abraham that he would save the city of Sodom if there were ten righteous people in it; but the ten could not be found, and there was no hope for its future. If civilization is to be preserved, there must be people whose lives contain the saving salt of Christian integrity.

My Lord and Master, keep my life from losing its distinctive flavor as thy follower. Strengthen my Christian convictions lest I conform so much to the standards of those around me that my life becomes insipid and worthless. Amen.

MONDAY—Week 14

THE LIGHT OF THE WORLD   Read Matt. 5:13-16

The modern hypocrite is not the man who goes around wearing a cloak of piety, but the one who pretends to be worse than he really is. He will not publicly acknowledge the ideals which he secretly cherishes in his soul. He still has Christian convictions, but he never defends them before others. He drinks with the crowd and appears to have a good time, although he doesn't enjoy it and the taste of liquor is unpleasant to him. There is still light in his heart, but he hides it under a bushel.

Back in the days of Queen Anne, every Englishman who lived in a village and owned a certain amount of property was compelled by law to put a lighted lamp in front of his house every evening from seven until eleven o'clock. Each person did his part toward having a community where people could walk without stumbling. Put your light out where others can see it. You will be glorifying God and helping to dispel the darkness.

Thou who art the Light of the World, illumine my life by a knowledge of thy truth. Make me a child of light, bravely letting my light shine in the night around me that others may see my good works and glorify our Father in heaven. Amen.

TUESDAY—Week 14

FULFILLING THE PAST   Read Matt. 5:16-37

We never outgrow the past; we grow out of it. One of our present needs is for wisdom enough to know what to keep from our heritage and what to throw away. Jesus said that he did not come to destroy the teachings of Moses and the prophets but to fill them full of new meaning. This is the attitude every generation should have toward its past.

You young people are radical and critical. Thank God that you are! You wish to go to the roots of things and appraise them by their present value. But in your impatience you are apt to cast away something you ought to keep.

When the French people revolted against Louis XVI, they threw away everything which belonged to the monarchy; but by breaking so violently with the past, they did not create a new nation. They brought the Reign of Terror and paved the way for Napoleon. You must learn to "prove all things" and "hold fast that which is good."

I thank thee, Lord, for the blessings which come to me from the past. Teach me to cherish my heritage, but give me the courage to look toward the future. May I never be held back by the past when I ought to launch my Mayflower in some new venture for thee. Amen.

WEDNESDAY—Week 14

THE SECOND MILE   Read Matt. 5:38-48

Do not overlook the "plus" element that runs through Jesus' teachings in the Sermon on the Mount. He asks people to do more than their duty, to have an overflowing generosity of spirit. "Whosoever shall compel thee to go a mile, go with him twain," says Jesus. If the hated Roman soldier impresses you into his service on a hot day and makes you carry his pack for a mile over the dusty road, do not do simply what you have been forced to do and then sullenly throw the pack at his feet as you hasten away. Go with him two miles, surprise him with your cheerfulness, and leave him as a friend instead of an enemy.

For many people life is joyless slavery, with duty as the task-master. They do what they know to be right, but only under a feeling of compulsion. Says Goethe: "It is not doing the thing which we like to do, but liking to do the thing which we have to do, that makes life blessed."

Dear God, help me to know the joy of walking with thy Son in the companionship of the second mile. Let me not, like Peter, follow him afar off. Keep me from being a minimum Christian. Grant me an overflowing enthusiasm for thy work and a boundless love for my fellowmen. Amen.

THURSDAY—Week 14

THE BEST INVESTMENT   Read Matt. 6:19-34

Everyone has something to invest. He has the money which he makes, his time, his ability, his enthusiasm, his life. What shall we do with this treasure so that we may run no risk of losing it and at the same time receive the largest dividends?

We have a choice between two types of investment. We can invest ourselves in the bank of the world or the bank of Christ. We can spend ourselves primarily on physical satisfactions or on character. The first means treasure on earth, the second treasure in heaven.

We sometimes hear people say, "No one can take his money with him when he dies." They are mistaken. If your money has been used for the enrichment of human minds, the strengthening of character, the development of goodwill, the spreading of the gospel of Christ, it has become immortal. It is treasure laid up in heaven and will pay dividends through all eternity.

I have but one life to live, my Father. Grant that I may spend it on the things that endure. Deliver me from the bondage of those fleeting pleasures which charm for a moment, but bring no lasting satisfaction. Help me to set my affections on higher values. Amen.

FRIDAY—Week 14

THE NARROW ROAD   Read Matt. 7:1-14

To walk in the narrow road does not mean that one becomes a narrow man. The very opposite is true. It is by traveling over a narrow road that we ourselves become broad. Our powers are enlarged, and our latent abilities are developed. Jesus advises us to follow the narrow way, not because he wants to make life hard or uncomfortable, but because it is the only path that leads to life's highest satisfactions.

The one who diligently seeks to perfect his ability as a scholar, a musician, a scientist, or an expert in any realm is always on a straitened path. He narrows his life to the pursuit of one major aim, but by so doing he becomes a man of broad powers.

Do not be deceived by the appearance of the other road, nor misled by the phrases that describe it. If you are traveling the wide and easy way, you are in danger of ending in a blind alley. If you are taking the narrow way, you will reach the abundant life.

O God, keep me from being like the vagrant who wanders aimlessly down the broad highway. Save me from self-indulgence and love of ease. Help me to choose a high goal and to put myself under the discipline that will enable me to attain it. Amen.

SATURDAY—Week 14

THE TWO BUILDERS Read Matt. 7:21-29

Jesus ended the Sermon on the Mount with an illustration which doubtless came out of his experience as a carpenter. He said that the one who followed his teachings, working them out in actual life, would be like a wise man who built his house on a rock foundation. The person who listened to his words and flattered him by saying "Lord, Lord" but did not seriously try to obey him would be like a foolish man building a fair-weather house on the sand.

A religion which goes no farther than words will not provide adequate undergirding for the life of an individual or a nation. Sermons and discussion groups have little value until they are translated into Christian conduct and social action.

The religion which stands the test is the one which consists of doing what Jesus said instead of being content with saying what Jesus did.

Father, I would build my life on enduring foundations. Grant that I may see in Jesus Christ a revelation of the truth which is eternal. May I faithfully obey his teachings, that I may victoriously face every situation that life may bring. Amen.

LOVING GOD WITH ONE'S MIND

SUNDAY—Week 15

BELIEF DETERMINES CONDUCT   Read Mark 12:28-34

When one of the scribes asked Jesus which was the first and greatest commandment, Jesus answered: "Thou shalt love the Lord thy God with all thy heart, and with all thy soul, and with all thy mind, and with all thy strength." He was quoting from Deuteronomy except that he added one phrase, "with all thy mind." In doing so Jesus gave to the Christian religion an intellectual content which has often been ignored by his followers. If we are to be his disciples, we must put our brains into our religion. Our minds must be dedicated to the service of God.

We frequently hear the statement, "I don't care what a person believes. The only important thing is what he does." How superficial! What a person does is the result of what he believes. His actions are the expressions of his thoughts. What we think about God will determine the way in which we live for him.

Give me an alert mind, O God, dedicated to thy service. Grant that I may serve thee with the understanding of a son or daughter rather than the ignorance of a slave. Amen.

MONDAY—Week 15

FIRSTHAND RELIGION   Read John 4:27-42

Most people start out in life with a secondhand religion. They accept the faith of their parents, or their pastor, or some of their teachers. Such a faith is not to be despised; but as you grow older, you should have the religious sincerity and mental energy to work out a faith which is based on your own thought and experience.

It is better to wear a secondhand suit, handed down from father to son, than to be entirely without clothes; but as you grow older you should think things through for yourself and be able to say with the Samaritans who lived near Jacob's well: "Now we believe, not because of thy saying: for we have heard him for ourselves, and know that this is indeed the Christ, the Saviour of the world."

You cannot climb very high on the ladder of spiritual life with borrowed faith. If your religion is to be vital, it must be your own.

69

Guide me by thy Holy Spirit, O God, and lead me into thy truth. Help me to have a faith that is free from sham and make-believe because I am loving thee with all my mind and seeking to express my religion in my daily life. Amen.

TUESDAY—Week 15

RELIGION MAY BE A CURSE OR A BLESSING
Read John 16:1-15

Whether religion becomes a joke, a curse, or a blessing depends on the degree of intelligence with which it is directed. Some people think they are most religious when they shout, roll over in the church aisle, or talk gibberish. They claim to be filled with the Holy Spirit, but seem not to know that Jesus said the function of the Holy Spirit is to lead people to a knowledge of the truth.

Other people, because of an intense faith in God, have hated and persecuted and killed. Rev. Cotton Mather was a conscientious minister, but he played a tragic role in burning helpless people as witches because he failed to use ordinary common sense in interpreting the verse in Exodus which says, "Thou shalt not suffer a witch to live."

If spiritual devotion is harnessed to ignorance, it discredits Christ and the church. We need a new type of saintliness which combines character and intelligence.

> O God, I offer thee my heart—
> In many a mystic mood by beauty led,
> I give my heart to thee. But now impart
> That sterner grace, to offer thee my head. Amen.

WEDNESDAY—Week 15

DOES YOUR MENTAL CLOCK NEED REWINDING?
Read II Tim. 2:1-15

"His clock stopped in 1819," wrote a biographer about the English statesman Sir Robert Peel. What did the author mean? Simply that Peel had stagnated mentally. As a young man he acquired a reputation as a financier. He was chairman of a special committee which made a report to Parliament on the Bank of England and brought about needed changes. Then he rested on his laurels. He was no longer interested in any national reform. He closed his mind, locked the door, and lost the key. The clock of his creative intellect ran down when he was in his early thirties.

The future of the postwar world depends on young people who faithfully rewind their mental clocks by reading and study. Constructive solutions are needed for the problems of racial antagonism and class cleavage, of national and international organization. Only thinking that is straight, critical, and unprejudiced can blaze the trail to a new world.

Thou God of all wisdom, give me a mind that is eagerly seeking the truth. Save me from prejudice and narrowness; keep me from shutting the door of my mind against facts which are unpleasant. May I know the truth that will make me free. Amen.

THURSDAY—Week 15

THE DEBT OF THE CHURCH TO ITS WISE MEN
Read Matt. 2

When Jesus was born in Bethlehem, the Magi came to worship at his manger and to present him with their treasures. Down through the centuries the cause of Christ has been advanced by wise men who have offered their learning to his service.

Think of the debt we owe to men like John Wycliffe and William Tyndale, who gave us our English Bible. Wycliffe was a fourteenth-century professor at Oxford and one of the greatest scholars of England. He made a complete translation of the Bible from Latin into English. A little over one hundred years later, Tyndale, an even more learned man, made a new English translation from the Greek and Hebrew. Both men suffered persecution; Tyndale was condemned as a heretic, strangled, and burned at the stake.

The great days of Christianity are those when it has the leadership of educated and dedicated minds. Whatever you have by way of education, offer it to Christ.

I thank thee, O God, for all the wise men who have brought the church the gifts of their wisdom and given it leadership in difficult times. Raise up among us today those who will grasp the shining sword of truth and go forth to do valiant battle for thee. Amen.

FRIDAY—Week 15

A BRILLIANT FAILURE
Read II Sam. 18

Aaron Burr was one of the most brilliant men America ever produced. He was the grandson of Jonathan Edwards, and the son of the president of Princeton College. He graduated from Princeton with the highest marks any student in that college had ever received. Talented and handsome, he was looked upon as a young man from whom great achievements might be expected. He ought to have held a place in our history like that of Washington or Jefferson; but he died a lonely and despised outcast. He intrigued against Washington during the Revolution, murdered Alexander Hamilton in a duel, and was tried as a traitor to his country though not convicted.

What was the reason for such a tragic ending to a promising career? He used his intellectual gifts only for the advancement of personal ambition. In his mind there was no love of God. A brilliant but undedicated intellect is a dangerous possession and often causes more harm than good.

O Thou who art the Light of the minds that know thee, the Life of the souls that love thee, and the Strength of the thoughts that see thee; help us so to know thee that we may truly love thee, so to love thee that we may fully serve thee, whose service is perfect freedom; through Jesus Christ our Lord. Amen.—A.D. 494.

SATURDAY—Week 15

THE CHURCH NEEDS TRAINED LEADERS Read Rom. 10

In his letter to the Romans, Paul refers to people who have "a zeal of God, but not according to knowledge." How often church people are zealous workers but will not spend their time in learning how to perform their service in the most effective way! A person assumes responsibility for a Sunday school class but knows little about teaching and less about the Bible. Young people accept the presidency of youth groups but give no earnest study to the way by which they can have better societies. The church needs people who will take time for training.

An ancient Norse legend tells how Odin as a young man became the leader of the gods. Knowing that only the wisest person was deserving of leadership, he exchanged his right eye for a drink from the well of wisdom. None but those who are willing to acquire knowledge at the cost of sacrifice are worthy of being leaders in the church.

O teach me, Lord, that I may teach
    The precious things thou dost impart
And wing my words, that they may reach
    The hidden depths of many a heart. Amen.

HOW CAN WE TELL RIGHT FROM WRONG?

SUNDAY—Week 16

THE CONFUSION ABOUT MORAL STANDARDS
Read I Kings 3:4-15

Old ideas of right and wrong are being challenged. People who seem to be equally sincere live by widely differing standards, and amid all the conflicting opinions people are asking the question, "How can I tell what is the right thing for me to do?" Let us remember that the experience of the ages has found that there are some things which are basic to decent living. As Washington Gladden said:

> While the anchors that faith had cast
> Are dragging in the gale,
> I am quietly holding fast
> To the things that cannot fail.
>
> I know that right is right,
> That it is not good to lie;
> That love is better than spite,
> And a neighbor than a spy.

Heavenly Father, when I stand at the crossroads and am in doubt which way I should go, help me to see the signs thou has placed for my guidance. And above the confused cries of men, may I hear the voice say, "This is the way, walk ye in it." Amen.

MONDAY—Week 16

THE TEST OF UNIVERSALITY
Read Exod. 19:1-9

When you are claiming the freedom to do as you please, ask yourself this question: "What would happen if everyone did what I wish to do? Would I want to live in the kind of world where such conduct became the accepted rule?"

An English tale of long ago tells about a young man named Beryn, who sailed on a ship which was blown off its course and came to port in the Land of Lies. It was an unhappy place where no one told the truth and every man cheated his neighbor. The innocent Beryn was accused of all sorts of crimes he had not committed; but, being a man of ready wit, he soon became the best liar

73

in the land and was made prime minister. His first act was to call a public meeting and explain that people could never live together in happiness unless they could trust each other. Sick of a civilization based on deceit, the people unanimously voted new laws and changed the Land of Lies into the Kingdom of Truth.

None can live to himself in thy world, O God. Grant that I may ask no special favors or exemption, but may so conduct myself that I would be glad to have all people follow my example. Amen.

TUESDAY—Week 16

CONSCIENCE CANNOT BE IGNORED   Read Acts 9:1-22

In a sophisticated company the remark "Let your conscience be your guide" is often greeted with a laugh; yet we need not discard conscience as too old-fashioned to be a moral guide. A bird flies south and goes unerringly to its destination; its instinct keeps it from going wrong. So there is something within a person that will urge him in the right direction *provided he is sincere in his desire for guidance*. To be sure, what conscience tells us depends largely upon environment and training; still the average American is following a fairly safe guide if he lives up to the best that he knows.

Dr. Stuart N. Hutchison tells of a small boy whose father explained to him that conscience is the little voice that warns against wrong, and that it speaks louder and clearer when obeyed and grows faint when disobeyed. That night the boy said in his prayer, "O God, make the little voice loud." That is a prayer we all need to make.

O God, sent out thy light and thy truth and let them lead me. Guide me by thy spirit that I may forsake the lower path and follow the highway which represents thy will. Amen.

WEDNESDAY—Week 16

HOW DOES YOUR CONDUCT AFFECT YOUR PERSONALITY?
Read Rom. 8:1-10

In this age when so much emphasis is placed on personality, let us ask about those practices about whose moral status we are in doubt: "What will they do to my personality? Will they gradually enrich or degrade it?" The result of any course of conduct must be judged over a period of many years. Its consequences are usually not seen in a few weeks or months.

Take the disputed question of drinking. For a moment it may add to the gaiety and satisfaction of life, but look at the people who have been using liquor for a long time. Can you see the slightest evidence that their drinking, even in moderation, has made their personalities more attractive? On the other hand, do you not know scores of people on whom it has obviously had a corroding effect?

Anything is wrong that has a harmful effect on your personality. Put that down as an incontrovertible fact.

Guide me, teach me, strengthen me, till I become such a person as thou wouldst have me be; pure and gentle, truthful and high-minded, brave and able, courteous and generous, dutiful and useful.—Charles Kingsley.

THURSDAY—Week 16

USE ORDINARY COMMON SENSE   Read Matt. 25:1-13

Jesus made common sense one of the signposts pointing toward character. He said that the trouble with many people was their foolishness, and he urged men to act with intelligent foresight. The man who stored up money for the sake of physical enjoyment; the five virgins who neglected the preparation that would have enabled them to enter into a happy experience; the man who built his house on the sand—these and many others Jesus called foolish.

Sinfulness often has its origin in ignorance. We sometimes say "as smart as the devil." It would be more accurate to say "as foolish." Said Ben Jonson, "The Devil is an ass." People who do not recognize and obey the moral and physical laws of the universe are dumb. It is foolish to make thievery a substitute for honest work, to neglect one's health and become a physical wreck, to indulge in sensual pleasures and destroy the basis for a happy home life.

Here is another guide to what is right: Don't be a fool!

Thou God of Wisdom, keep me from playing the fool. Open my eyes to see more clearly the nature of the universe in which I live, that I may understand and obey thy laws and not be destroyed through ignorance. Amen.

FRIDAY—Week 16

ARE YOU AFRAID OF PUBLICITY?   Read I Cor. 3:11-17

Newspaper editors say there are two types of people who frequently come to their office—those who wish to get their names in the paper and those who are anxious to keep them out because they have become involved in some matter of which they are ashamed.

This suggests another test of whether a matter is right or wrong. Would you be willing to have everyone know what you have done? How would you feel if the daily paper made it a feature story with big headlines? Phillips Brooks once said some plain words about this matter: "To keep clear of concealment, to keep clear of the need of concealment, to do nothing which he might not do out on the middle of Boston Common at noonday, I cannot say how more and more that seems to me the glory of a young man's life. It is an awful hour when the first necessity of hiding anything comes.—Put off that day as long as possible."

Grant that I may do my duty faithfully, O God, and be conscious of thy approval. Help me to make my life an open book, that I may never be haunted by the dread that some hidden deed will be revealed. Amen.

SATURDAY—Week 16

WHAT WOULD JESUS HAVE ME DO?   Read John 1:35-51

There is a final authority for those who are in doubt as to what is right. Submit your conduct to the judgment of Christ and ask what he would have you do. Say what else we will about the life of Christ, we must admit that he is widely accepted as the noblest personality whom the world has ever known. His life has stood the test of time, so that George Matheson was voicing the opinion of mankind when he said: "Son of Man, whenever I doubt life I think of thee. Thou never growest old to me. Last century is old. Last year is obsolete fashion but thou are not obsolete. Thou are abreast of all the centuries and I have never come up to thee, modern as I am."

> O Lord and Master of us all
> Whate'er our name or sign,
> We own thy sway, we hear thy call,
> We test our lives by thine.

Thou living Christ, I thank thee that thou has given us an example of the stainless life. Help me to make my heart the dwelling place of thy spirit. Mold me into thy likeness and transform my weakness into thy strength. Amen.

FINDING JOY IN YOUR RELIGION

SUNDAY—Week 17

THE JOY OF JESUS   Read Luke 2:8-20

The Creator must have a sense of humor, for he made the world the kind of place in which the average healthy person finds frequent cause for laughter.

Jesus, who revealed the character of God, was one of the most joyous individuals who ever lived. His birth was heralded to the shepherds by an angel who proclaimed good tidings of great joy. His first public appearance was at a wedding, where he turned water into wine to save the host from embarrassment and add to the enjoyment of the guests. His last meeting with the disciples, according to John's Gospel, was around a campfire on the shore of Galilee.

Nothing is more false to the spirit of Jesus than to make him a gloomy person who interfered with people's good times. You are not a true follower of our Lord unless your religion puts a smile on your face and a song in your heart.

Open my eyes, O God, that I may see the beauty and joy of the world which thou hast made. Give me the spirit of Jesus, who said that sorrow could be turned into joy and who promised his disciples a joy that no one could take from them. Amen.

MONDAY—Week 17

HOW OFTEN DO YOU LAUGH?   Read Matt. 9:10-17

A newspaper article tells about an eighty-year-old man who kept a detailed record of what he had done during each hour of every day and then figured out how he used his time during the entire period of his long life. He spent over 26 years in sleep, 21 years working, 228 days shaving, and 140 days paying his bills. He also spent over 26 days scolding his children and 2 days yelling at his dogs. Only 26 hours were spent in laughing.

How unpleasant it must have been to live with a man who spent more days in scolding his children than hours in laughing!

Could it be said of you that you do more "grouching" than laughing? If so, you are no true follower of the Christ who compared himself and his disciples to a joyous wedding party on a prolonged honeymoon.

Give me a sense of humor, Lord,
　Give me the grace to see a joke,
To get some pleasure out of life,
　And pass it on to other folk. Amen.
　　　—From the Refectory, Chester Cathedral

TUESDAY—Week 17

DON'T CHEW YOUR PILLS   Read Ps. 100

On the bottle containing a certain brand of chocolate-coated cod-liver oil pills are these instructions: "These pills are to be taken preferably with milk or fruit juice. However, they can be chewed if desired." One cannot imagine why any person would wish to chew cod-liver oil pills and have the bitter taste linger in his mouth. But evidently some people enjoy chewing their pills, or such directions would not be given.

Jesus was not the kind of person to let unpleasant experiences remain in his memory. During the last night of his life, when he was facing the cross, he talked with his disciples about the joy he had found in life and expressed the hope that a similar joy would be theirs. When troubles came, he swallowed them and then went forward without bitterness. He never chewed his pills.

Forgive me, Father, that so often I become discontented and unhappy over trivial matters. Keep me from finding fault with others and blaming them for my unhappiness when the cause is in myself. Amen.

WEDNESDAY—Week 17

THE VALUE OF A SMILE   Read Ps. 95:1-6

A few years ago a Brooklyn girl was left a million dollars by a woman who explained the bequest by saying in her will: "She brings sunshine and happiness into my daily life."

A smiling face may not bring you a fortune, but it can be one of your greatest assets in making friends and achieving success.

The thing that goes the farthest toward making life worth while,
That costs the least and does the most, is just a pleasant smile.

It's full of worth and goodness, too, with manly kindness blent—
It's worth a million dollars, and it doesn't cost a cent.

Give us to awake with smiles, give us to labor smiling. As the sun returns in the east, so let our patience be renewed with dawn; as the sun lightens the world, so let our loving-kindness make bright this house of our habitation. Amen.—Robert Louis Stevenson.

THE DEVIL'S FAVORITE TOOL   Read John 16:20-33

It is said that the devil, prospering as a result of war and convinced that hell was already firmly established on earth, decided he no longer needed to work so hard and advertised most of his equipment for sale. However, he refused to part with one favored tool, which was labeled "discouragement." He knew that he would want it if he ever returned to active work. Said he, "When I get people downhearted and discouraged, they soon give up trying to lead good lives and easily come under my power."

The New Testament pictures Jesus as a cheerful person who habitually looked on the bright side of life. He counted his blessings instead of his misfortunes and frequently urged people to be of good cheer.

O thou Eternal Gladness, dwell within me with thy spirit of joy and hope. Teach me to be like the sundial, which records the sunshine but not the clouds and the rain. So may I go about with a smile on my face and scatter joy in the lives of others. Amen.

LIGHT SHINING IN DARKNESS   Read Ps. 38

Fanny Crosby, the blind hymn writer, was known among her friends for her cheerful outlook upon life. The affliction, which might have embittered her, was transformed into a source of sweetness and radiance. When only eight years old, she began to turn her darkness into light and wrote the words:

> O what a happy soul am I!
>   Although I cannot see,
> I am resolved that in this world
>   Contented I will be;
>
> How many blessings I enjoy
>   That other people *don't*.
> To weep and sigh because I'm blind,
>   I cannot, and I won't.

Give me grace, dear God, to belong to the glorious company of those who have a song in their hearts even when the night around them is dark. Grant that I may be able to make any affliction a stairway by which to climb into thy presence. Amen.

THE FELLOWSHIP OF SINGING HEARTS

Read Mark 14:12-26

Mark ends the account of the Last Supper by saying, "When they had sung a hymn, they went out into the Mount of Olives." The last act of Jesus before leaving the upper room to go out into the darkness of his arrest and crucifixion was to join his friends in a hymn. He belonged to what someone has called "the fellowship of singing hearts."

Great Christians have usually been great singers. John and Charles Wesley, Martin Luther, Isaac Watts, John G. Whittier, and many other shining souls have been lovers of music and have enriched our spiritual heritage with their hymns.

The early Christians were always singing. When cast into jail or thrown to the wild beasts in the arena, they met their fate with a faith that expressed itself in song. Surely this is an indication that a true Christian life is a source of inner joy!

For the sunshine and the gladness of the world, for beautiful flowers, for birds and souls that sing, for all that makes life glad and happy, I give thee thanks, O God. Help me to live in the light of thy love and to make my life a reflection of the joy that I see in the world around me. Amen.

THE PURSUIT OF HAPPINESS

SUNDAY—Week 18

HAPPINESS IS NOT FOUND BY SEARCHING

Read Ps. 34:1-8

The Declaration of Independence declares it a self-evident truth that the pursuit of happiness is one of the inalienable rights of mankind. While everyone has the right to pursue happiness, no one overtakes it simply by going after it. The one who chases pleasure never catches it.

Maeterlinck likens the search for happiness to the quest of a boy and girl who left home to find a bluebird. They said farewell to their father and mother and their bird at home and traveled through the land of memory and the kingdom of the future.

Failing to discover the object of their quest, they finally returned to their parents and for the first time noticed that the bird in their own house was blue.

If you cannot find happiness at home, you will hardly find it anywhere, for it depends not so much on where you live as on how you live.

Forgive me, dear Father, that I am so blind to the sources of happiness that are ever round about me. May I find happiness wherever I go because I carry it in my heart. So may I be a blessing to my family and friends. Amen.

MONDAY—Week 18

A HAPPINESS CLUB

Read Ps. 19

Alice Freeman Palmer, early president of Wellesley College, had a Happiness Club composed of girls in the poorest section of Boston. The girls asked how to be happy, and Mrs. Palmer gave them the following rules which she observed herself and said must be faithfully followed each day:

(1) Commit something good to memory each day.
(2) Look for something beautiful each day.
(3) Do something kind for someone every day.

Follow the rules persistently, and they will produce the desired results. If you study the life of Jesus you will find that his happiness came from sources similar to those of Mrs. Palmer.

Spirit of God, descend upon my heart and give me the happiness which no one can find by seeking but which is the fruit of a kind and loving life. May I keep the example of Jesus' goodness and love ever before me that I may learn from him. Amen.

TUESDAY—Week 18

A NEGLECTED SOURCE OF HAPPINESS

Read Luke 18:18-30

Dr. Wilfred T. Grenfell spent his life on the coasts of Labrador as a physician to fishermen who had lived and died without medical attention until he went to make his home among them. He cut himself off from his friends and the associations in England that meant so much to him during his early life. Traveling over the island with a dogsled, he faced biting cold and stormy weather and was several times in danger of death. Many people would have retreated from these hardships, but to Grenfell life in Labrador was a privilege and a joy.

A short time before he died, he spoke at the New York State Christian Endeavor Convention. He told of the happiness he had found in serving Christ among lonely folk who needed his help. On his weather-beaten face was a radiance which spoke louder than his words. He had learned what Jesus meant when he said, "It is more blessed to give than to receive."

Guide my feet, O God, along paths that will lead me to spiritual likeness to the Savior. May I not hesitate to carry a cross, knowing that I will receive from thee the crown of happiness. Amen.

WEDNESDAY—Week 18

GLOOMY CAESAR AND HAPPY JESUS Read Luke 16:17-26

Compare the life of Jesus with that of Tiberius Caesar, who was emperor of Rome during the time when the Master was doing his work in Palestine. Tiberius was the most powerful man of his day, with servants scurrying to do his bidding and unlimited wealth to gratify his desires. He had all of the things for which people usually long, and in the possession of which they think they would be happy. What was the result? Pliny, a Roman writer of the first century, refers to Tiberius as "the gloomiest of mankind."

Jesus, on the other hand, lacked the sources of amusement open to the Emperor. He spent most of his life working at hard manual labor as a carpenter; during his last years he was a homeless wanderer. Yet on the night before the crucifixion he was able to talk to his disciples about the joy he had found in life and to say, "Be of good cheer, I have overcome the world."

O Master, let me walk with thee
In lowly paths of service free;
Tell me thy secret; help me bear
The strain of toil, the fret of care. Amen.

THURSDAY—Week 18

THE MOUNTAIN OF MISERY

Read Ps. 37:1-9; Lam. 3:22-40

Addison's essay about the mountain of misery gives a humorous setting to an important truth. Jupiter issued a proclamation that all people might bring their miseries to one place and put them in a common heap. All sorts of people brought all sorts of troubles. Some brought their diseases; others brought their poverty; one man brought his wife.

When the pile was complete, Jupiter made a second decree saying each person should now choose some affliction in place of the one he had brought. Each person reluctantly made his choice until all the troubles were redistributed.

The people then made a sorry sight, for they were unhappier than before. They filled the plain with their complaining until Jupiter took pity on them and allowed each one to take back his own rightful burden. At the same time he sent a goddess named Patience to teach people how to adjust their loads and carry them in the easiest manner. Soon they were returning home in happiness.

Forgive me, O God, that I become unhappy so easily and often have a complaining spirit. Teach me thy patience and help me to keep closer company with thee. Grant that I may share with others my satisfactions in life and not my grievances. Amen.

FRIDAY—Week 18

HAPPINESS IN FORGETFULNESS OF SELF

Read Matt. 13:44-53

An English newspaper editor once offered a prize for the best answer to the question, "Who are the happiest people on earth?" The four winning answers were the following: a mother bathing her baby; a craftsman, or an artist, whistling over a job well done; a little child building castles in the sand; a doctor who has finished a difficult operation and saved a human life. Notice that all four people had one thing in common. None of them was engaged in a selfish pursuit of pleasure. Each was absorbed in some task that seemed important and that caused him to forget himself.

Jesus said happiness comes from devotion to some noble purpose. To illustrate the joy that one finds in doing the work of God's kingdom, he told the story of the man who gladly sold all that he had in order to buy the pearl of great price.

O Lord, renew our spirits and draw our hearts unto thyself that our work may not be a burden to us, but a delight. Oh, let us not serve thee with the spirit of bondage as slaves, but with the cheerfulness and gladness of children, delighting ourselves in thee and rejoicing in thy work. Amen.—Benjamin Jenks.

SATURDAY—Week 18

SOURCES OF HAPPINESS OPEN TO ALL
Read Luke 10:17-24

The main sources of joy are open to all on equal terms, whether they are rich or poor, of high or low estate. Jesus, who was the happiest of men, found satisfaction in the enjoyment of nature, in the ministry of helpfulness, in the love of friends; and back of it all was his abiding faith in the goodness of God. No one ever learns the first lesson in happiness until he starts to enjoy the simple blessings which provide the setting for the average life.

Dante, in his imaginary trip through hell, came to a great mudhole with bubbles oozing up through the slime. His guide explained that under the mud were the people who lived on earth without enjoying the lovely things made by God. They had been blind to the blessings around them and now their eyes were filled with mud.

Happy you are if you have eyes to see the ordinary things that should give you joy!

Heavenly Father, grant that I may not be deceived by the lure of glittering pleasures which last but for a moment and then fade away. May my eyes be ever bright with happiness because I find delight in simple joys whose lasting satisfactions all may share. Amen.

AS A MAN THINKETH

SUNDAY—Week 19

YOUR MIND IS THE RUDDER

Read Jas. 1:1-8

Mind is the rudder that steers the ship of life. Says the Book of Proverbs, As a man "thinketh in his heart, so is he." If you can control your thoughts, you can determine your destiny. You will be the master of your fate and the captain of your soul. If you do not learn how to govern your thoughts, you will be like a vessel with a broken helm which, tossed about by wind and tide, finally crashes on the rocks. Do you remember Longfellow's description of the way Hiawatha sailed his birch-bark canoe?

> Paddles none had Hiawatha,
> Paddles none he had or needed,
> For his thoughts as paddles served him,
> And his wishes served to guide him;
> Swift or slow at will he glided,
> Veered to right or left at pleasure.

Father, I thank thee that in making us in thy own image thou has endowed us with a mind and given us the capacity to think and choose for ourselves. Help me to control my thoughts and direct them toward noble ends. Amen.

MONDAY—Week 19

THOUGHTS AFFECT PHYSICAL STRENGTH
Read Matt. 21:18-22

A British scientist conducted a series of experiments on some young men to find out the extent to which the strength of their bodies was controlled by their thoughts. He first gave them tests to discover their physical strength under normal conditions. Then he hypnotized them, told them they were puny weaklings, and repeated the same tests. Their strength was reduced 30 per cent. While still under hypnotic influence, they were told emphatically that they were physical giants and had unlimited powers. Then the tests were given a third time. Not only did their strength go back to normal; it rose to 40 per cent above it.

Where did the extra strength come from? Not from the hypnotist but from within themselves. They had reserves of strength which they were not ordinarily using. What we do, and what we become, depends upon what we think.

Set me free, O Lord, from paralyzing thoughts of weakness and failure. Grant that by waiting upon thee in prayer I may renew my strength. May I find all things possible through my faith in thee. Amen.

TUESDAY—Week 19

VICTORY BY A CHANGE IN MENTAL OUTLOOK

Read Ps. 31

When Beethoven first became aware of his deafness, he was plunged into the depths of despair. "What a sorrowful life I must now live!" he wrote in a letter. "How happy I would be if my hearing were completely restored; but as it is I must draw back from everything, and the most beautiful years of my life will take wings without accomplishing all the promise of my talents and powers!"

Why was it that his pessimistic predictions for himself were not fulfilled? Not because his deafness was cured, but because he was able to control his inner life and acquire a different mental outlook. In a later letter he said: "There is no greater joy than for me to pursue and produce my art. I will seize fate by the throat; most assuredly it shall not get me wholly down. Oh, it is so beautiful to live life a thousandfold!" A change, not in his physical condition, but in his thinking, enabled Beethoven to fulfill his destiny.

Save me, my Father, from moods of pessimism and melancholy. Let not worry and despair make me their captives. Give me the faith to believe that thy grace is sufficient for my needs. So may I have courage to go forward and do my best for thee. Amen.

WEDNESDAY—Week 19

KILLED BY AN ILLUSION

Read Matt. 15:1-20

A story from Russia tells how a railway employee accidentally locked himself in a refrigerator car. Unable to escape or attract attention, he resigned himself to his fate. As he felt his body becoming numb, he recorded the story of his approaching death in sentences such as these, scribbled on the wall of the car:

"I am becoming colder. . . . Still colder. . . . I am slowly freezing. . . . Half asleep. . . . These may be my last words."

When the car was opened the man was dead, but the temperature of the car was 56 degrees. The freezing apparatus was, and had been, out of order. There was sufficient air in the car, and the man had not suffocated. There was no physical reason for the man's death. He was the victim of his own illusion. How carefully we need to guard the door of our minds, knowing the power that our ideas have over us!

O God, help me to banish the foolish fears that seek to undermine my life. Give me an abiding sense of thy presence and help me to know that I am never alone, for thou art with me. Because thou are my companion, may I face every situation in life without fear. Amen.

THURSDAY—Week 19

WHAT IS YOUR BIG IDEA   Read Phil. 3:7-14

The daily schedule of a boy's camp had a fifteen-minute period immediately after breakfast which was listed as "The Big Idea." During this interval every camper was expected to make out his program for the day, and especially to decide on the one activity which was to have his major attention. Said the camp director: "The value of your day depends on the idea you select and the way you work it out."

The camp director wanted the boys to learn that their usefulness to society would depend on the ideas which gripped their minds and which were released through them into the life of the world.

Is it not true that the greatness of every life depends on the ideas by which it is controlled? Think of the early followers of Christ. They were only ordinary men, but they became the channels through which Jesus' great ideas of love and brotherhood flowed out into society.

Keep me, O Christ, from becoming the victim of petty ideas. Give me a larger vision of right and duty and truth. Lead me into an understanding of thy purposes for mankind, and grant that my life, such as it is, may be an agency for their fulfillment. Amen.

FRIDAY—Week 19

THOUGHT IS CREATIVE   Read I Cor. 2

When Dwight L. Moody was holding evangelistic services in Chicago, he called the head usher to the platform and glanced toward one of the assistant ushers as he said: "Who is that man? I don't like his looks. His face repels me." The name of the assistant was Charles J. Guiteau, who later assassinated President Garfield. Disappointed in not being appointed to a coveted political office, Guiteau allowed his mind to become unbalanced by hate and selfish ambition.

The evil in a person's mind will reveal itself in his face and actions. The opposite idea is equally true. Good thoughts will inevitably make a good life. "He is always thinking about helping someone," said a minister of one of his church officers, "and see what radiance he has on his face."

Thinking is creative. Every thought finds some way to express itself. This is the reason Jesus laid so much emphasis on the quality of the inner life.

> Take thou our minds, dear Lord, we humbly pray;
> Give us the mind of Christ each passing day;
> Teach us to know the truth that sets us free;
> Grant us in all our thoughts to honor thee. Amen.

SATURDAY—Week 19

SAVED BY THE RENEWING OF HIS MIND

Read Eph. 4:13-31

A king summoned one of his subjects who was a notorious miser and placed before him a jeweled casket filled with gold. The miser's face gloated with greed. He was told that he must accept the money as a gift, but that his life would be forfeited if ever again a greedy look came on his face. At first the miser planned to control his expressions when in the presence of others, but to exult over his gold in secret.

He feared, however, that in some unguarded moment his face would reflect his thoughts. He decided that the only way to protect himself was to drive all selfish thoughts from his mind so that the forbidden expression could never appear on his countenance. He began to give away his money to those in need and to fill his heart with sympathy and kindness. Soon the face that had been repulsive with greed was transformed by love.

Forgive me, dear God, that my mind so often becomes filled with greedy and selfish desires. Help me to center my thoughts on thee and thy goodness, that my life may be controlled by thy spirit of love. Amen.

YOUR DUTY TO YOURSELF

SUNDAY—Week 20

CARING FOR YOUR BODY
Read Mark 5:25-34

Out of the two million men who were the first to be examined for the United States Army under the selective service system approximately half were rejected for physical reasons. The record shows that at the age of forty-five only three out of twenty men could pass the rigid examination; out of the same number only six could pass at the age of thirty-six, fourteen at the age of twenty-one, and fifteen at the ages of eighteen and nineteen. The physical examinations were afterward made less exacting, but the statistics plainly reveal that people are not caring for their bodies as they should. A Christian should keep at his best physically as well as morally and spiritually. Said Emerson, "A gentleman should be a good animal."

To be "whole" or "holy," one should be healthy. The religious man is not the anemic individual who tries to become a saint by neglecting his body. He is the one who dedicates his whole self—body, mind, and spirit—to the service of God.

O Eternal God, let my body be a servant of my spirit, and both body and spirit servants of Jesus; that, doing all things for thy glory here, I may be partaker of thy glory hereafter, through Jesus Christ our Lord. Amen.—Jeremy Taylor.

MONDAY—Week 20

LIVING WITH YOURSELF
Read Luke 15:11-24

When the prodigal son was feeding swine in the far country, "he came to himself." He had tried to run away from himself by traveling a long distance from home. He had supposed that his discontent was due to the people with whom he lived, but he found that the trouble was in his own life. Always and forever that is true of human experience. We keep coming back to ourselves and make no progress until we have solved our personal problems. In spite of all the complexities of our times, the basic duty of every man is to discover how to live happily with himself. This is essentially a religious matter, for in the last analysis it means learning how to live with God.

Jesus depicted the kingdom as a place of ideal relations with other people, but he also pointed out that it cannot come in the world until it comes in the individual heart. He said, "The kingdom of God is within you."

O Lord, come quickly and reign on thy throne, for now ofttimes something rises up within me and tries to take possession of thy throne; pride, covetousness, uncleanness, and sloth want to be my kings. O King of Peace, come and reign in me, for I will have no king but thee.—St. Bernard.

TUESDAY—Week 20

LOVE YOURSELF
Read Luke 10:25-28

One of the earliest sermons—perhaps the first—to be preached in America was that of Robert Cushman to the Pilgrim Fathers on "The Sin and Danger of Self-Love." Such a sermon is probably more needed in the prosperous America of today than it was three centuries ago on the bleak shores of New England. There is always a temptation to selfish living; but at the same time, there is too little of the self-love which results in the strengthening of character and the enrichment of personality.

A man's first duty is not to others but to himself. The greatest contribution you can make to a better world is the influence of yourself at your best. As Shakespeare says:

> to thine own self be true,
> And it must follow, as the night the day,
> Thou canst not then be false to any man.

My Father, while I seek to fill my heart with love for others, may I not forget to love myself. Save me from easygoing self-indulgence, and from becoming my own worst enemy. Help me to preserve my self-respect by being true to the best that I know. Amen.

WEDNESDAY—Week 20

KNOW YOURSELF
Read II Tim. 2:15-26

A dwarf was brought to a royal tea party to dance for the entertainment of a little princess. He was greatly elated at the applause he received and thought he was a marvelous dancer. He did not realize that the company was merely being entertained by his curious antics. Later in the day he made his way unnoticed into the palace and waltzed along until he saw a funny little man dancing at the other end of the hall. As he came closer he found that he was looking into a mirror and that the funny person was himself.

Have you ever seriously tried to follow out Socrates' great

maxim, "Know thyself"? You may be funnier than you have realized. Be honest with yourself and face the truth without any attempt at concealment. Only as you begin to realize your limitations, can you begin to strengthen yourself at your points of weakness.

Dear Father, help me to see myself, not only as others see me, but as thou dost see me. Then I shall rightly appraise my weakness and my strength, my wisdom and my folly, and begin to make my life more acceptable to thee. Amen.

THURSDAY—Week 20

ACCEPT YOURSELF
Read II Cor. 12:1-10

After you have studied your personality and abilities, you must accept what you find without evasion, self-pity, or conceit. You may wish you were more talented or beautiful, but it does no good to spend your time in whining or daydreaming. In the lives of many of the world's most successful men there have been handicapping facts that could not be escaped. Beethoven and Edison had their deafness; John Milton and George Matheson, their blindness; Paul, his thorn in the flesh; Franklin D. Roosevelt, his lameness; Abraham Lincoln, his gangling ungainliness.

Think of Lincoln, for a moment, as a single example. He knew he was homely and awkward, but he did not rebel against this. Probably it was hard for him when his political enemies called him a gorilla, but he went ahead with his career and did the best he could; and lo! he became the best-loved man of American history. As soon as you have accepted yourself, you can start on the road to achievement.

O Lord, thou knowest what is best for us, let this or that be done, as thou shalt please. Behold, I am thy servant, prepared for all things; for I desire not to live unto myself but unto thee; and oh, that I could do it worthily and perfectly! Amen.—Thomas à Kempis.

FRIDAY—Week 20

DEVELOP YOUR HIDDEN RESOURCES
Read Exod. 3:10-15

Oliver Wendell Holmes spoke of people who "die with all their music in them." He referred to the many people who have splendid potentialities which are unrealized. They never use their hidden resources to make themselves into the people they might be. The "possible you" is never developed.

Centuries ago when parchments for writing were scarce, one

which had already been used would be covered over and written on a second time. On such manuscripts, known by librarians as palimpsest, the original writing could be deciphered only after the letters which appeared on the surface had been scraped away. So every person has qualities which lie so deep within that they can never be released by living only on the surface of life. You can become the man you might be only when you find a high cause to stir your hidden devotion, a great affection to arouse your love, a spiritual Master to energize your soul.

Forgive me, dear Lord, for trying to satisfy myself with the superficial things of life and making no effort to discover its deeper values. Help me to know the power which is released by unselfish enthusiasm for some cause that commands my complete allegiance. Amen.

SATURDAY—Week 20

YOUR OWN PLACE
Read Acts 1:15-26

The Book of Acts, in describing the suicide of Judas, says that he went to his own place. His ultimate abode was peculiarly his own because it was determined by his own deeds. Was there ever a truer or terser summary of any man's life than this? Everyone goes to the place which belongs to him because he makes it for himself.

What one finally becomes, and where one goes, depends upon one's own choices and the course followed by one's own feet. Circumstances may help us on our way or conspire to hold us back, but we are never their slaves. We are free moral agents and not puppets in the hands of relentless fate.

Judas went to the place created by his treachery and his love of money. Jesus went to the place fashioned out of his steadfast loyalty to God's will. You go to your own place, and I go to mine. We owe it to ourselves to make it as beautiful as we can.

Thou hast made me for thyself, O God, and I am restless until I rest in thee. Grant that in my restlessness I may seek thee and find thee. Then may I abide in thy presence until it becomes the true home of my soul. Amen.

SOME PERSONAL QUESTIONS

SUNDAY—Week 21

WHAT IS YOUR NAME?   Read Gen. 32:24-32

"A good name is rather to be chosen than great riches," says the author of Proverbs; but no one has a chance to select his own name. It is given to him by his parents. Yet everyone can say what his name is to stand for, and in that sense he makes his own name. When Jacob became a transformed man, God gave him the name "Israel," which meant "a fighter for God." Your name takes on a new meaning when you begin to live for God and struggle for righteousness. Your name is worth something when it stands for character.

Robert E. Lee was a poor man after the Civil War. He was offered a salary of fifty thousand dollars a year by an insurance company to become its president. He was told that he would not need to do any work. All the company wanted was to use his name. Lee refused the offer, saying that if his name was so valuable, he must guard its integrity.

O God, make me worthy of the name given to me by my parents, and help me to keep it unsullied. May I make my life so kind, so friendly, so helpful to others, that they will come to think of my name as one to be loved and cherished. Amen.

MONDAY—Week 21

HOW OLD ARE YOU?   Read Gen. 5:21-27

Old people become proud of their age. Let a man live for one hundred years and he will pride himself on his attainment, although a long life is not necessarily an interesting or useful one. Methuselah lived 969 years and captured the long-distance record for human existence, but what did he accomplish? The Bible gives no evidence that he did anything of lasting value to mankind. Jesus died while still a young man, yet he filled his life with such glorious achievements that he has been gratefully remembered for nineteen hundred years. Says Philip James Bailey in "Festus":

We live in deeds, not years; in thoughts, not breaths;
In feelings, not in figures on a dial.

We should count time by heart-throbs. He most lives
Who thinks most—feels the noblest—acts the best.

Thou who art my Creator, help me to remember thee in the days of my youth. Grant that each year may be nobly and usefully lived. Let me not fritter away my time on trivial things but devote myself to the enduring cause of thy kingdom. Amen.

TUESDAY—Week 21

WHERE DO YOU LIVE?   Read John 1:35-42

Two men in a certain city were next-door neighbors. One was a Y.M.C.A. secretary, and the other a liquor dealer. Though they dwelt side by side, they lived in the realm of interests that were as far apart as the east is from the west. One was concerned about helping young men become good Christians; the other had no purpose except to make money regardless of how many promising careers he ruined. Where a person really lives is not a matter of his street number but of the ideas and purposes that control him.

Someone made fun of Goldsmith because he lodged in a basement. "Your soul must live in a basement!" was the stinging challenge. The main question is not whether you live in a mansion or a cottage, but where you feel most at home. Is it in a church or a poolroom, a library or a saloon, a flower garden or a mudhole? Jesus felt at home wherever he found goodness and beauty and the search for truth. Do you feel at home with him?

Heavenly Father, whatever may be my earthly surroundings, grant that my soul may find its home in thee. Forgive my earth-bound ways; make me fit for thy fellowship, and lift me above all baseness into the beauty of thy presence. Amen.

WEDNESDAY—Week 21

HOW TALL ARE YOU?   Read I Sam. 10:17-27

The Hebrews chose Saul to be their king partly on the basis of his height. He was the tallest man in Israel, standing head and shoulders above his fellows, but he was not big enough to overcome his jealousy of David and become the spiritual leader of his people.

How tall were Abraham Lincoln and George Washington? Though Lincoln was the tallest president ever to sit in the White House, and Washington measured over six feet, their true height was not in their physical stature, but in the lofty moral principles which made them men who lived "above the fog in public duty and private thinking." Napoleon Bonaparte was five feet, three inches high, but his smallness was in his shriveled and conceited soul rather than in his diminutive body.

Your height is determined by the upreach of your ideals. Nature may have made you short, but you can make yourself tall by stretching the muscles of your soul and reaching up toward God.

> Christ of the Upward Way, my Guide Divine,
> Where thou hast set thy feet may I place mine;
> And move and march wherever thou hast trod,
> Keeping face forward up the hill of God. Amen.

THURSDAY—Week 21

HOW MUCH ARE YOU WORTH?   Read Ps. 52

When Li Hung-chang, who later became prime minister of China, visited the United States during the presidency of General Grant, the first question he asked of the famous people whom he met was, "What are you worth?" The Chinese gentleman was reputed to be the richest man in his own country, and he thought he was paying a compliment to people by inquiring about their wealth. The day is past, however, when intelligent people judge a man's value on the basis of the material possessions he has inherited or accumulated.

A scientist figured out that the average man would be worth less than a dollar if his body were reduced to its chemical constituents. Some women would probably be worth even more if one also figured the cost of the cosmetics on their faces. A person may own millions of dollars' worth of property and be morally bankrupt. Jesus insisted that one is a fool if one is not "rich toward God."

Dear Savior, who became poor for our sakes that we might become rich through thee, give me wisdom to discern the true sources of enrichment. May I prefer moral worth to worldly wealth and so have the eternal treasure which no one can take away. Amen.

FRIDAY—Week 21

WHERE ARE YOU GOING?   Read John 6:59-71

At a football game in the Rose Bowl some years ago a player grabbed the ball and made a spectacular seventy-yard run. A deafening roar went up from the spectators, and the runner supposed he was being applauded for his brilliant performance. When he was a few yards from the opponents' goal posts, he suddenly discovered his mistake. How many times a young man rushes through life and thinks he is a great success only to awaken to the fact that he has been headed the wrong way!

According to an ancient legend, the Apostle Peter started to leave Rome during a time when Christians were being bitterly persecuted. He escaped by the Appian Way but a short distance from the city met one whom he recognized as the Master. "*Quo vadis, Domine?*" exclaimed Peter. Jesus answered, "To Rome to be crucified again." Peter turned and went back with the Master. Are you going with Jesus or in the opposite direction?

O Christ, as I go forward in life, give me courage to choose the high way. Thou art ever calling to me to follow thee. May I be willing to accept thy leadership, knowing that I cannot miss the road if I am traveling as thy companion. Amen.

SATURDAY—Week 21

WHAT DO YOU WANT?

Read Ps. 106:1-15

The god Bacchus, in gratitude to King Midas for a favor, offered to grant the king one great wish. Midas chose that whatever he touched should be turned into gold. All his food became shining metal when he tried to eat; finally, in danger of starving, he implored Bacchus to deliver him from the consequences of his request.

What would you ask of life if you could make one wish and have it gratified? Answer with care, for in this universe you are likely to get that which you most deeply desire! Education, money, fame—whatever you make your dominant purpose and seek with your whole heart, that you can achieve. But beware lest, having been granted your wish, you find yourself starving. Says the Psalmist of God's dealings with the Israelites in the wilderness: "He gave them their request; but sent leanness into their soul." If your wish is for an understanding heart, inner integrity, and outreaching helpfulness, your soul will be in no danger of starvation.

Dear Lord, life offers me so many things that I am torn by conflicting desires. Grant that I may not be satisfied with that which is good but may set my heart earnestly on the attainment of the best. Amen.

DEVELOPING YOUR PERSONALITY

SUNDAY—Week 22

THE PERSONALITY OF JESUS   Read Mark 1:35-45

What a personality Jesus must have had! The Bible gives no description of his appearance, but it is evident that he was the kind of man who was sought after by all sorts of people. The common people heard him gladly. A multitude followed him into the wilderness to hear him preach. He was a popular guest at dinner parties and was entertained by both rich and poor. Nicodemus and the rich young ruler sought interviews with him.

What was the source of his attractiveness? No one can give a completely adequate answer, but two facts need to be especially noted. He sought to do the will of God, and he had a genuine love for people. He combined a deep religious faith with an unselfish and outreaching interest in others. His personal charm was the result of something deep within which expressed itself in all that he was and said and did.

Grant, O Heavenly Father, that I may be able to love thee with all my soul and mind, and my neighbor as myself. So may the spirit of love, shining forth from my life, reflect the love which is eternally in thy heart. Amen.

MONDAY—Week 22

DO YOU HAVE AN INFERIORITY COMPLEX?
Read II Cor. 10:10-18

You do not need to worry over the fact that you do not look like a Hollywood star. People who have achieved distinction in business and professional life, and who have been blessed with a large circle of friends, represent all types. Some are tall, and others tubby. Some are fat, and others thin. Some have been favored by fortune, and others have been handicapped. One's inner attitude and personal outlook upon life are far more important than external appearance.

Dr. Charles W. Eliot, former president of Harvard University, was sensitive over a birthmark on the right side of his face. In having his picture taken he always turned his left side toward the camera. Yet he need not have been disturbed about his face. It did not prevent him from becoming a noted educator and one of the most admired college heads of his day. Personality depends on something far more important than inherited face and form.

O God, the Beloved, give me beauty of the inward soul; and may the outward and the inward man be as one. May I reckon the wise to be the wealthy, and may I have such a quantity of gold as none but the temperate can bear and carry. Amen.—A prayer of Socrates.

TUESDAY—Week 22

THE ART OF CONVERSATION   Read Job 15:1-13

Nietzsche said that conversation was a major factor in the success or failure of marriage. Surely it is an important aspect of personality, and one which can be cultivated. No one need sit silently when in the company of other people. Some people talk too much; their stale jokes and secondhand wisecracks are boring rather than entertaining. If you want to please others, you must not monopolize a conversation or try to make yourself the center of attention, but neither should you sit tongue-tied with nothing to say.

The ability to engage in an interesting conversation is largely a by-product of a well-furnished mind and a wide range of interests. Read good books, subscribe to some of the best magazines, develop some hobbies, enlarge your mental horizons, take a sincere interest in other people, and you will be providing soil for the growth of your personality.

Like the people of Nazareth, O God, I marvel at the gracious words which came from the mouth of our Savior, words which arrested attention and made people think, words filled with sympathy and healing and hope. May my words be like his. Amen.

WEDNESDAY—Week 22

CLEANLINESS NEXT TO GODLINESS   Read Matt. 6:16-18

During the Middle Ages there were people who made the mistake of thinking they became more saintly by dressing in rags and going about dirty and disheveled. Holiness should never be confused with sloppiness. A Christian ought to be clean outside as well as inside. An otherwise fine personality can be ruined by slovenly habits.

Every person ought to have enough self-respect and consideration for his friends to dress neatly, keep his fingernails clean, his hair combed, his shoes shined, and to attend to other little details that will make him acceptable to civilized people. The wise person will avoid the clothes that make him conspicuous but will be careful not to discredit himself by being careless of his appearance. Said John Wesley: "Certainly this is a duty, not a sin. Cleanliness in indeed next to godliness."

O Christ, my King, I would be a worthy representative of thee. Save me from any carelessness or negligence that might rob my Christian life of its beauty and attractiveness. Amen.

THURSDAY—Week 22

PERSONALITY PLUS
Read Ex. 6:1-13

William Wilberforce, the English philanthropist, was a hunchback; but his physical handicap did not keep him from leading a successful fight for the abolition of slavery and for the adoption of many social reforms. When he arose in Parliament to plead the cause of the black people, he became a person transfigured. No one thought of his deformed body, for everyone gazed at the light on his face. He became one of the most loved men in the British Empire and was buried in Westminster Abbey. His funeral procession was one of the longest ever to pass through the streets of London.

The secret of his amazing hold on multitudes of people was his complete forgetfulness of self and his devotion to great causes of human justice. If you will become totally absorbed in some project, and will undertake it without thought of personal reward, you will acquire "personality plus." You will take on some of the nobility of the cause you represent.

O God, who art the Father of all men and the special Friend of the poor and afflicted, give me greater sympathy for those who are victims of race prejudice and other forms of injustice. May I give myself to the service of those in need and find my own life ennobled by the love I give away. Amen.

FRIDAY—Week 22

A FINE PERSONALITY CAN BE LOST
Read Ps. 38

One of the stories told about Leonardo da Vinci's picture of the Last Supper relates how the artist painted the faces of Jesus and Judas from living models. In one of the church choirs of Milan he found a young man of such noble face that he immediately engaged him to sit as his model of the Savior.

He then sought without success for somebody with such a debased look that he could pose as the traitor. Years passed before he met in the slums of the city a repulsive beggar who seemed so completely lost to the finer things of life that he hired him as his Judas. As he paid him for his time, Leonardo remarked that he had a recollection of having seen him somewhere before. The begger replied, "You ought to know me. I also sat for your picture of Christ."

The legend may not be historically true, but it is an accurate description of what can happen in life. A few years of dissipation quickly show themselves in a person's face. What you will look like as you grow older depends in part on the kind of character you develop.

O God, thou hast made me in thy likeness. Let not the divine image within me be marred or disfigured. Keep me strong and pure and true. Deliver me from evil and let no sin have dominion over me. Amen.

SATURDAY—Week 22

YOU CAN HAVE A CHRISTIAN PERSONALITY

Rev. 3:14-22

A new pastor of a little church in a French village started to call upon the members of his congregation. When a workingman came home one evening, his wife said, "The new minister was here today." "What did he have to say?" asked the husband. The wife answered: "He didn't talk very much. He was peculiar. All he did was to stand in the doorway after I answered his knock and say, 'Does Jesus Christ live here?' "

Both the husband and wife were angry and inclined to resent the question which the pastor had asked. But as they talked about the matter and then prayed over it, their mood of irritation gave way to an effort to humbly open their hearts to Christ in order that they might answer the question in the affirmative if it should ever be asked them again.

"Behold, I stand at the door, and knock!" says Jesus. Welcome him into your heart and allow him to live in you. Then your personality can rightly be called Christian.

> O Lord, with shame and sorrow
> We open now the door;
> Dear Saviour, enter, enter,
> And leave us never more. Amen

THE SACREDNESS OF THE TRUTH

SUNDAY—Week 23

ALL HIGH RELIGIONS EMPHASIZE THE TRUTH
Read John 18:28-40

For thousands of years, as far back as there is any recorded history, people of many different religions have thought it wrong to lie and right to tell the truth. On an ancient Egyptian temple is the inscription: "God findeth his satisfaction in truth." Confucius, the wise man of China, said, "I do not know how a man is to get on without truthfulness." The Buddhist teaching says, "Hold fast to the truth as to a lamp." Mohammed wrote in the Koran, "God speaketh the truth." Jesus said, "To this end was I born, and for this cause came I into the world, that I should bear witness unto the truth."

If you are ever tempted to think there is no harm in lying, meditate upon the fact that wise people of every age and religion have considered truth a basic virtue in every life and a necessity to civilization.

Thou art the truth, O God, and I would make my life like thine. May I be truthful in my words and sincere in my actions. Keep me free from any desire to deceive and above every need for concealment. Amen.

MONDAY—Week 23

THE FUNDAMENTAL SIN
Read Rev. 22:1-15

A clever boy, asked to give a definition of a lie, replied, "It is an abomination to the Lord but an ever-present help in time of trouble."

Does not this describe the attitude which many people take toward a lie today? They believe in telling the truth but will resort to prevarication or a half-truth for the sake of avoiding an unpleasant situation. They forget that a lie is the fundamental sin, for it destroys the basis of confidence and mutual trust on which men can live and do business together. Listen to these words of John Ruskin: "Do not let us lie at all. Do not think of one falsity as harmless, and another as slight, and another as unintended. Cast them all aside; they may be light and accidental, but they are an ugly soot from the smoke of the pit for all that: and it is better that

101

our hearts should be swept clean of them without our care as to which is largest or blackest."

Dear God, the world is filled with falsehood and deceit, but save me from being like the world. Place thy Spirit within me and give me the courage to be like thy Son, in whose name I pray. Amen.

TUESDAY—Week 23

JESUS' INSISTENCE ON THE TRUTH   Read Luke 9:57-62

Jesus wanted men to be his followers, but he would not let them go with him under false impressions. He insisted that they fully understand the sacrifices they might be called upon to make.

A scribe attracted by Jesus' works of healing, offered to be his disciple. Jesus reminded him of the hardships he would be compelled to face in living away from home, perhaps having no place to sleep but under the open sky. "Foxes have holes, and birds of the air have nests," he said, "but the Son of man hath not where to lay his head."

Jesus told the truth to all men, whether friends, strangers, or enemies. There are no circumstances under which we can imagine his practicing any kind of deception.

Thou God of Wisdom, grant that I may be able to love thee with all my mind. Instill in my heart a scorn for deceit. May I seek a knowledge of the truth that I may obey it as the law of my life. Amen.

WEDNESDAY—Week 23

RESPECTING A PROMISE TO AN AFRICAN CHIEF
Read Col. 3:1-17

David Livingstone, the famous missionary and African explorer, wanted to find a way from the interior of the continent to the coast. He persuaded a chief to let some of the members of his tribe go with him and serve as guides. The chief agreed to allow the men to accompany him only on condition that Livingstone would promise to come all the way back with them.

When they reached the coast they found a british ship, and its captain urged the missionary to return to England with him. Livingstone's family was in England, and he had not seen them for a long time. But, much as he wanted to accept the captain's invitation, he refused to do so because of his promise to the African chief. He returned to the jungle and led the black men safely back to their own huts.

O God, our Father, I thank thee for faithful people who have sacrificed their own immediate desires for the sake of maintaining their integrity and of keeping faith with others. Make me like them in maintaining my honor and respecting the sacredness of my word. Amen.

THURSDAY—Week 23

WHAT ABOUT A BAD PROMISE?   Read Matt. 14:1-12

In a rash moment, after he had been drinking heavily, Herod promised to give the daughter of Herodias anything she requested. When she asked for the head of John the Baptist, he regretted his agreement but remained true to his word.

It is not unusual for a person to make a hasty promise and then be in doubt whether he should keep it or break it. A high-school boy agreed to go to the movies with his friend and then found that his parents needed his help at home. He sneaked away and kept the date, afterward giving his parents the excuse that he felt duty-bound to keep his engagement.

Would it not have been better for Herod to break his evil promise? Should not the boy have explained the situation to his chum and asked to be released from the date? You must be careful about giving or breaking your word, but you should not allow a promise to lead you into wrongdoing.

O God, give me such loyalty to my high standards that I will not become involved in moral entanglements. Although I may commit one sin, may I not make it worse by committing another, but frankly seek forgiveness and seek to make restitution. Amen.

FRIDAY—Week 23

ESTABLISHING A REPUTATION FOR VERACITY
Read John 8:25-32

During a critical stage of the Civil War, General Robert E. Lee was discussing the future movement of the Confederate army with one of his officers. A farmer's boy overheard Lee remark that he had made up his mind to march on Gettysburg instead of Harrisburg. The boy sent the information to Governor Andrew G. Curtin of Pennsylvania.

Said the governor on receiving the message, "I would give my right hand to know if the boy tells the truth." An army corporal spoke up and said, "I know that boy. There is not a false drop of blood in his veins. It is impossible for him to tell a lie."

The boy's word was accepted in a crucial situation because he had previously established a reputation for veracity, and Union soldiers were soon marching toward Gettysburg. If you want people to believe your word without question, begin now to make yourself worthy of their confidence.

Thou dost desire truth in the inward parts, O God. Take from my heart any seeds that might grow into falsehoods and deceptions. May I be so honest and straightforward that I will not be tempted to excuse my conduct by evading the truth. Amen.

SATURDAY—Week 23

A PAGAN WHO HONORED HIS WORD

Read Prov. 12:13-28

Regulus, a Roman general, was taken prisoner by the armies of Carthage. The leaders of the Carthaginians asked him to go back to Rome and tell his people that Carthage was ready to grant the terms of peace. They made him promise that he would return if the conditions of peace were not accepted.

Regulus went to Rome and advised his friends to keep on fighting. He told them that Carthage had been weakened by war and that Rome could finally win if she refused to give up now. Then he bade farewell to his wife and children and started back to the death which he knew the enraged Carthaginians would inflict upon him.

Some of the Romans urged him not to go back, but Regulus would not even consider it. "I am a Roman," he said, "and a Roman must keep his word."

As followers of Christ, we ought to have as much integrity as this old pagan. Can we not say: "I am a Christian, and a Christian must tell the truth"?

Teach us, good Lord, to serve thee as thou deservest; to give and not to count the cost; to fight and not to heed the wounds; to toil and not to seek for rest; to labor and not to ask for any reward, save that of knowing we do thy will; through Jesus Christ our Lord. Amen.—Loyola.

THE NOBLEST WORK OF GOD

SUNDAY—Week 24

HONESTY INSPIRES CONFIDENCE   Read Prov. 19:1-9

Abraham Lincoln, as a young lawyer in Springfield, was so poor that he hardly knew where his next meal was coming from. Yet he could never defend a man in court unless he honestly believed that right and justice were on the side of his client. "I could not do it," he said. "All the time I was talking to the jury, I would be thinking, 'Lincoln, you're a liar.' "

His unswerving honesty made people believe in him and choose him as their leader in a time of national crisis. Back of his election as president was the conviction of a majority of the voters that he could be trusted to do what he believed to be right.

Lincoln belonged to a later century than Alexander Pope, but his life gave new meaning to the poet's words: "An honest man's the noblest work of God."

I would be honest with myself, O God, that I may be honest with others and with thee. Give to me the inner integrity that enables me to stand in the presence of all men unashamed and unafraid. Amen.

MONDAY—Week 24

AN OPEN OPPORTUNITY   Read Luke 19:1-10

When Theodore Roosevelt was out West running a ranch, he found that one of his cowboys was putting the Roosevelt brand on stray cattle that did not belong to him. It was a common practice, and the man thought he would be winning the approval of his employer. Roosevelt discharged the man. "If you will steal for me, you will steal from me," he said. Roosevelt would not allow one of his employees to do wrong under the cloak of loyalty.

What a transformation would occur in economic life today if all the heads of business and industrial enterprises would make absolute honesty the unchanging rule for all their transactions! One of the Christian opportunities facing modern youth is to put higher ethical standards into commercial life.

Thou God of righteousness, grant that I may never ask or expect another to do wrong for the sake of protecting me or advancing my interest. May I make it easy for others to do right and never tolerate wrongdoing when it is possible for me to prevent it. Amen.

TUESDAY—Week 24

WINNING THE APPROVAL OF GOD   Read John 8:12-30

The final test of character is whether a man is loyal to an ideal for the sake of the ideal; that is, whether he will do right even when he knows he could be dishonest without any danger of discovery.

A village merchant, wanting to find out the character of the people who were his regular customers, tried the experiment of giving excess change to twenty-five different persons. Six carelessly put the money in their pockets or purses without counting it. Eight counted it and returned what did not belong to them. Eleven counted the money, knew that they had an extra amount, but said nothing about it as they had no idea that anyone would be aware of what they were doing.

The greatest incentive to honesty, and the only one adequate to all situations, is the desire for the approval of God. Jesus revealed a controlling motive of his life when he said, "I do always those things that please him."

Almighty God, unto whom all hearts are open, all desires known, and from whom no secrets are hid; cleanse the thoughts of our hearts by the inspiration of thy Holy Spirit, that we may perfectly love thee, and worthily magnify thy holy Name; through Christ our Lord. Amen.—Book of Common Prayer.

WEDNESDAY—Week 24

THE WEAKNESS OF JUDAS   Read John 12:1-11

The beginning of Judas' treachery seems to have been in his dishonesty. He was treasurer of the band of disciples and had been stealing from the money which belonged to the group as a whole.

Probably he started by borrowing money from the common fund with the idea that sometime later he would put it back. As time went on, he found it easier to yield to the temptation to borrow again than to restore what he had already taken.

Any form of wrongdoing serves as an entering wedge which gradually opens the door to the forces of evil. We must not allow ourselves to be careless with other people's money.

> In vain we call old notions fudge
> And bend our conscience to our dealing;

The Ten Commandments will not budge,
And stealing will continue stealing.

Strengthen me in the hour of temptation, dear Father. Give me the courage to say "No" to the suggestion of evil. Grant that I may obey every prompting toward goodness and honor and so have a conscience which guides me aright and truly becomes thy voice. Amen.

THURSDAY—Week 24

AN INEVITABLE CHOICE   Read Luke 16:1-13

When Jacob Riis was a young man, just beginning to make his way as a newspaper reporter in New York City, he was offered a much larger salary to become private secretary to one of the nation's great financiers. The new position held many attractions. Not only did it bring more money, it offered the possibility of further advancement; it meant social prestige and interesting associations.

As a newspaper man, Riis had already learned something of the unscrupulous practices of the financier and knew that he would be forced to sacrifice his own personal integrity if he took the new position. He decided he would rather remain poor, if necessary, than to win material advantages by giving up his moral standards. Everyone may sometime face the choice between money and character.

Make clear to me the path of duty, O Lord, and give me the will to pursue it. Help me never to compromise my ideals. May I place worth before wealth and inner peace before outward plenty. May I prefer my own self-respect to any honor or advantage the world may hold before me. Amen.

FRIDAY—Week 24

A GOOD NAME MORE THAN MONEY   Read Prov. 22

When the name of Admiral Dewey was being acclaimed throughout the country after his victory at Manila Bay in the war between the United States and Spain, his son was offered two hundred dollars a month to sign his name to a daily article which an experienced newspaperman was to write. The editor of the paper wanted to use the name of the son of the famous naval hero for advertising purposes.

Young Dewey was then earning only twenty dollars a month at his first job. The chance to make ten times as much was an alluring offer, but he refused to be a party to such deceit and dishonesty. He decided he would rather keep on doing hard work at a small wage than be false to his father's name and lose his own self-respect.

What if you have a chance to make easy money by slight dishonesty? Can you still retain your inner integrity?

Dear God, give me the courage to be poor rather than sell my soul. Deepen my conviction that a good name is more to be desired than money, and help me to acquire the inner wealth which no one can take from me. Amen.

SATURDAY—Week 24

TRIFLES THAT REVEAL CHARACTER Read Luke 19:11-26

A man dropped a dime out of his pocket as he was hurrying down the street. A boy picked it up and ran after the man, who did not even know that he had lost the money. Not only did he thank the boy; he took down his name and address.

When the boy graduated from high school, the man offered him a position which involved handling large sums of money. He felt sure that a boy who returned a dime could be trusted with hundreds of dollars.

It is the trifle that indicates our character. If we are always careful about giving back pencils and books which we have borrowed and about repaying small sums of money, we will be cultivating habits of honesty. The little things we do every day determine our character and control our destiny.

O God, may I never for a moment forget that every act of mine has power to help or hinder my future happiness. Teach me to be ever faithful in that which is least that I may be considered worthy of greater responsibilities. May I seek today the kind of character I wish to have tomorrow. Amen.

QUALITIES THAT REVEAL CHARACTER

SUNDAY—Week 25

HONOR   Read John 5:36-44

Dr. Henry Hitt Crane tells of a young man who was fortunate enough to have as a family acquaintance an elderly man who was an author of distinction and held in high regard both for his literature and his life. The youth went to him one day and said: "You have written many things for a great many men. Will you write something especially for me? I want one word which I may hold in my heart as though it were the priceless jewel of life—one word from you to me that shall always be the touchstone of my life." The old man took a sheet of paper and on it wrote the word "honor."

We need to have the word written not only on paper but in our hearts. There could be no better compass by which to steer our lives than the great affirmation which forms the beginning of the Boy Scout oath, "On my honor, I will do my best."

Heavenly Father, help me to keep the white plume of my honor unsullied. Grant that I may live above all sham and pretense. Give me a wholehearted devotion to the right, and keep me away from the perilous edge of doubtful practices. Amen.

MONDAY—Week 25

HUMILITY   Read Matt. 12:13-21; Isa. 42:2

Humility is an unpopular virtue with most Americans. We are a nation of publicity seekers and believe in advertising ourselves. Such an attitude is not that of Jesus. To describe him, Matthew takes this thought of Isaiah's: "He shall not strive, nor cry; neither shall any man hear his voice in the streets." It was the Oriental way of describing a person who does not call attention to himself.

The Christian patterns his character after Christ and does the best work of which he is capable; then he lets his life and achievements speak for themselves. Though he appreciates the commendations of others, he does not go around seeking them and is not disturbed if he is overlooked by those who control the channels of publicity. There is food for thought in the inscription honoring a woman in Westminster Abbey:

She had great virtues,
And as great a desire of concealing them.

Dear Father, take away my love of applause and make me more like thy Son, who was meek and lowly of heart. Help me to escape from myself and to find a new center for my life through obedience to thy will. Amen.

TUESDAY—Week 25

SINCERITY

Read Ps. 26

The word "sterling" is stamped on the backs of many knives, forks, spoons, and other articles of silverware. It means that they are made of silver all the way through. They are of the same quality underneath as on the surface and so are far more valuable than similar pieces which are made of some other metal and then plated or coated with silver.

You may not always be able to tell by looking at people whether they are sterling or plated; but if you associate with them long enough, you will find out their real value which is revealed by the way they wear. Some show that they are made of baser metal underneath the polished surface, while others are of solid worth. Does a person talk but not perform; promise but not fulfill? Do his spontaneous words and acts reveal a lack of inner quality? Then the mark of "sterling" is not on him. He has put a coating of religion on a life that lacks integrity, but his true character will finally show itself.

Give us, O Lord, a mind after thine own heart, that we may delight to do thy will, O our God; and let thy Law be written on our hearts. Give us courage and resolution to do our duty, and a heart to be spent in thy service. Amen.—John Tillotson.

WEDNESDAY—Week 25

FAITHFULNESS

Read Luke 13:31-35

Jesus was warned that Herod, who had already beheaded John the Baptist, had threatened to kill him. The Master paid no attention to the threat. Regardless to what others might do to him, he was determined to be faithful to his daily duties. He continued to perform his works of healing and helpfulness; persistently he went forward in his customary course. He said, "Nevertheless I must walk today, and tomorrow, and the day following."

Few tests are more exacting than those which are imposed by the tasks of each day. Most people are quick to use any excuse to slight their work or to run away from any situation that is monotonous or unpleasant. To do our work faithfully at home, in school, in office or shop, whatever the situation, is one of the best indications that we are followers of Christ. William E. Gladstone wrote in his diary on his twenty-second birthday, "It matters not whether the sphere of duty be large or small, but may it be duly fulfilled."

I thank thee, O God, for those who do not become weary in their well-doing but stay faithfully at the place of duty even though they stay alone. Help me to be, like them, truehearted and wholehearted in my loyalty. May I never be found wanting in the hour of thy need. Amen.

THURSDAY—Week 25

GENTLENESS Read Gal. 5:16-26

War always tends to brutalize people. Even those who do not take part in the actual fighting are affected by the spirit which pervades the whole life of a nation. As Christians, we need to be on our guard that the virtues of gentleness and tenderness are not crowded out of our lives.

In the annual round-up of cattle during his ranching days, Theodore Roosevelt found a cow with a calf a little over a week old. Usually calves were left behind because they could not keep up with the herd. Roosevelt took the calf up on his saddle and proceeded at a walk. The other cowboys objected to going so slowly, and Roosevelt put the calf down but left the mother cow to take care of it. It meant that he would never have the cow, as she would be free to run wild on the plains. "It doesn't seem right to leave the calf to die on the prairie," he said. Roosevelt was a daring soldier, but his gentleness was a part of his greatness.

> The bravest are the tenderest,—
> The loving are the daring.

Father of all mercy, make my life as gentle and kind as thy own. Create within me the tenderness which is one aspect of courage and a distinguishing mark of all those who become spiritually great. Amen.

FRIDAY—Week 25

REVERENCE FOR PERSONALITY Read Matt. 25:31-46

The late Dr. John McDowell, well-known Presbyterian clergyman, spent his boyhood working in a coal mine. An accident, for which he was in no way responsible, killed a mule and crushed Dr. McDowell's arm so that amputation was necessary. The company records refer to the purchase of a new mule, but make no reference to the boy's injury. Boys were easily replaced and were less valuable than mules.

Reverence for human personality was a basic element in Jesus' teaching. Nothing aroused his wrath so much as the violation of human rights and the neglect of human need. In his parable of the last judgment Jesus said he would be eternally present in the needs of the sick, the hungry, and the outcast, and that all who ministered to them would be rendering a service to him also. Here is the supreme test of Christian character: Faced by human need, do you act like the priest and the Levite, or do you act like the good Samaritan?

Dear Father, save me from the sin of treating any person with contempt. Help me to remember that all the forlorn and sinful people are made in thy image and are entitled to respect as human beings. Amen.

SATURDAY—Week 25

PERSEVERANCE   Read Matt. 10:1-22

The verse which says, "He that endures to the end shall be saved," occurs three different times in the Gospels and there are many other passages that emphasize the same idea. Jesus insisted that perseverance is an essential Christian quality. One reason for our moral failures and our meager spiritual achievements is our lack of endurance. There is too much truth in the following revised version of Longfellow:

> Toiling—rejoicing—sorrowing,
>   So I my life conduct;
> Each morning sees some task begun,
>   Each evening sees it chucked.

Our modern demand for "pep" involves the danger of having a superficial zeal for all sorts of enterprises, regardless of their value, instead of a lasting devotion to the more worthwhile causes. Foundations are laid and fine structures built, not by spurts of enthusiasm, but slowly by adding brick after brick. We talk about executive ability, but more important is "consecutive ability," the capacity to keep on going.

Make me to remember, O God, that every day is thy gift, and ought to be used according to thy command. Grant me, therefore, so to repent of my negligence that I may obtain mercy from thee, and pass the time which thou shalt yet allow me in diligent performance of thy commands. Amen.—Samuel Johnson.

ADD COURTESY TO CHARACTER

SUNDAY—Week 26

BEAUTY AND STRENGTH   Read I Kings 7:13-22

The pillars which supported the porch of Solomon's temple at Jerusalem were not complete until they had been decorated with lily work. Skillful workmen were employed to ornament the columns in order that the temple might be beautiful for the worship of the Creator.

If decoration has its place in the church, surely it is fitting that Christian people, as living temples, should make themselves as attractive as possible! Character, to be complete, needs to have courtesy and gentleness added to strength and honor. Good manners are no substitute for inner worth, but they are needed as the proper setting for a good life.

Jesus is described by John as one who was "full of grace and truth." His life combined graciousness with moral integrity. If Christ comes into our hearts, he will bring with him both strength and beauty.

Thou God of all graciousness, mold me into thy own likeness. Save me from the sins of rudeness, peevishness, and impudence. Help me to grow like the tree, which becomes graceful as well as useful, beautiful as well as strong. Amen.

MONDAY—Week 26

COURTESY ON THE CROSS   Read Luke 23:32-44

Sir Philip Sidney, an English nobleman, was seriously wounded when fighting in the Netherlands against Spain. He lay on the battlefield in great pain and suffered intense thirst. When a canteen was brought to him containing only enough water for one person, he motioned toward a private soldier who lay dying near by. "Give it to him," he said. "His need is greater than mine."

Even greater was the courtesy shown by Jesus on the cross. In spite of his own suffering, he prayed that the soldiers who had crucified him might be forgiven and spoke a comforting word to the penitent thief. Such courtesy is so amazing that we can hardly understand it. It has nothing in common with superficial politeness

113

but springs from a great depth of character which enables one to forget oneself for the sake of others.

Grant, O God, that trouble and suffering, if they come into my life, may not make me selfish. May a sense of thy companionship bring me comfort and peace, and may I be able to ease my own burden by trying to lighten the burden of another. Amen.

TUESDAY—Week 26

GOD IS NO RESPECTER OF PERSONS   Read Jas. 2:1-18

General Robert E. Lee was once riding on a train filled with Confederate officers and soldiers when a woman who was poorly dressed boarded the train at one of the stations and walked down the aisle looking for a seat. No one offered to give her one until General Lee, in the far end of the car, arose and motioned to her to take his place. Immediately, several of the soldiers jumped up and offered their seats to the General.

"No, gentlemen," said he. "If you could not rise out of ordinary courtesy to an unknown woman, you need not do so for me."

His courtesy was like that of the early Christian leaders who insisted that God is no respecter of persons and that all people should be given the same treatment whether rich or poor.

Heavenly Father, make me thoughtful of the needs of other people, treating them all with Christian courtesy and giving special consideration to those weaker than myself. If I can add to the comfort of others, or ease their burden, may I do it gladly regardless of any personal inconvenience. Amen.

WEDNESDAY—Week 26

SAYING "THANK YOU"   Read Luke 17:11-19

Jesus was disappointed when nine of the lepers whom he had healed failed to thank him for their restoration to health. Doubtless they did not intend to be unkind or discourteous. They were merely thoughtless.

It is easy to be careless about such matters, but few things are more rude than to accept a favor from another and not thank him for it. To express our gratitude to those who have helped us will cost us nothing and take but a moment of our time. Said Emerson: "Life is not so short but that there is always time enough for courtesy."

> Hearts, like doors, will ope with ease
> To very, very little keys;
> And don't forget that two of these

Are "I thank you" and "If you please."

Forgive me, O God, for my careless ingratitude. Thou hast surrounded me with blessings, but I forget to praise thee for thy goodness. Make me thankful not only to thee, but to all who have enriched my life by their kindness. May I never be too busy or too bashful to say "Thank you." Amen.

THURSDAY—Week 26

COURTESY AT HOME   Read Col. 3:16-25

An Eastern legend tells how a messenger came to Dama, the jewel merchant, seeking to buy his finest gems for the breastplate of the high priest in Jerusalem. Dama showed the man some of his jewels. "Have you none better than these?" the man asked. "My choicest ones are in a cabinet in my father's room, and I will get them for you," replied Dama. He went out a moment, but came back without the jewels. He explained that his aged father was asleep and that the messenger must wait until he awakened. "My business requires haste," urged the messenger. "What if you do awaken the old man. I will make you rich with my gold." Dama answered: "My father is not well, he needs his rest, and he is much dearer to me than gold."

So the messenger departed without buying the jewels and reported to the high priest that Dama's courtesy to his father was rarer than any gem he had ever seen.

Dear Father, give me the spirit of courtesy toward those in my own home. Keep me from insisting on my own rights and forgetting the needs of others. Make me patient and thoughtful. Help me to have love which suffers long and is kind. Amen.

FRIDAY—Week 26

COURTESY TOWARD LITTLE CHILDREN
Read Mark 10:13-27

The way young people act toward little children is a revealing sign of their character. Children often thoughtlessly interrupt those who are older, but a person who speaks to them harshly or treats them roughly shows the littleness of his own soul. An older and stronger person should always feel responsible for those who are younger and weaker, and deal gently with them.

The scripture reading for the day contrasts the difference between Jesus' attitude and that of his disciples toward the mothers who brought their little ones to the Master. The disciples thought Jesus was too busy to be bothered by children and spoke rudely to

115

the mothers. Jesus was indignant at the conduct of his disciples. He took the little children up in his arms and blessed them. He was never in too much of a hurry to be courteous.

Dear God, I remember that I was once a baby in my parents' arms and that for years I was dependent on the care of others. Forgive me if my strength has now made me thoughtless or rude toward anyone younger than I. Make me like the Good Shepherd, who deals tenderly with the lambs of the flock. Amen.

SATURDAY—Week 26

THE SOURCE OF TRUE COURTESY   Read Matt. 7:15-23

The courtesy which comes from studying books on good manners and imitating the words and actions of others is merely a veneer or an ornament added to the outside of life. It should not be confused with the higher type of courtesy which springs from kindness and unselfishness of character.

Just as a good tree will bring forth good fruit, so a loving heart will express itself in courtesy of conduct. The gracious manners of the true Christian are the natural expression of the inner quality of his life. He will have the kind of courtesy which Tennyson attributed to King Arthur and Sir Launcelot:

> These two
> Were the most nobly mannered men of all;
> For manners are not idle, but the fruit
> Of loyal nature and of noble mind.

Dear Lord, forgive me if my life has not been producing the fruit of Christian courtesy. Help me to yield myself to thee that thy love may possess my heart. So may my inner life be bright with thy presence and my outward life an expression of thy grace. Amen.

WHEN YOU ARE CRITICIZED

SUNDAY—Week 27

MOST CRITICISM CAN BE IGNORED

Read II Sam. 16:1-14

A man named Shimei, who for some unknown reason had a grievance against David, swore at the king and threw stones at him. A member of David's bodyguard asked for permission to capture Shimei and cut off his head. David merely replied, "Let him curse."

The best way to treat a person who curses you, or criticizes you, is to ignore him. Do not let him know that you are disturbed by his remarks. Refuse to give him the satisfaction of having you answer back. Argument is generally useless and a waste of time. When we try to get even, we consume our energy and gradually embitter our spirits. Worst of all, we are in danger of descending to the level of the one who attacked us.

In most cases, when a person treats you unfairly, you do not need to defend yourself. Intelligent people will judge your life by what you do, not by what some slanderous gossip has said.

Dear Father, help me to keep sweet in spirit and not to become bitter because of what others may say or do. Grant that my own integrity may ever be my chief defense against those who make mean and false statements about me. Amen.

MONDAY—Week 27

DON'T TRY TO PLEASE EVERYBODY

Read Neh. 4

Some people are so sensitive to criticism that they are continually changing from one course of action to another. Aesop has a fable about a man and boy who were leading a donkey to town. A passerby laughed at them for walking while the donkey had no load, so the man had the boy get up and ride. Soon they met a man who criticized the boy for riding while his father walked. The boy got off the donkey and the man climbed on. Soon another person called the man selfish because he was making the little boy walk. When both started to ride, they were accused of cruelty to the donkey. Then they tied the donkey's legs, put a pole between them, and shouldered the pole. People laughed at them so much that they started to let the donkey down; it began to kick, rolled over into the river, and was drowned.

We make ourselves wretched by being too sensitive to the opinions of others. Sir Walter Scott used the word "Naboclish" as slang for "Never mind; it makes no difference." We need Scott's attitude, if not his word.

Save me, Lord, from becoming sensitive and touchy. Keep my spirit bright through a consciousness of thy presence. Teach me to be kind and helpful toward others and to preserve my faith in my fellowmen regardless of their treatment of me. Amen.

TUESDAY—Week 27

GIVE HEED TO INTELLIGENT CRITICISM

Read Prov. 10:1-17

When Apelles, an early Greek artist, put his paintings on public exhibition, he hid behind a curtain where he could hear the comments of those who looked at them. A shoemaker studied one of the canvases thoughtfully and remarked that Apelles had made a mistake in the way he painted a shoe. The artist decided a cobbler was a better judge of shoes than a painter, so that night he corrected the error.

The next day the shoemaker looked at the picture again. Flattered that his comment had been heeded, he made an unfavorable criticism of another aspect of the picture. This time Apelles knew the man was talking in conceited ignorance. Rushing from behind the curtain, he exclaimed, "Cobbler, stick to your last!" He meant that one should limit one's criticisms to matters on which one has accurate information.

Intelligent suggestions should always be welcomed, but the comments of the ignorant can be safely ignored.

Lord, help me to be charitable in my attitude toward others. Make me thoughtful of their happiness, and keep me from speaking an unpleasant truth except in the spirit of love. Amen.

WEDNESDAY—Week 27

MAINTAIN YOUR POISE

Read Mark 11:15-26

Whatever else you do in the face of criticism, you must learn to maintain your poise and self-control. If you fly off the handle, allow another person to "get your goat," become angry and resentful, you will be unfit for the ordinary tasks of life and you run the risk of losing the respect of those who have been your loyal friends.

No man ever suffered more bitter criticism than President Lincoln, but he kept himself free from resentment. Everyone can profit by his example and words. He said: "No man resolved to make the most of himself can spare the time for personal contention. Still less can he afford to take all the consequences, including the vitiating of his temper and the loss of self-control." On another occasion he remarked: "You have more of that feeling of personal resentment than I have; perhaps I have too little of it, but I never thought it paid."

Heavenly Father, I thank thee for the example of thy Son, who blessed them that cursed him, prayed for them that persecuted him, and returned good for evil. Grant that I may set myself earnestly to be his follower. Amen.

THURSDAY—Week 27

DON'T GET MAD
Read II Cor. 2

Michelangelo was unsurpassed as an artistic genius, but he was only an ordinary man in his resentment of criticism. He was commissioned by the pope to make the paintings on the walls of the Vatican chapel and included several undraped figures in his pictures. Biagio, the papal master of ceremonies, criticized them as inappropriate for a place of worship and asked that they be changed. Michelangelo's reply was to paint another figure on the wall—one of Biagio with horns, a serpent twined about his waist while he writhed in eternal torment.

Biagio appealed to the pope, but the latter jokingly said: "Had the painter sent you to purgatory, I might have used my influence to get you out, but I have no power in hell." So the picture of the horned and snake-entwined priest remains on the chapel wall because a great artist could not take criticism without getting mad.

O God of patience and consolation, give us such good-will, we beseech thee, that with free hearts we may love and serve thee and our brethren; and, having thus the mind of Christ, may begin heaven on earth. Amen.— Christina G. Rossetti.

FRIDAY—Week 27

BE SURE YOU ARE RIGHT AND GO AHEAD
Read Matt. 21:1-27

The story of Jesus' last week in Jerusalem shows him going steadfastly forward in the fulfillment of his mission, unaffected by either praise or criticism. He came into the city on Palm Sunday amid the acclaim of an enthusiastic multitude. By the next day his popularity had waned. Instead of being surrounded by an admiring crowd, he was being questioned and criticized by the Pharisees.

How did Jesus conduct himself in the face of these shifting attitudes? He had the same reaction to seeming failure that he had previously had to apparent success. He was seeking to carry out God's will, and he remained quietly indifferent to the praise and blame of men.

No one can fill any position of leadership or take an open stand in behalf of any cause without having some people approve of what he does and others disapprove of him. There is only one Christian course. Make your plans carefully and prayerfully, and go ahead.

O God, give me the steadfastness of Jesus, that I may walk in the path of duty without faltering. If others praise me, may I not become conceited; if they blame me, may I not be cast down. Grant that my only concern may be to hear thee say, "Well done!" Amen.

SATURDAY—Week 27

PROTECT THE CHURCH FROM ITS CRITICS
Read Phil. 2:1-16

One of the favorite indoor sports of the American people is to criticize the Christian church. They judge the church by its weaknesses and mistakes, not by its attainments. They condemn it because its officials do not practice their religion in their everyday relationships, pointing out the inconsistencies in the lives of its members.

A well-known author and critic of the church is said to have had his whole religious attitude colored by the fact that a leading man in one of the churches the critic attended as a boy could not be trusted in business transactions. What a foolish and partial way for an intelligent man to judge one of the great historic institutions of mankind!

And yet, let us face the facts. There is too much truth in these charges to ignore them. The best way to answer the critics is for those of us who love Christ and his church to make our lives honestly Christian so that we are living refutations of what the critics say.

Father, make me like salt which has not lost its savor. Grant that I may let my light shine before men in such a way that others, seeing my good works, will glorify thee and honor the church of thy Son. Amen.

OVERCOMING OUR WORRIES

SUNDAY—Week 28

THE FACE OF THE CAPTAIN   Read Ps. 107:23-43

Robert Louis Stevenson tells of one of his voyages to the South Sea Islands when a terrible storm arose. The passengers were all frightened, and feared the ship would be lost. One of the men finally went out in the wind and rain and climbed to the upper deck, where he saw the captain quietly pacing the bridge. With calm and undisturbed face he looked out across the sea and gave orders for the handling of the ship. The man made his way back again to the cabin where the passengers were huddled together. In response to their questions he answered, "I have seen the captain's face and all is well."

Amid all the anxiety and confusion of our time, and amid all our uneasiness over what may lie ahead, we need to take time to go apart from our comrades and gaze upon the face of the Captain. We will rise from our knees with calmer minds and fresh courage.

Dear Father God, give me the peace that passes the understanding of men because it comes only to those who trust in thee. Above the roar of the storm may I hear the voice of my Savior saying, "Peace, be still." When the night is dark, may I still be conscious of the light of thy love. Amen.

MONDAY—Week 28

ANALYZE YOUR WORRIES   Read Ps. 62

A doctor who was frequently consulted by people whose ills were mainly the results of their anxieties made a catalog of the worries of his patients. He found that forty per cent of them worried over things which never happened. Thirty per cent of the worries were over past matters which were now beyond their control. Twelve per cent were anxious over their health, although their only illness was in their imagination. Ten per cent worried over their families and friends and neighbors, although in most cases these people were endowed with enough common sense to look after themselves. Eight per cent of the worries had real causes which needed attention.

If the doctor's analysis was correct, nine tenths of our worries are entirely useless and are unworthy of our concern.

Forgive me, Father, for having so many foolish anxieties. Grant that I may face life with earnestness, and make careful plans for the future, without having my energy sapped by worry which is useless and sinful. Amen.

TUESDAY—Week 28

FORGET THE PAST   Read Phil. 3:13-21

There is an Oriental proverb which says, "My skirt with tears is always wet; I have forgotten to forget." Too many people worry about the mistakes and disappointments of the past, and by so doing unfit themselves to deal wisely with the future.

Did you ever watch a canal boat go through a lock? Before water can be let in to lift a boat to a higher level, the gates must be closed behind it. How like life! You must forget the past if you would press on toward a better future. Says Sidney Lanier:

> Old Past, let go, and drop i' the sea
> Till fathomless waters cover thee!
> For I am living, but thou art dead;
> Thou drawest back, I strive ahead,
>   The Day to find.

My Father, thou knowest that I cannot change the past. Keep me from fretting about it. May I confess my sins and my mistakes to thee and go forward with the faith that thou wilt lead me in safe paths if I put my hand in thine. Amen.

WEDNESDAY—Week 28

DON'T CROSS IMAGINARY BRIDGES   Read Phil. 1:12-21

More people worry about the future than about the past. They are burdened by a vague dread of evil things ahead and spend their time crossing imaginary bridges. They look forward to difficulties which never arise.

Many of our expected troubles are like the lions in *Pilgrim's Progress*. Christian heard them growling in the distance when on his journey to the heavenly city. As he came nearer he found they were chained and powerless to hurt him. Said Ralph Waldo Emerson to the worriers of his day:

> Some of your hurts you have cured,
>   And the sharpest you still have survived,
> But what torments of grief you endured,
>   From evils which never arrived!

Save me, O God, from worry about the future. May I commit myself to thy keeping and accept the truth taught in the Bible that all things work together for good to those who love thee. May I do my best and leave the rest to thee. Amen.

THURSDAY—Week 28

WORRYING OVER SUCCESS   Read Eccles. 2:1-15

Augustine, as a young man, worried because he had not achieved honors as great as he desired. He was far more successful than most people of his own age, for he became a professor of rhetoric in the university at Milan when he was in his early thirties. Yet he craved greater fame and honor.

One day on his way to a reception by the emperor where he was to deliver an oration, he saw a beggar who was rejoicing over the fact that he had just been given a good meal. Impressed by the happiness of the beggar in comparison with his own discontent, he realized how foolish it was to worry so much about the honors and material rewards that he sought so eagerly.

Many young people worry too much over the attainment of their ambitions. If you study and work and keep your standards high, you can safely leave success in the hands of God.

Thou God of Wisdom, keep me from judging my life by low standards of worldy success. May I desire worthiness before wealth, peace rather than power, and care more for thy approval than for the praise or blame of men. Amen.

FRIDAY—Week 28

A SCOT WHO WAS THRIFTY BUT LACKING
IN FAITH   Read Luke 12:13-21

Ian Maclaren tells a story about a Scotsman who was continually worrying whether he had enough money to last him the rest of his life. He had no one to support except himself but lived in daily anxiety that he might finally starve.

After his death, papers were found in his cottage on which he had figured how long he could live on the money he already possessed if he spent five shillings a week and how much longer it would last if he reduced his expenditures to a smaller amount. He was richer at the time of his death than he had ever been before, for he was spending less than his income. He had enough money to be absolutely free from want for a much longer time than he stood any chance of living, but he made himself wretched by worrying about how much it cost to live.

Such worrying is utterly useless. Young people need to make

the best provisions they can for the future, but anxiety over tomorrow should not be allowed to spoil the enjoyment of today.

Thou art the giver of every good and perfect gift, O God. Thou openest thy hand and suppliest the needs of all thy children. Increase within me the spirit of gratitude and take away my fears. May my present happiness be undisturbed by vague anxieties. Amen.

SATURDAY—Week 28

SECURITY WHERE GOD IS

Read Ps. 23

A party of shipwrecked sailors succeeded in getting ashore on a rocky coast which had high cliffs rising sharply a few hundred feet out of the water. The tide was coming in, and they were afraid they would be overwhelmed by it with no further chance of escape.

Suddenly one of the sailors gave an exclamation of joy. He had found a little plant and was naturalist enough to know that, while it made its home on rocky coasts, it always kept beyond the reach of the highest tide. The sea might roll in and dash its spray upon them, but they were safe from harm.

Similar is the security of the person who knows that he is standing with God in the place of truth and duty. He need not fear what men can do unto him, for no one can harm his soul.

Like the disciples of old, I come to thee saying, "Lord, increase my faith." May I rest my troubled soul in thee, who remainest ever the same amid the sweeping uncertainties of time. Make me calm and unafraid because I know thy everlasting love is round about me. Amen.

FACING LIFE COURAGEOUSLY

SUNDAY—Week 29

THE HEROISM OF JESUS   Read Luke 4:16-30

Physical valor is the most commonly found form of courage. It is shown by animals and all races of men. From the beginning of recorded history, soldiers have shown themselves brave on the field of battle. Ordinary men often act like heroes in times of fire and flood. Policemen and firemen risk their lives as part of their daily duty.

Such bravery can never be too loudly applauded. Jesus possessed it in the highest degree. He faced mobs and crazy men and went to the cross without flinching; but he showed a higher form of courage when he dared to challenge many of the traditional ideas of his people. He attacked their race prejudice and intense nationalism, and ventured to preach a gospel of love in a world of hate. The prize for courage should go to those who have a moral and intellectual heroism like that of the Master.

Thou God of all courageous souls, make me willing to suffer hardship as a good soldier of Jesus Christ. Make me brave to seek and proclaim the truth even though it be unpopular. May I be willing to belong to a minority when I believe it to be on thy side. Amen.

MONDAY—Week 29

THE HOME OF THE BRAVE   Read Josh. 1:1-9

America has rightly been called the home of the brave. Our country was discovered by a brave man who faced the terrors of an unknown ocean and continued to steer his course "due west" when his crew threatened to mutiny unless he turned back. Brave men settled America. If the early colonists had not been stouthearted, they would not have faced the danger from wild Indians and the hardships of pioneer life. Brave men signed the Declaration of Independence and fought for our freedom. Brave men preserved the Union during the Civil War, and equally brave men fought for their convictions on the Confederate side. Brave men fought in both World Wars for democracy and righteousness.

Never in her history has America lacked people who were brave in her defense. The physical courage of our nation needs now to be matched by a moral courage which dares to abolish the color line, wipe out social injustice, bring an end to greed, and create a Christian brotherhood.

O beautiful for patriot dream
That sees, beyond the years,
Thine alabaster cities gleam,
Undimmed by human tears!
America! America!
God shed his grace on thee,
And crown thy good with brotherhood
From sea to shining sea! Amen.

TUESDAY—Week 29

COURAGE TO DEFY THE STANDARDS
OF THE CROWD
Read Dan. 3

Charles Kingsley, English author and clergyman, once wrote a letter to the young men of his congregation in which he said in part: "My dear young men: The human race may, for practical purposes, be divided into three parts—honest men who mean to do right and do it; knaves who mean to do wrong and do it; fools who mean to do whichever of the two is pleasanter. And these last may be divided into black fools and white fools—black fools who would rather do wrong than right, but dare not unless it is the fashion; white fools who would rather do right than wrong, but dare not unless it is the fashion."

What an accurate description of those who are only as good as the crowd they are with, "white fools who would rather do right than wrong, but dare not unless it is the fashion"! The courage most needed in a democracy is that which enables one to do right regardless of whether it makes one popular or unpopular.

Give me the courage, O God, to live by the highest and best that I know. May I be willing to face ridicule rather than lower my standard. Save me from being afraid of what others may say. May I be content to know that my conduct is approved by thee. Amen.

WEDNESDAY—Week 29

ACCEPTING THE INEVITABLE
Read Luke 22:39-52

Margaret Fuller once said, when discussing her philosophy of life, "I accept the universe." "Egad, she'd better!" said Thomas Carlyle when the statement was reported to him. There are difficult situations that must inevitably be faced by every person. The way we meet them is a test of our courage. It is easy to play the coward, to run away from hardship instead of facing it courageously. George Matheson, as a student for the ministry, found that he was losing his eyesight. He went bravely ahead, and his life is still an inspiration to every clergyman. Think of him when you sing his hymn:

> O Light that followest all my way,
>   I yield my flickering torch to thee;
> My heart restores its borrowed ray,
> That in thy sunshine's blaze its day
>   May brighter, fairer be.

Almighty God, who hast placed me in a world where nothing can be achieved without courage, make me brave to face the necessities of life. May I not spend my time complaining about circumstances or fretting about difficulties, but do my best where I am with what I have. Amen.

THURSDAY—Week 29

COURAGE TO GRAPPLE WITH SOCIAL INJUSTICE
Read Exod. 4:1-17

In the year 404 a Christian monk by the name of Telemachus went from Syria to Rome to protest the cruelty of the gladiatorial combats. He leaped over the railing of the Colosseum into the arena, tried to wrest the swords from the gladiators, and called upon the emperor, Honorius, in the name of Christ to stop the bloody combat. "Back, back, old man!" shouted the spectators. Telemachus refused to move. "Cut him down!" yelled the crowd, and he was killed by the gladiators, who continued to fight over his dead body. But the monk's heroic sacrifice stirred the consciences of the Roman people, and the emperor decreed that the combats should be forever abolished.

A similar bold and sacrificial spirit is needed by modern Christians in grappling with some of the deeply intrenched evils of our day.

> In paths our bravest ones have trod,
>   O make us brave to go;
> That we may give our lives to God
>   By serving men below. Amen.

FRIDAY—Week 29

RECKLESSNESS IS NOT COURAGE   Read Acts 27

A man who had his summer home on the top of a mountain advertised for a chauffeur. Several persons applied for the position and were taken out to a steep cliff not far from the house. Each

127

prospective chauffeur was asked how near he could drive to the edge of the precipice without running over. One man said he could go within five feet of it without danger; another said two feet; a third man confidently stated that he would not be afraid to go within six inches. The man who got the job was a quiet-spoken youth who said he always kept as far away from dangerous places as possible.

Recklessness must not be confused with true valor. The bravado of the man who puts his head in the lion's mouth or the woman who does a sky dance on a pole 150 feet from the ground merely for the sake of money and applause is no comparison to the kind of courage shown by Jesus and the heroic souls of history.

Give me the courage and strength to be brave, O God, but save me from playing the fool by placing my body or soul in needless peril. Keep me from dangerous paths and lead me in ways of righteousness for thy name's sake. Amen.

SATURDAY—Week 29

THE SOURCE OF COURAGE IN CHRISTIAN FAITH
Read Ps. 27

No people have ever shown themselves braver than the Chinese during the years of the Japanese invasion. Back of their courage was the faith of the Chinese Christians, which expressed itself in these words sung by soldiers, students, and all classes of people:

> I will not be afraid;
> I will not be afraid.
> I will look upward,
> And travel onward,
>   And not be afraid.
>
> His arms are underneath me;
> His arms are underneath me.
> His hand upholds me,
> His love enfolds me,
>   So I'm not afraid.

Father of love, give me the faith that casts out all fear. May I feel thy presence round about me and make thee my refuge and strength. Help me to have the calm assurance that no permanent harm can come to me when I am with thee. Amen.

THE GREATNESS OF LITTLE THINGS

SUNDAY—Week 30

A WORLD OF LITTLE THINGS   Read Gen. 11:1-9

Someone has said that "Jumboism" has become our national religion. As the crowds once flocked to see P. T. Barnum's elephant, which was advertised as the largest animal in captivity, so now our enthusiasm is aroused by everything which is big. We admire a city with a big population, a university with a big student body, an industry which has a big production and makes big profits. We are impressed by a man with a million-dollar income and think a church is successful if it has a big membership.

God's standards of value are far different. His world is made up of little objects. Immense as the universe is, it is composed of infinitesimal atoms. More and more scientists are turning from the telescope to the microscope to learn about God's ways of working. We will be in harmony with the methods used by the Creator only when we give more attention to the small things we often despise as trivial.

Forgive me, O God, that so often I crave the opportunity for spectacular service in thy kingdom and am slow to respond to the call of humble duty. Help me to remember that Jesus spent much of his time in doing good in unnoticed ways. Amen.

MONDAY—Week 30

TRIFLES MAKE PERFECTION   Read Luke 8:4-15

"I cannot see where you have made any progress since the last time I was here," said a caller in the studio of Michelangelo. The great sculptor pointed to different parts of the statue and replied: "I have retouched this part, polished that, softened this feature, brought out that muscle, given more expression to the lip, and more energy to the limb." "But those things are all trifles!" exclaimed the visitor. "That may be," said Michelangelo, "but trifles make perfection and perfection is no trifle." Without the capacity for detail which enabled him to spend a long time on a seemingly unimportant part of a statue, he would not have been the prince among sculptors.

It is easy to understand how neglect of trivial matters can ruin the work of an artist and yet overlook the application of this truth to the rest of life. Little things well done are the secret of all worthy achievement. Dickens said that the genius is the one who pays attention to trifles.

My Father, I would be true to thee in small duties. Help me to remember the words of my Savior: "He that is faithful in that which is least is faithful also in much: and he that is unjust in the least is unjust also in much." Amen.

TUESDAY—Week 30

THE MINUTES ARE IMPORTANT   Read Matt. 24:42-51

"Dost thou love life?" asked Benjamin Franklin, and answered his question by saying, "Then do not squander time, for that is the stuff life is made of." Some people amaze us by their ability to get things done. Others disgust us because they never complete any task they undertake. The controlling factor is the use of time.

One of the worst practices of the human race is "killing time." Time is so valuable that when anyone kills ten minutes he has comitted a serious sin. The excuse most frequently given by young people for failure to pray and read the Bible and go to church and Sunday school is lack of time. Many persons neglect the culture of their souls because they dawdle around and do nothing. They have twenty-four hours a day, which is all any man ever had. Their failure comes from not using the fragments of time more wisely. Time is broken up into minutes, and each one is sacred before God. Budget your time and make a place for the things that are really important.

Take my moments and my days, O God. Help me to dedicate them to thee, knowing I cannot serve thee at all unless I place my time in thy control. May each morning find me ready to do thy will, and each evening find me looking back on hours well spent. Amen.

WEDNESDAY—Week 30

BEAUTY IN THE COMMONPLACE   Read Ps. 36:5-10

Nothing in all nature is more beautiful than a brilliantly colored sunset, yet few things have a more commonplace explanation. Its beauty is caused by the light of the sun coming through countless particles of dust in the atmosphere close to the earth. The sun is more beautiful near the horizon than when above our heads, because it shines through more dust, which provides greater opportunity for the reflection and refraction of light.

There is beauty even in the dust if one gets it out of the house and scatters it through the air so the sun can irradiate it at the close of day. Any of the ordinary things of life can be made beautiful if they reflect the divine light. The secret of glorifying the trivial is to link it with the larger purposes of God. Edwin Booth gave this advice to young actors: "The king sits in every audience; play to the king." Does your part in the drama of life seem insignificant? Play to the King!

> Give me not scenes more charming; give me eyes
> To see the beauty that around me lies. Amen.

THURSDAY—Week 30

ANGELS IN THE KITCHEN   Read Zech. 14:16-21

Murillo has a picture called "Angels in the Kitchen." What an unusual place in which to find angels! How can one be an angel if one has to spend one's time in the humdrum and common task of cooking meals and washing dishes to cook more meals, which make it necessary to wash more dishes? Yet out of such an experience, made a service to Christ, comes this poem by Cecily Hallack:

> Lord of the pots and pipkins, since I have no time to be
> A saint by doing lovely things and vigilling with Thee,
> By watching in the twilight dawn, and storming Heaven's gates,
> Make me a saint by getting meals and washing up the plates.

. . . .

> Warm all the kitchen with Thy love, and light it with Thy Peace,
> Forgive the worrying and make the grumbling words to cease.
> Thou, who laid breakfast on the shore, forgive the world which saith,
> "Can any good thing come to God out of poor Nazareth?"

Dear Father, help me to make my daily task, monotonous though it may be, an open door into thy presence. May I grow in grace, not only by withdrawing to kneel before thee, but by learning to labor in the same spirit in which I pray. Amen.

FRIDAY—Week 30

THE DECISIVE FACTORS IN CIVILIZATION
Read Mark 10:13-16

In the year 1809 Napoleon was at the height of his power. Whenever people met, they talked about his campaigns. Nothing else seemed so important as the activities of the military dictator.

At the same time forces of a different sort were at work. In that same year a boy was born in a log cabin in Kentucky, and the mother expressed her ambition for him by saying she would rather have him learn to read the Bible than own a farm. Some months later a baby was born in a wealthy home in Liverpool and dedicated in Christian baptism.

Abraham Lincoln and William E. Gladstone were the babies, both destined to be great Christian statesmen—one in America, and the other in England. What happened in the lives of these boys was more important for civilization than the campaigns of Napoleon. The influences that quietly determine the destinies of unknown young people may be more far-reaching in their effects than the noisy clash of the world's armies.

O God, let me not forget that the birth of a tiny baby in the little town of Bethlehem was the greatest event in history, and that civilization still marches forward on the feet of little children. When the present is discouraging, help me to put my hope in the forces of the future. Amen.

SATURDAY—Week 30

THE HINGES OF THE DOORS OF DESTINY
Read Luke 14:15-24

Not long before his death, Robert Lincoln, who lived to be an old man and had a summer home in Vermont, was discussing the assassination of his father, President Lincoln. He said: "If I had gone to the theater with my father, as I was asked to do, he would not have been shot."

Young Lincoln had just returned to the White House from the army. He had ridden a long distance and was tired. The president asked him to go to the theater, but the son asked to be exused so that he could go to bed. Robert Lincoln said that if he had been in the president's box at Ford's theater, he would have been sitting at the back and could have blocked Booth from getting at his father.

The course of life may be changed by what seems an unimportant decision. Every act a person makes is fraught with endless consequences. Little things are hinges on which turn the doors of destiny. Cultivate, then, the habit of submitting all life to the guidance of God.

Dear Lord, I would put my hand in thine and walk through life in thy company that I may have light and guidance all my way. Keep me from trusting my own wisdom; grant that I may humbly seek to do thy will. Amen.

GUARDING OUR LANGUAGE

SUNDAY—Week 31

THE CONSEQUENCE OF OUR WORDS

Read Matt. 12:22-37

Our modern standards of estimating the importance of our words are in striking contrast to those of Jesus. "Talk is cheap," we often say. Not so did Jesus. He told his disciples emphatically: "By thy words thou shalt be justified, and by thy words thou shalt be condemned."

"What a man says doesn't count" is a remark that is often heard, but from Jesus comes the unhesitating statement, "Every idle word that men shall speak, they shall give account thereof in the day of judgment."

According to Jesus, the words we utter have more far-reaching consequences than we usually realize. Our words have endless power to bless or blight other lives, and they are an accurate index of our own character. They reveal what we are in our inner lives, and they exert a lasting influence upon others.

O Christ, touch my lips with thy kindness that my words may go forth as thy messengers of love into other lives. May others be cheered and strengthened by what I say as well as by what I do. Keep me from speaking harshly and causing needless pain to any person. Amen.

MONDAY—Week 31

A PERSON IS KNOWN BY HIS SPEECH

Read Matt. 26:57-75

The servants in the palace of the high priest identified Peter as a disciple of Jesus because his accent was like that of the Galileans rather than that of the people who lived in Judea. "Thou also art one of them; for thy speech betrayeth thee," said the bystanders. Our speech is always giving us away to the people around us. We can tell a Southerner or a New Englander as soon as we hear him talk. Not only do our words indicate the section of the country we come from; they also give accurate information about our character and the quality of our spiritual life. The boastful man reveals his egotism; the profane person, his irreverence; the critical one, his lack of sympathy.

The speech of the true Christian will at once show the gracious kindness of his spirit. Said Emerson, "Use what language you will, you can never say anything but what you are."

O God, grant that the words which I utter may reveal me as one who has been in the company of thy Son.
> Lord, speak to me, that I may speak
> In living echoes of thy tone. Amen.

TUESDAY—Week 31

WORDS CANNOT BE RECOVERED   Read Jas. 3

A European peasant, who had told an unkind and untrue story about an acquaintance, went to a monk and asked him what he could do to atone for it.

"Fill a bag with chicken feathers," said the monk. "Then go to every house in the village and drop a feather in each dooryard."

The peasant followed the monk's instructions and returned to ask if he had done sufficient penance for his folly.

"Not yet," said the monk. "You must now take the bag, go back to every house, and pick up every feather you dropped."

The peasant protested that it would be impossible because most of the feathers would already be blown by the wind.

"And so it is with your slanderous stories and evil words," rejoined the monk. "They are easily spoken; but no matter how hard you try, you cannot bring them back again."

Dear Father, help me to love my neighbor with my conversation. Knowing that my words can never be recalled, may I send them forth only when they are true and kind. Teach me to keep silent rather than to speak falsely or foolishly. Amen.

WEDNESDAY—Week 31

BY ORDER OF GENERAL WASHINGTON   Read Jas. 5:1-12

"The General is sorry to be informed that the foolish and wicked practice of profane cursing and swearing, a vice heretofore little known in an American army, is growing into fashion. He hopes the officers will, by example as well as influence, endeavor to check it, and that both they and the men will reflect that we can have little hope of the blessing of Heaven on our arms if we insult it by our impiety and folly. Added to this, it is a vice so mean and low, without any temptation, that every man of sense and character detests and despises it."

This was a general order issued by George Washington to the American army from his headquarters in New York City in the month of July, 1776. Washington was no prig. Much of his life was spent among soldiers and workingmen, but he had no use for irreverence and vulgarity.

Lord, save me from the mistake of thinking that profanity is a sign of manliness. May I remember that Jesus said, "Swear not at all." Help me to set a seal upon my mouth that I may keep my tongue from evil and my lips from speaking guile. Amen.

THURSDAY—Week 31

CLEAN HUMOR   Read Matt. 15:7-20

During the Civil War, General Grant and several of his officers were gathered in a Virginia farmhouse for the evening. As they sat around the fireplace in conversation, one of the younger officers said, "I have a good story"; then, looking around to see if the door was closed, he added, "I think there are no ladies present." The other men laughed in anticipation of a racy joke, but General Grant said quietly, "No ladies, but there are some gentlemen."

Those who think it makes no difference whether a story borders on indecency so long as it is funny should recall the case of Harold Lloyd, a favorite movie comedian of a previous decade, who refused a million-dollar contract because the story he was asked to play contained scenes he considered off-color. He said, "If I can't be funny and clean, then I'll just be clean."

Guard us against flippancy and irreverence in the sacred things of life. May we find genuine pleasure in clean and wholesome mirth and feel inherent disgust for all coarse-minded humor.—From a prayer of the West Point Cadets.

FRIDAY—Week 31

WORDS OF APPRECIATION   Read Deut. 34

The children of Israel wept for Moses thirty days after he was dead. But think how meanly they treated him when he was alive! They murmured and criticized and made his life wretched with their complaints. How often this experience is repeated! We find fault with our friends and family while they are alive and neglect to say a word of gratitude which would bring joy to their hearts. After they are gone, we are lavish with our praise. Said Henry Ward Beecher: "Do not keep the alabaster boxes of your love and tenderness sealed up until your friends are dead."

It's better to buy a cheap bouquet
And give to your friend this very day

135

Than a bushel of roses, white and red,
To lay on his coffin after he's dead.

Heavenly Father, teach my stammering tongue how to express the gratitude that is in my heart. May I never withhold the words of praise and thankfulness that would brighten the lives of my friends, and may I never speak the words of complaint that would make them unhappy. Amen.

SATURDAY—Week 31

THE ARROW AND THE SONG

Read Prov. 8

An idle word may be a power for evil, but a helpful word can be an equally strong influence for good. So Longfellow sings:

> I shot an arrow into the air,
> It fell to earth, I knew not where;
>
> . . . .
>
> I breathed a song into the air,
> It fell on earth, I knew not where;
>
> . . . .
>
> Long, long afterward, in an oak
> I found the arrow, still unbroke;
> And the song, from beginning to end,
> I found again in the heart of a friend.

Courage in the midst of despair, comfort in a time of sorrow, hope in the place of doubt, good cheer that dispels the darkness—these are the rich fruit of the expressions of kindness and gratitude.

Guide me, teach me, strengthen me, till I become such a person as thou wouldst have me be; pure and gentle, truthful and high-minded, brave and able, courteous and generous, dutiful and useful.—Charles Kingsley.

BOOKS AND READING

SUNDAY—Week 32

JESUS WAS EDUCATED BY HIS READING
Read Matt. 13:53-58; John 7:14-17

"How knoweth this man letters, having never learned?" was the question asked about Jesus by the people of his own generation. Biblical scholars today are still asking how a man brought up in a humble home, spending his working hours as a carpenter, could acquire the wisdom which has made his ethical teachings the loftiest the world has ever known. How did he acquire the ability to speak in such a way that many of his parables and short stories are among the flawless gems of literature?

The answer is that Jesus' wisdom came, in part, through his familiarity with the best literature of the Hebrew people. He had read the scrolls of the Old Testament, memorized many passages, meditated upon them until their truths had dominated his mind. Again and again he quoted from the Psalms and the Prophets. His mind was a storehouse of the best literary treasures of his race.

Dear God, I thank thee for the wisdom as well as the goodness of Jesus. Stir me to a more searching study of the Scriptures, that my mind may be nourished on the thoughts that make men wise. Amen.

MONDAY—Week 32

ONE TEST OF A GOOD BOOK
Read II Kings 22:8 23:3

One of the best and simplest ways by which to judge any book or work of art is to note what you remember longest about it. Look at one of the famous statues of Lincoln, such as the one in the Lincoln Memorial in Washington, and the chances are that you will not remember many of the details, but an impression is stamped on your memory of nobility of character of a great soul humbled with a great responsibility but carrying it bravely because of an all-embracing love for his fellow men.

If you have read Dickens' *Tale of Two Cities*, you have probably forgotten the details of the plot and the names of many of the characters; but you will still recall the noble figure of Sidney Carton as he mounts the guillotine to give his life for another. Like

137

food which leaves a good taste in the mouth, the best literature is that which flavors our lives with some high enthusiasm.

I thank thee, O God, that there are so many books which, in giving enjoyment, open my eyes to the beauty of the world in which I live and create within me a deeper love for my fellow men. Teach me to make such books my friends. Amen.

TUESDAY—Week 32

LINCOLN'S READING
Read Prov. 1:1-7

Abraham Lincoln spent his boyhood in a frontier environment that provided little intellectual stimulus. Cut off from libraries and schools, he is said to have had the following books available for his reading: The Bible, *Pilgrim's Progress, Aesop's Fables, Robinson Crusoe,* Weems's *Life of Washington,* and a history of the United States. Limited as the list is, it includes many different types of literature—fiction, history, biography, works of moral and religious inspiration. Lincoln read these books, not only once, but many times. He mastered them and made them yield up their last drop of intellectual nourishment.

Notice that four of these books have stood the test of time and are among the recognized classics of the world. The quality of Lincoln's reading, in a home on the edge of the wilderness, was better than that of many people today who have access to the best libraries.

Thou who art ever seeking to lead us into the truth, grant that I may hunger and thirst after knowledge; may my mind be filled with the treasures of thought which come from reading the good books that are ever available. Amen.

WEDNESDAY—Week 32

MAKE FRIENDS OF THE GREAT
Read Mark 9:1-8

In the ocean are many creatures like the sponge which fasten themselves to rocks and get their food by opening their mouths and swallowing whatever the waves wash in. So there are people who use little discrimination in what they read. Trashy and poorly written stories, cynical novels that undermine one's faith in life, magazines with vulgar jokes—all are swallowed, and the person becomes like that which he feeds on.

It is not enough that the books you read do you no harm. You need to choose those which will introduce you to the world's great minds. When Michael Pupin came to this country as a young Serbian immigrant, immigration officials asked him if he had any

riends in America. He replied that he did and named Benjamin
Franklin, Abraham Lincoln, and Harriet Beecher Stowe. The offi-
ials let him in; they were sure that a boy who was familiar with
uch people would make his way. The great minds of the world
await your companionship. Take their books and read.

All through life I must make choices, O God. Teach me not only to choose
right between good and evil, but to discriminate between the best and the
second best. Help me to set high standards for my reading and friendships,
and never to lower them. Amen.

THURSDAY—Week 32

LET THE SUNSHINE IN!   Read Ps. 119:105-112

When Hamlin Garland, as a young man, was lecturing on literature in Philadelphia, he went to call on Walt Whitman, who lived
across the river in Camden. The old poet talked for an hour about
the men who were America's leading authors; then Garland asked
him for some advice to give to the younger writers of his day.

"Somewhere in your play or novel, let the sunshine in!" was
Whitman's message.

Does not that suggest a standard which can be used by any reader,
as well as by any author, to determine whether a book is worthy
of attention? Does the book darken one's outlook on life, obscure
the light which shines from one's ideals, or make it more difficult
to have faith in God and one's fellowmen? Then it has no rightful
claim upon a Christian's time. The work may be clever and witty,
but it makes no helpful contribution to life. The world is already
dark enough; books are needed which will let in the sunshine.

Heavenly Father, help me to keep my life radiant with faith. Let not the
light that is in me be turned into darkness! Guide me to books and magazines which will give me a wholesome outlook on life and will keep me
aware of thy presence. Amen.

FRIDAY—Week 32

WHY PAUL WANTED HIS BOOKS   Read II Tim. 4

Do you remember one of the urgent desires of the Apostle Paul
when he was in prison in Rome? He wrote to Timothy, asking him
to come for a visit and to bring some objects he greatly wanted. He
needed a cloak for the cold weather, but most of all he craved food
for his mind. He said, "Bring . . . the books, but especially the
parchments."

What a blessing a good book is when we are shut up in some
prison of illness or loneliness! It allows us to escape from the limi-

tations of our environment. But Paul had a more serious reason for reading. The parchments were the scrolls of the Old Testament; in them were stories of men whose faith in God enabled them to face death without flinching. Such writings would bring him inspiration and courage.

De Quincey divided literature into two classes: one type gives information, the other is a source of power. Some books are like an intellectual storage battery; they renew our strength. In this field the Bible is without rival.

O God, help me to find courage for life's difficult situations in the stories of brave men who have learned how to turn their hardships into blessings. Grant that my reading may become a source of moral power. Amen.

SATURDAY—Week 32

HAVE YOU STARTED A LIBRARY?   Read Ps. 119:1-16

Every young person ought gradually to be developing his own library. But you must choose the books with care. Best-selling novels are, with a few exceptions, a bad gamble, for most of them are soon forgotten. The books to make your own are those that have become recognized as literature—books which, like a fine violin, have the richness of age.

The first book to put in your library is a well-bound Bible, printed with good type and containing a concordance. Do not hesitate over the price, for you will use the Bible all your life. Then choose as you will from the deathless and timeless literature of the world, but choose with discretion; for it frequently happens that the course of one's life is determined by what one reads.

Said Henry Ward Beecher: "A little library growing larger each year is an honorable part of a man's history. It is a man's duty to have books. A library is not a luxury, but one of the necessities of life."

Lord of life, help me to throw open the doors of my mind and extend a welcome to all beauty and truth. Teach me how to create an environment in which it will be easy for me to do what is right. Amen.

THE CHRISTIAN AND HIS MONEY

SUNDAY—Week 33

JESUS' CONCERN OVER MONEY   Read Matt. 25:14-30

A young man fell heir to over a million dollars not many years ago and refused to accept it. He felt that he had done nothing to earn it and could be a better follower of Jesus without it. Whether or not he was right or wrong is a question on which opinions will differ, but the incident serves to remind us that there are few more difficult problems for the Christian than those which are connected with money.

Jesus was deeply concerned about the way people made and used their money. Throughout the Four Gospels one verse in every eight deals with the proper use of material possessions, and sixteen out of the thirty-eight parables deal with the same theme. His main concern was that in making money people should not lose their personhood. He warned them that it can be secured at too high a price and that one makes a bad bargain if one gets money in such a way that one loses one's soul or harms the soul of one's neighbor.

O God, make me strong to win the victory over any temptation to use my blessings wrongly. May I seek to lay up treasure in heaven instead of on earth. Give me an unselfish heart and a deeper devotion to the cause of thy kingdom. Amen.

MONDAY—Week 33

MONEY TALKS   Read Luke 19:2-9

When Zacchaeus was defrauding others and hoarding his wealth for himself, his money proclaimed his dishonesty and stinginess. When he returned four times as much as he had taken from others in unjust taxes, and gave half of his wealth to the poor, his money announced his honesty and largeness of heart.

Yes, money talks. It seems hardly on speaking terms with some people and keeps saying "Goodby" to others, yet it speaks a language which describes the one who possesses it. The means by which you get your money tells whether you are a worker, a beggar, or a thief. The way you spend it reveals whether you are wise or foolish. The amount you contribute to Christian causes proclaims whether you are a tightwad or a liberal giver. What does your money say about you?

O God, when my money talks about me, may it always describe me as a true follower of Jesus Christ. Grant that I may consider my money as a trust from thee, who art the owner of all. Whether my money is given to me by my parents or earned by my own labor, may I use it in a way that will meet with thy approval. Amen.

TUESDAY—Week 33

IS MONEY YOUR FRIEND OR YOUR ENEMY?

Read I Tim. 6

Our attitude toward money is one of the great forces for the making or unmaking of character. Rightly used, money is one of our best friends; wrongly used, it is our worst enemy. Money in itself is neither good nor evil, but it can become a blessing or a curse according to the way it is handled. This idea has been put into the following lines by an unknown poet:

> Dug from the mountainside, washed from the glen,
> Servant am I or master of men.
> Steal me, I curse you,
> Earn me, I bless you;
> Grasp me and hoard me, a fiend shall possess you;
> Live for me, die for me,
> Covet me, take me,
> Angel or devil, I am what you make me.

Grant, O Lord, that I may use whatever money I have in such a way that it remains my servant and does not become my master. Knowing that the love of money is the root of all evil, may I never seek it for its own sake, but always as a means of helping me to live at my best and of doing good to others. Amen.

WEDNESDAY Week 33

THE MONEY MICROBE

Read Luke 12:1-15

Two scientists made a series of bacteriological experiments on paper money after it had been in circulation a short time. Nineteen hundred germs of various kinds were found on the average bank note, and one microbe was discovered which was peculiar to paper money in that it had never been found anywhere else. It seemed to thrive and multiply only on the kind of paper out of which money is made. So it might be said, by way of a parable, that there is a money microbe.

Whatever may be true of real microbes, there is a germ called covetousness, which often goes with money and is a deadly peril to the soul. "Thou shalt not covet" was the tenth commandment of Moses, and Jesus emphasized it by saying, "Take heed, and beware of covetousness." The person who is envous of the riches of others or allows his thoughts to be dominated by the desire for gain has been infected by the money microbe and is in danger of becoming sick with a deadly disease.

Our Father, I thank thee that Jesus, though he was poor, was never envious or discontented. Help me to understand that true happiness depends, not on the money in my pocket, but on the love in my heart. Amen.

THURSDAY—Week 33

MONEY IS NOT YOUR OWN   Read II Cor. 8

No one ever has a right to say that money is his to spend as he pleases. We are indebted to God as the Creator and Owner of the earth and its resources, and in all our enterprises we are dependent on the help given by other people. Whether one is a capitalist or a newsboy one must recognize that money is not secured simply by one's own efforts.

Listen to what Fritz Kreisler says about the money he made with his violin: "I never look upon money I earn as my own. It is public money. It belongs to the public. It is only a fund entrusted to my care for proper disbursement. So I never spend the money I earn in high living for personal pleasure. If I did, I should feel guilty of a heinous crime. How can I squander money on myself while there is so much misery, so much hunger in the world?"

Creator of all things, make me a faithful steward of the money and material possessions which thou hast entrusted to my care. May I never think of them as my own but remember that I must render account unto thee. Amen.

FRIDAY—Week 33

CARELESS SPENDING   Read Gen. 41:25-57

A father agreed to give his son a regular allowance on condition that he keep a careful account of the way he spent it. After a few months the father looked over the boy's record. He found various amounts listed under appropriate headings but was puzzled at the last and largest item of all, which was put down as T.L.O.K. The boy explained it by saying: "I forgot how I spent a lot of my money, so I put everything I couldn't remember under T.L.O.K., which means "The Lord only knows."

No one realizes how much money he spends needlessly and

carelessly until he begins to make out a budget and keep an accurate record. Many high-school students, by being careful with their money, could save enough in four years to pay a considerable part of a year's expenses in college. This might prove to be the determining factor in the ability to get a college education.

O most liberal Distributer of thy gifts, who givest us all kinds of good things to use, grant to us thy grace, that we misuse not these thy gracious gifts given to our use and profit. Amen.

SATURDAY—Week 33

GIVING TO THE CAUSE OF CHRIST   Read Mark 12:28-44

It is a historical fact that King Louis XI of France once made out a deed in which he gave the province of Boulogne to the Virgin Mary but expressly stated that all the income and revenues should forever be paid to himself and his heirs. He gave everything for his religion but did it in such a way that he made no personal sacrifice.

Do not many people today go through a similar form of pious hypocrisy when they say they dedicate their lives to Christ but have no intention of allowing Christian principles to control their attitude toward money? It is not uncommon for a person to stand up in church and sing, "All to Jesus I surrender," and then give less than the price of a theater admission or a package of cigarettes when the collection plate is passed.

During his last week in Jerusalem "Jesus sat over against the treasury and beheld how people cast money into the treasury." He still watches the way we give to the church and the agencies of his kingdom.

Giver of all good gifts, I thank thee for thy boundless goodness. Grant that out of true gratitude I may give freely to the church and its worldwide work. With the offering of my money may there go the dedication of my life to the doing of thy will. Amen.

144

RECREATION AND AMUSEMENTS

SUNDAY—Week 34

CHRISTIANS NEED TO PLAY   Read Matt. 11:15-19

Those who try to divorce religion from healthy forms of amusement and recreation are not being true to the spirit of Jesus. An early church legend about the Apostle John, who was the disciple Jesus most dearly loved, correctly reflects the Master's attitude.

The aged saint was playing with a flock of doves, which flew around him and perched on his shoulders and hands while he talked to them as if they were human friends. A hunter came by and expressed his amazement that anyone so religious as the saintly John would spend his time in such a useless pastime. John pointed to the bow in the hunter's hand and asked why he carried it with a loosened string. "Because it loses its strength unless it is given a chance to unbend," said the hunter. John laughed and said: "If even a piece of wood needs to unbend to retain its usefulness, why should you be surprised that a servant of Christ should sometimes relax and so keep himself stronger for his work."

Dear Father, whenever I think about thy Son, may I remember that he went about Palestine with a cheerful face and that others rejoiced to have him join their company. Keep me from associating religion with dullness. May I make it a source of health and joy. Amen.

MONDAY—Week 34

RECREATION SHOULD HAVE POSITIVE VALUE
Read Eph. 6:10-18

A young woman went to a minister to talk about becoming a Christian and uniting with the church. She mentioned certain aspects of her social life and said, "I would hardly be willing to give these things up." The clergyman answered: "You must be willing to marshal all your resources to keep yourself at your best. If you think Christ is asking you to give up these pleasures, you must be willing to do so, or you will not truly be committing your life to him."

Your recreation, like every other aspect of your living, should help you to become positively and actively a Christian. It is not enough to say that some practice does you no harm. It should

145

make a contribution to your health and your wholesome outlook on life. Your recreation ought to be recreating: it ought to give tang and zest to your life and make it easier for you to be a whole-hearted follower of Christ.

O God, I would bring my life to thee that I may live in all the fullness of my powers. Give me the kind of faith that will make me stronger in body, keener in mind, purer in heart, and better fitted to do my share of the world's work. Amen.

TUESDAY—Week 34

"BLEACHERITIS"   Read I Tim. 4:12-16

Too many people are afflicted with "bleacheritis." They get all their amusement by watching others. From seats on the grand-stand they shout instructions to a few hardworking players; their lungs get exercise but not their legs. We need to be participants and not spectators. Movies and other forms of passive entertain-ment have their place, but they are not adequate substitutes for taking active part in some type of recreation. Play at its best can never be experienced vicariously; like eating, it is something that cannot be done by proxy.

That you are not an expert player is no reason for not getting into some game. You ought not to be bashful about taking part in a sport because of inexperience. Be encouraged by G. K. Chester-ton's remark that anything worth doing at all is worth doing badly.

Thou Captain of my soul, if I have been sitting on the grandstand, help me now to respond to thy call to play the game. Grant that I may not timidly stand aside from the joys and struggles of life but wrestle with all life's reali-ties. Amen.

WEDNESDAY—Week 34

DO YOU HAVE A HOBBY?   Read I Sam. 16:14-23

The finest type of recreation is in the cultivation of some kind of hobby which you can follow through life with an interest that does not diminish as you grow older. President Roosevelt was a long-time stamp collector; toward the end of his term in office, he re-marked to a friend that he was longing for the time when he could give more attention to his stamps. John Erskine, famous author and professor of literature, was a skilled pianist. Dr. Frederick Banting, the Canadian doctor who developed insulin as a treat-ment for diabetes, was an artist of no mean ability. A well-known clergyman has become an expert photographer, and another is an enthusiastic student of birds. Such people know how to amuse themselves without being dependent on the entertainment of others.

The late William Lyon Phelps said that the happiest person is the one who thinks the most interesting thoughts. A good hobby will help to make you happy by enriching your inner life.

I thank thee, Father, that I live in an interesting world that has endless opportunity for creative activities. Grant that my life may never be drab and colorless. Make it like that of thy Son, who was alive to the beauty of the world as well as to the needs of men. Amen.

THURSDAY—Week 34

SUNDAY AMUSEMENTS   Read Mark 2:23-28

Historically, Sunday was the time when the early Christians celebrated the resurrection of Jesus. So it was the most joyous day of the week—happy and religious, quiet and gay, a time for activities which could be enjoyed in companionship with a living Lord. This gives us a clue to the kind of pleasures to be enjoyed on Sunday. The ones in keeping with the spirit of the day are those which strengthen us physically, mentally, morally, and make us better all-round Christians.

Jesus says the Sabbath was made for man. Notice he does not say that it exists for spiritual laziness, self-indulgence, money, and commercialized pleasure; he says that it exists to serve the higher interests of those made in the image of God.

There are fifty-two Sundays in a year. By the time you are fifty years old you will have lived more than seven years of Sundays. What you do on these days will go a long way toward determining the quality of your life. Learn to make wise use of your Sundays.

Dear God, grant that Sunday may ever be a joyous day because it calls me to the house of worship and to thoughts of thee. As the disciples walked through the cornfields with their Master on the Sabbath, so may I feel that I can rightly go wherever I have his companionship. Amen.

FRIDAY—Week 34

SUNDAY SHOULD NOT BE COMMERCIALIZED
Read Exod. 16:22-30

The observance of the Sabbath as a day of rest and worship has been one of the citadels of civilization. The idea of making the seventh day different from the rest of the week is far older than Christianity; it is older than Moses, for references to it are found in the records of Babylonia. Originally it grew out of the needs of mankind. It is significant that the League of Nations recommended that all countries recognize the Sabbath. The statesmen knew that a civilization is endangered when the Sabbath ceases to be a day of worship and rest.

What does this mean for the Christian? Surely he or she will oppose the increasing commercialization of the day and will make it a personal principle not to patronize Sunday amusements maintained primarily for profit! To have the Sabbath dominated by commercialized recreation is to crowd out its higher values and throw away something vital to the national life.

O God, grant that the Sabbath Day may be preserved from the taint of commercialism. May it never become an ordinary day but be reserved for the recreating activities which are always in danger of being pushed aside during the week. Amen.

SATURDAY—Week 34

THE EFFECT OF OUR PLEASURE ON OTHERS
Read I Chron. 11:10-19

Another standard by which to test our recreations is this: Is this thing which provides enjoyment for me a source of happiness and moral health to all who are affected by it?

Aesop has a fable about a boy throwing stones at some frogs, one of whom lifted his head above the water and asked, "Why are you throwing these stones?" "Just for fun," the boy replied. And the frog said, "What is fun to you is death to us." The scripture reading for the day tells how David refused to drink the water that had been brought from the Bethlehem well at the risk of his soldiers' lives. He said: "God forbid it me, that I should do this thing: shall I drink the blood of these men that have put their lives in jeopardy? for with the jeopardy of their lives they brought it."

God forbid that our pleasure should be purchased at the price of another person's welfare or by killing someone's self-respect!

O Lord, grant that in my desire for pleasure I may never thoughtlessly or selfishly cause harm or unhappiness to others. May I spend my money only on wholesome recreation and never add to the profit of any business that endangers human welfare. Amen.

SOME ENEMIES OF THE HIGHER LIFE

SUNDAY—Week 35

LIQUOR WEARS A FALSE FACE Read Prov. 20:1; 23:29-35

"Whosoever is deceived thereby is not wise," says the Book of Proverbs about those who use wine and strong drink. Could any word more aptly describe liquor than "deceiving"? It hides behind a false face; it poses as a friend when it is an enemy. It pretends to be a stimulant when it is really a depressant.

If you think a drink is a stimulus to your mind, you are under an illusion. Drink removes inhibitions, loosens the tongue, weakens self-control, and destroys good judgment. The sense of self-satisfaction created by liquor is subtly deceptive; it will make you think you are more of a man when you have become something less than your normal self.

There is nothing a person can do better after taking a drink. He cannot be more intelligent in conversation; nor can he become a better student or soldier, a better athlete or chauffeur, or a better anything.

Heavenly Father, keep me from being deceived by any evil masquerading as good, and save me from deceiving myself. Help me to look at all life in the light of thy truth and to square my daily conduct by the standards of thy Son. Amen.

MONDAY—Week 35

WHAT IS TEMPERANCE? Read II Pet. 1:1-11

Do you know the original meaning of the word "temperance"? It was applied to a steel blade that had been subjected to the proper temperatures of heat and cold until it represented the best possible combination of strength and flexibility. It was neither too hard nor too soft; it could hold the keenest cutting edge and was so pliable that it could not readily be broken. To say that a sword was finely tempered meant that it had been brought to the highest degree of efficiency.

The temperate character, then, is one which is so self-controlled that it is best able to meet all the demands that life may place upon it. Since the athlete, the railroad engineer, the Greyhound bus driver, and other people in highly responsible positions are not allowed to drink, the logical conclusion is that anyone who wishes to be finely tempered and keep at his best will be a total abstainer from alcoholic beverages. Peter gave good advice when he told us to add "temperance" to knowledge.

Dear God, in these days when strong bodies and clear minds are needed, make me ashamed to be anything less than my best. Help me to discipline my desires and to bring them all into obedience to thy will. Amen.

TUESDAY—Week 35

TESTIMONY OF THE WORLD'S FASTEST RUNNER
Read Isa. 5:11-23

Glenn Cunningham, of Kansas, was called the world's fastest human being. He held the world's record as a mile runner, having covered the distance in the Dartmouth gymnasium in 4:04:4. He had amazing speed; more than that, he had courage and the capacity for self-discipline. During boyhood days he was so badly burned in a schoolhouse fire that doctors said he would never walk again. Cunningham fooled them. He got out of bed and fell on his face, but he walked. Day by day he walked farther; then he ran. He rigidly abstained from liquor and tobacco. He said: "An individual cannot use alcoholic beverages and expect to perform as efficiently, physically or mentally, as he would otherwise. If young people would clear their minds of cobwebs, they would understand the motives of those who try to induce them to drink. All I can say is that any person is better off without alcohol. I have known some athletes who used alcoholic beverages. They don't last."

O Lord, help me to develop all the possibilities of my manhood. Give me a vision of what I may become by accepting the guidance of thy spirit and relying upon thee as my source of strength. Amen.

WEDNESDAY—Week 35

FOR THE SAKE OF OTHERS
Read Rom. 14:13-23

No thoughtful person takes the position that he is entitled to use liquor without restraint. He will, therefore, decide to be either a moderate drinker or a total abstainer. Entirely apart from the consequences of moderate drinking on ourselves is the question of our influence. Jesus' severest condemnation was on those whose conduct was injurious to others. He said it were better for a man to have a millstone hung about his neck and be cast into the sea than to harm a child. But how many children have been denied a deent chance in life because of drunken parents whose first drinks were taken at a social gathering.

Dr. William J. Mayo, in a bulletin of the Mayo Clinic, said that three out of every ten drinkers become alcohol addicts and find it almost impossible to break the habit. Is it not the Christian attitude to abstain from drinking for the sake of these people and their families? "For their sakes I sanctify myself," said Jesus.

O God, let me never forget that I am my brother's keeper. Grant that I may make it easier for others to do right and harder for them to do wrong. May my influence be to others a source of strength and not of weakness. Amen.

THURSDAY—Week 35

LET EVERY BUSINESS JUSTIFY ITSELF
BY THE TRUTH
Read I Cor. 10:23-33

Is there not something wrong about a business that resorts to false propaganda in its advertisements? Until stopped by the government, several liquor and tobacco companies were using endorsements by famous athletes, implying that they smoked or drank.

The magazine of the Amateur Athletic Union came out with this rebuke: "Considerable harm has been done to the youth of the nation by misleading advertisements proclaiming that this or that athlete smoked or drank while on the way to a championship. On the face of it, that could not be. Not only is it bad taste for athletes to give these testimonials but some of them are lending their names to outright lies. Some of them never have smoked and certainly those who did smoke never did it while in training!"

Is any business worthy of a place in the life of the nation, or deserving of patronage, if it cannot do business under the banner of truth?

Thou God of truth, help me to recognize deceitful propaganda for what it is. Teach me to discern truth from falsehood and make me fearless in seeking the facts in every situation. Amen.

FRIDAY—Week 35

SMOKING HANDICAPS THE CHRISTIAN RUNNER
Read Heb. 12:1-17

The author of Hebrews compares the Christian life to a race and calls upon his readers not only to avoid the things which are definitely sinful but those which would be a "weight" or handicap. He says, "Let us lay aside every weight, and the sin which doth so easily beset us."

Is not smoking one of the habits which hinder rather than help the Christian runner in his race for a healthy and wholesome life? Gene Tunney, former heavyweight boxing champion, insists that smoking is bad not only for athletes but for everybody.

He says: "No boxer, no athlete in training, smokes. He knows that whenever nerves, muscles, heart, and brain are called upon for a supreme effort, the tobacco user is the first to fold. But how about the ordinary citizen? Does smoking affect his vitality, shorten his life and nudge him down the trash skid before his time? The grim monosyllabic answer, based on medical testimony, is 'yes.' "

Father, keep me from allowing any habit to make me its slave. Knowing that the Christian life is a long, hard race, may I lay aside everything which might hinder me from reaching the goal. Amen.

SATURDAY—Week 35

WHAT IS WRONG ABOUT GAMBLING?

Read Acts 20:32-38

"What is wrong about gambling? Everyone does it," said a young man brought before a judge after being arrested as a member of a youthful gambling ring. "The same thing that is the matter with stealing; it is trying to get money from someone without giving him any value in return," answered the judge.

Gambling was once allowed in all states, but experience showed it was an enemy of thrift, honesty, and hard work; and so laws were passed to suppress it. Lotteries were used to raise public funds in the early history of our country, but the practice was abandoned because it was found to be contrary to social and moral welfare. It is significant that when Monte Carlo was in its heyday, before the war, the ruler of Monaco never gambled and permitted his subjects to do so only one day a year. He knew that a nation of gamblers would not be fit for useful living.

Lord, teach me the sacredness of money. May I see it not merely as paper or metal, but as part of somebody's life. Save me from the sin of trying to get money without work, and help me to see that honest toil of hand or head is a part of thy plan for all people. Amen.

RACIAL AND RELIGIOUS PREJUDICE

SUNDAY—Week 36

"GOD MUST LOVE COLORED PEOPLE"
Read Luke 13:23-30

The relations of the various races to each other constitute a baffling problem in the world today. Said H. G. Wells: "There is no more evil thing in the world than race prejudice. It justifies more baseness and cruelty than any other sort of error in the world."

White people are in a minority. Over two-thirds of all the people in the world have colored skins. This means that if we have faith in humanity we must believe in dark-skinned peoples, as they form the majority of mankind. We might paraphrase the words of Lincoln about poor people by saying, "God must love the colored people or he would not have made so many of them."

Christian people have an inescapable responsibility for taking the lead in wiping out race prejudice. We make a mockery of our religion if we pray to God as the Father of all mankind and then refuse equal opportunities to brothers whose skins are a different color.

God of men and nations, give us the human love which alone can bridge the chasm of race that divides us. Guide us in making a new declaration of interdependence with all mankind. We live in one world; make us one in spirit. Amen.

MONDAY—Week 36

THERE ARE NO SUPERIOR RACES Read Acts 17:16-34

Many people still believe in the myth that some races are superior to others. This is the heart of Nazi philosophy; it has also been the basis of imperialism and colonial exploitation on the part of many nations. White people have thought the colored races belonged to a lower order of humanity and so felt justified in subjugating them.

What is the actual fact? The American Psychological Association is on record as saying, "There are no innate mental differences between the races." Franz Boas, famous anthropologist, says: "If we were to select the most intelligent, imaginative, energetic, and emotionally stable third of mankind, all races would be represented." Some races are backward because they have thus far had little opportunity for education, but none are inferior. God has made of one blood all the races of mankind, and there is no inherent difference in their capacities.

Dear Father, forgive the conceit which makes us think we are better than others because our skins have a whiter hue. Transform our pride into a humble desire to use our strength in the service of the weak. Amen.

TUESDAY—Week 36

OUR AMERICAN MIXTURE
Read Ps. 133

Did you ever stop to consider the mixture of races and religions we have in America? From the standpoint of racial origins, our population is as follows: Anglo-Saxon, sixty million; Teutonic, fifteen million; Negro, thirteen million; Irish, ten million; Slavic, nine million; Italian, five million; Jewish, five million; Scandinavian, four million; French, two million; Finnish, Lithuanian, Greek, and Mexican, one million each; Indian and Oriental in smaller numbers.

From the religious standpoint there are about thirty-nine million Protestants and nearly twenty-three million Roman Catholics. A little less than five million are Jews; one million, Greek Catholics; two-thirds of a million, Mormons; and all sorts of cults and sects.

Is it not plain that racial and religious prejudice contains enough dynamite to blow our democracy to pieces? We must be true to our Declaration of Independence, which says all men are created equal and are endowed by the Creator with inalienable rights.

O God, give our beloved America thy blessing. Help us to remember that, though we represent many races and creeds, we all belong to thy holy family. Make us one in our service to thee and in our loyalty to our country. Amen.

WEDNESDAY—Week 36

LOOK AT ALL THE FACTS
Read Num. 23:11-26

The old story of Balaam and Balak has a needed lesson for our own day. Balak, king of Moab, was afraid his kingdom would be invaded by the Israelites on their way from Egypt to Canaan. So he hired a wizard by the name of Balaam to pronounce a death-dealing curse on the foreigners. Balaam started to curse Israel but was overruled by the spirit of the Lord. The king then suggested that Balaam go to a spot on the mountain where he could not see all the Israelites but only the utmost part of them"—the sick and infirm who brought up the rear. He thought the wizard could more readily curse the Israelites if he saw their weakness instead of their strength.

How often we judge people on a partial basis! We treat a race or group as though all its members were alike, making snap judgments and mistaking a half truth for the whole truth. Should we not look at our fellowmen from some high spot where we can see all the facts?

Eternal Truth, make me fearless in facing facts, and save me from the sin of distorting them to suit my own convenience. Keep me from believing idle statements made by unthinking people, and give me a mind without prejudice. Amen.

THURSDAY—Week 36

CHANGING PLACES Read Acts 26:24-32

How can we break down the walls of misunderstanding that divide people of different groups and classes? One thing we can all do is use our imaginations to put ourselves in the place of those with whom we disagree and try to empathize with their viewpoint.

A king and a cobbler changed places for a week. The king envied the simple life of the cobbler, while the cobbler was jealous of the king's power and wealth. The king pricked his finger with the needle, banged his thumb with the hammer, and became weary from sitting on a wooden bench; the cobbler, on the other hand, was driven to despair by the people who came to solicit his help and ask him to change the laws. Before the week was over, the cobbler was glad to go back to his shop, and the king was ready to return to his throne. Because of their insight into each other's problems, the cobbler became a better subject and the king a kinder ruler.

Dear Father, I pray for the gift of an empathetic heart. When I know that others are being wronged, grant that my soul may burn with indignation and that I may seek to right the injustice that is being done to them. Amen.

FRIDAY—Week 36

ARE YOU A TRUE PROTESTANT? Read Acts 24:10-21

Too many people have an "anti" religion. They are against some other group. Lacking any positive convictions or any depth of personal devotion to God, they become critics of the religious practices of others. They are anti-Jewish, anti-Catholic, or anti-Protestant.

That we are Protestants does not mean that we should allow ourselves to become protesters and nothing more. The word Protestant comes from two roots, "pro" and "test." "Pro" means not "against" but "for." "Test" means "to testify." So a Protestant, in the true sense of the word, is one who makes a great testimony *for* something which he believes.

What is the chief affirmation of the Protestant faith? It is the right of the individual soul to find God for himself. People who have a different background of ancestry and education may find God in a way that is strange to us, but every person must be allowed to worship according to the dictates of his own conscience.

O God, keep me from having a negative attitude toward life. May I always work with the builders and not with the wrecking crew. Give me a stalwart faith, but make me a defender of the rights of others to worship as they please. Amen.

SATURDAY—Week 36

RESPECTING THE CONVICTIONS OF OTHERS
Read Rom. 14:1-12

Albert Schweitzer, world-famous organist, who astounded the world by studying medicine and going to Africa as a missionary, has told what a lasting impression one aspect of his boyhood religious experience left upon him. His father was a Lutheran pastor, whose people worshiped in the same church that was used at a different hour by Roman Catholics. Afterward, in writing about the friendly spirit of the two congregations, he said: "One thing more I have taken with me into life from this little church that was Catholic and Protestant at the same time—I mean religious tolerance." That is something we all ought to learn and take through life.

> You go to your church, and I'll go to mine,
> But let's walk along together;
> Our Father has built them side by side,
> So let's walk along together.

Almighty and ever-blessed God, I thank thee for the heritage of religious freedom. I pray that it may never mean for me the liberty to ignore the church. May all thy children be faithful to the truth as thou hast revealed it to them. Amen.

GETTING ALONG WITH OTHERS

SUNDAY—Week 37

A SIMPLE RULE GIVEN BY JESUS   Read Luke 6:27-38

When William Penn first came to America as the governor of the Quaker colony of Pennsylvania, he called a conference of all the Indian chieftains within his territory. They met under the branches of a spreading elm tree on the bank of the Delaware River and made what was called "A Treaty of Friendship." Running through it was the controlling idea that white men and red men should never take advantage of each other and should live together as brothers. It was the practical application of the Golden Rule given by Jesus: "Whatsoever ye would that men should do to you, do ye even so to them." The treaty was faithfully kept. Fighting occurred between other white men and the natives, but not a drop of Quaker blood was ever shed by an Indian.

If you will manage your relationships with others on the basis of the Golden Rule, you will have little difficulty in getting along harmoniously with normal people.

O God, I would play the game of life fairly and never violate the rules. Help me to apply the principles of good sportsmanship in all my dealings with others and to do unto them only what I am willing to have them do unto me. Amen.

MONDAY—Week 37

ARE YOU ADAPTABLE?   Read I Thess. 5:8-23

Thomas B. Macaulay, the English historian, is said to have made it the first aim of his life to get along happily with the people who were most intimately associated with him. The result was that he had an unusually satisfying home life and a large circle of friends. If you will adopt the same principle, you will find that you have gone a long way toward solving one of the most perplexing problems which life presents.

The world is filled with all sorts of people, no two of whom are alike. No two fingerprints are the same; temperaments, personalities, and tastes differ even more widely. The ways of our neighbors may not be as our ways; we must therefore learn to appreciate and enjoy them for what they are, not for what we wish they were. Paul

157

urged the Thessalonians to be patient toward all men. Even more than patience we need adaptability. Without sacrificing our moral standards, we need to cultivate the flexibility of character which can adjust itself to the ways of others.

Gracious God, help me to understand my own limitations, and make me grateful for the people who are different from me. Grant that thy children may live together in patience, learning from each other and in honor preferring one another. Amen.

TUESDAY—Week 37

LEARN TO SPEAK TACTFULLY   Read Jas. 3:10-18

An Oriental king had a dream and called upon one of his wise men to explain what it meant. The vizier gave the following interpretation: "O King, your dream unfortunately means that every single solitary relative of yours will die before you, leaving you the lone survivor of your family." The king was so angry at such a prediction that he executed the one who made it. Later he had the same dream a second time and asked another counselor to interpret it. This man tactfully replied, "O King, this dream means that you are a very fortunate man; you are destined to outlive all your relatives." The king was so pleased that he made the man his prime minister.

Many times the way in which we say something is more important than what we say. Whatever the situation, nothing is ever lost by being courteous. Said Dr. Samuel Johnson, "A man has no more right to say a rude thing to another than to knock him down."

My Father, teach me the importance of my words and help me to say the right thing at the right time. Give me such an understanding heart that I will never thoughtlessly hurt others by my speech but will make my words messengers of healing and hope. Amen.

WEDNESDAY—Week 37

ENVY AND SENSITIVENESS MUST BE OVERCOME
                                          Read Luke 15:25-32

The elder brother in the parable of the prodigal son was hard-working and thrifty. He stayed late in the field and evidently was a successful farmer, but he made a tragic failure of handling his personal relationships. He is typical of many industrious and otherwise efficient people who find it difficult to make and hold friendships because they antagonize their associates in various ways.

They are to be pitied as well as blamed, for they make themselves wretchedly unhappy.

Only a jealous and peevish churl would have refused to attend the party given by the father for the returned prodigal. The elder brother should have joined in the merrymaking for the sake of the family. The one who cannot overcome his envy and sensitiveness and rejoice in the good fortunes of others will always be a forlorn figure who shuts himself out from much of the joy of life and remains his own worst enemy.

O Lord, cast out of my heart all jealousy and malice and whatever keeps me from living in the spirit of brotherly kindness. Save me from littleness and make me bighearted enough to rejoice in the good fortune of others. Amen.

THURSDAY—Week 37

PEOPLE LIKE TO BE APPRECIATED   Read Mark 14:1-9

When Mary showed her deep regard for Jesus by anointing him with costly ointment, some people criticized her, saying that the ointment should have been sold and the money given to the poor. Jesus would doubtless have told her to use the ointment in that way if she had gone to him seeking advice, but since the deed had already been done, to criticize Mary was not only useless but rude. So Jesus called attention to the loving motive which prompted the deed and said it would be long remembered as her memorial.

Most people need far more appreciation than they receive. Critics are never lacking to point out our mistakes, but there is a scarcity of those who see our good points and give us friendly encouragement. Do you want people to like you? Then do not overlook the many opportunities when you can speak an honest word in commendation of their efforts.

God of love, give me true kindness of heart that I may be sympathetic and not critical. Teach me how to speak words of appreciation to those whose spirits have been bruised by the unfairness of others, that they may have new faith in their fellowmen. Amen.

FRIDAY—Week 37

BEGIN AT HOME   Read Mark 6:1-6

One of George Eliot's books has a disagreeable character by the name of Mrs. Waule, who thought there was no need to behave agreeably when only members of the family were present. It is easy to think that those who know us intimately do not mind our rudeness because they know we have good intentions. Actually, kindness and gentleness are more important in the home than anywhere; we ought not to show our worst side to those we love best. Moreover, let it be remembered that what one is in the habit of doing at home one will keep on doing wherever one is.

Jesus is said to have grown "in favour with God and man." This was while he was in Nazareth in a family with four younger brothers and at least two sisters. Because he learned to live happily as a member of a large family, he afterward found favor with others. Are you agreeable and unselfish enough to live without quarreling with those at home? If so, you should find it possible to get along amicably anywhere.

O God, make me cheerful and thoughtful, quick to do my part in common tasks but slow to ask favors for myself. Help me to develop the disposition that enables me to live happily with all. Amen.

SATURDAY—Week 37

WHEN TO GET MAD
Read Matt. 23:23-39

There are some people with whom a sincere Christian cannot live on peaceable terms. Recognition of this fact is contained in Paul's words to the Romans: "If it be possible, as much as lieth in you, live peaceably with all men." Followers of Christ can have nothing in common with those whose lives are willfully and impenitently evil.

Jesus was intolerant of the legalized graft in the temple. He drove out the money-changers and vehemently denounced the scribes and Pharisees. His wrath was one aspect of his love. But notice that Jesus did not become angry over what was done to him personally. He is described in the Epistle of Peter as one "who, when he was reviled, reviled not again; when he suffered, he threatened not."

If we would be Christian in our relations to others, we must learn when to get mad. We will be wrathfully indignant at people who deliberately harm those too weak to defend themselves, but we will not become resentful over personal injuries.

Dear God, give me the power to rule my own spirit that I may not easily be angered at what others say about me or do to me. But grant that, like Christ, I may be stirred with righteous wrath whenever I see some weak or innocent person being unjustly treated. Amen.

CHOOSING OUR FRIENDS

SUNDAY—Week 38

CHOOSE WISELY   Read Mark 4:14-20

"What is the secret of your life? Tell me, that I may make mine beautiful, too," said Elizabeth Barrett Browning to Charles Kingsley. "I had a friend," was the simple reply.

Friendships help to determine our destiny, and one of the first questions every person needs to ask himself is this: "Who are to be my friends?" A group of young men once asked William E. Gladstone, prime minister of England, to give them some suggestions which would enable them to make a success of life. The great statesman sent back this message: "Choose wisely your companions, for a young man's companions, more than his food or clothes, his home or his parents, make him what he is."

Nearly a century before the time of Gladstone, George Washington wrote in his book of boyhood maxims: "Associate yourself with men of good quality, if you esteem your reputation; for 'tis better to be alone than in bad company."

Almighty God, who hast placed millions of people upon the earth, guide me by thy spirit of understanding so that I may find the companions who will help me to order my life by thy laws and become a useful member of thy kingdom. Amen.

MONDAY—Week 38

HOW JESUS CHOSE HIS FRIENDS   Read Luke 6:12-16

What was the standard by which Jesus chose the twelve disciples? It was not occupation, wealth, or social position. Peter and Andrew, James and John, were fishermen; the last two evidently came from a family of means, for the Gospel refers to their father's hired servants. Matthew was a tax collector; we presume that Judas was a businessman, since he was made treasurer of the group. Not only did the twelve come from all walks of life; they were people of different temperaments: quiet Andrew, rough-and-ready Peter, hot-tempered James and John, pessimistic and doubting Thomas. Simon was a zealot who preached rebellion aganst Rome.

Jesus chose these men because they were willing to stake every-

161

thing on his revelation of the good life and stand for it in the face of a hostile world. History shows that he chose wisely. Can we do better than follow his lead? It is the heart of a person that determines his or her worth as a friend.

Eternal Wisdom, teach me to judge people by their inner worth. Let me look not upon the outward appearance but upon the heart. So may I have friends who share my vision of eternal values and who are not afraid of following the best they know. Amen.

TUESDAY—Week 38

JESUS WAS EVERYONE'S FRIEND   Read Luke 7:31-50

While Jesus had his circle of intimate companions, he was always friendly with everyone. He treated the Samaritans and Romans, who were foreigners, with the same courtesy that he showed toward the members of his own race. He was never too proud to associate with people who were poor or unpopular. In spite of the sneers of the Pharisees, he accepted invitations to the homes of publicans and sinners whenever he felt there was a chance of helping them by his presence. But wherever he was, Jesus always held to his own high ideals. He never descended to a low level of conduct for the sake of winning the favor of others.

What a fine standard of friendship we have in the example of Jesus! We all need to have our special friends, what we call "our crowd." But unless you are content to be a snob, you will not give yourself exclusively to your inner circle.

I turn to thee , O Comrade of my soul, seeking to become like thee in thy friendliness and sympathy. Save me from loveless ways. As I go about among my fellowmen, may I be a channel of thy love and thy grace. Amen.

WEDNESDAY—Week 38

THEODORE ROOSEVELT'S ADVICE TO HIS SONS
Read Prov. 10

When Theodore Roosevelt lived in New York City and his children were small, a woman told them they ought not to be playing with all sorts of children on the streets but should select their playmates more carefully. The boys told their father, and Roosevelt, who detested the thought of having his sons grow up to be snobs, said: "Remember this always: there are only two classes of boys, good boys and bad boys. If you choose your companions among the good boys, you need not worry whether they are rich or poor, or who their fathers and mothers are."

It would be hard to give a simpler or better rule by which to de-

cide on the persons who are worthy of being welcomed as our closest friends. A person's ideas and ideals are far more important
than his race, nationality, or ancestry. It is not important that your
friend live on the right side of the railroad track, but it is essential
that he or she be on the right side of moral questions.

I thank thee, O Christ, for the people through whom I catch a glimpse of
what life at its best can be, and for those who reveal to me the inner resources by which life is made strong and pure. Grant that I may have such
people as my friends and may become worthy of their companionship.
Amen.

THURSDAY—Week 38

THE FRIENDSHIP OF SERVICE   Read Matt. 19:16-22

Jacob Riis, as a police reporter on a New York newspaper, often
went into the city's slums and tenements. Distressed at the wretched
places which poor people were forced to call their homes, he
determined to start a movement to remedy such conditions. In
order to arouse public opinion, he wrote a book entitled *How the
Other Half Lives*, setting forth all the facts as he had personally
observed them.

One of the first persons to read the book was Theodore Roosevelt, who went at once to the newspaper office and left his card for
Mr. Riis. Underneath his name were the words, "Have read your
book and have come to help." That was the beginning of a lifelong
friendship in which the two men worked together to improve the
conditions of New York's poor. Could there be a better foundation for true friendship than the desire to be of service to others?

O God, give me compassion for all who suffer wrong and injustice. Stir me
from my lethargy that I may respond more swiftly to the call of duty. If others need my help, may I give myself to them without counting the cost. So
may I show forth thy love for all mankind. Amen.

FRIDAY—Week 38

FRIENDSHIP A GIFT OF GOD   Read John 15:14-27

Consider carefully this thought from Emerson: "My friends
have come to me unsought. The great God gave them to me." Is it
not true that many of our best friends have come to us without any
conscious effort on our part? We did not set out to win their
friendship. Something about the other person attracted you to
him. Something about you made you the kind of person he liked.
As Montaigne said about his friend, "If a man should importune

me to give a reason why I loved him, I could only answer—because it was he, because it was I."

The secret of having friends is to make ourselves worthy of them. Like attracts like. Develop a natural capacity for friendship, a sincere desire to be helpful to others, and you will never need to go out looking for friends. The great God will give them to you.

I thank thee, Lord, for the providence through which human souls are brought together in warmth of comradeship. Thou has bestowed many gifts upon me, but greatest of all is a friend with an understanding heart. Make me worthy of such a blessing. Amen.

SATURDAY—Week 38

A SCIENTIST'S GREATEST DISCOVERY
Read John 14:15-24

Robert Burns lamented that he could not pour out his inmost soul without reserve to any human being without danger of one day repenting his confidence. All earthly friendships have their limitations. This is the reason we need to cultivate the friendship of Christ until he becomes for us the closest and most constant companion of our souls.

James Simpson, the Scottish surgeon and scientist who discovered the use of chloroform as an anesthetic, was asked what was the greatest discovery he ever made. Without hesitation he replied, "That Jesus Christ is my personal friend." The simplest description of what it means to be a Christian is that one accepts Jesus' offer of friendship and leads a life that enables one to keep faith with one's Friend.

Heavenly Father, bind me more closely to my friends in true love and comradeship, but grant that I may come to know thy Son as the Friend who sticketh closer than a brother. May all my relations to other people be enriched by my companionship with him. Amen.

KEEPING OUR FRIENDSHIPS IN REPAIR

SUNDAY—Week 39

BEING CAREFUL OF OUR WORDS   Read Matt. 12:31-37

"Don't flatter yourself that friendship authorizes you to say disagreeable things to your intimates. The nearer you come into relation with a person, the more necessary do tact and courtesy become." These words of Oliver Wendell Holmes remind us that we must discipline our tongues if we would keep our friendships in a healthy condition. After hasty words have been uttered, you cannot completely heal the wound that has been made, even though you ask, and receive, your friend's forgiveness.

> Boys flying kites haul in their white-winged birds;
> You can't do that way when you're flying words.

. . . .

> Thoughts unexpressed may sometimes fall back dead;
> But God himself can't kill them when they're said!

O God, I thank thee for all the words of kindness, appreciation, and love that have been spoken to me. Without them my soul would have been starved. Grant that my words may be a source of continual inspiration to my friends. Amen.

MONDAY—Week 39

ADVICE FROM THE ANCIENT NORSEMEN
Read Matt. 20:20-28

The *Poetic Edda*, which is a collection of Norse poems going back at least to the thirteenth century, has some lines which stress the idea that you lose your friends if you make too great demands upon them.

> Forth shall one go, nor stay as a guest
> In a single spot forever;
> Love becomes loathing if long one sits
> By the hearth in another's home.

The ancient tendency to overstay a visit is only one of many ways of imposing on a friend. If you require too much of your friend's time, or take it for granted that he will lend you money or let you wear his clothes, you will find that his friendship soon loses its warmth.

Friendship cannot long endure after one person has started using the other for his own advantage. Enjoy your friend and help him. But don't use him.

Dear Father, teach me to enjoy my friend for what he is and not for what he can do for me. May I find joy in giving myself to him without asking or expecting favors in return. Amen.

TUESDAY—Week 39

DAVID AND JONATHAN   Read I Sam. 20

One of the greatest friendships of all history was that between David and Jonathan. It was based on the complete unselfishness of two men between whom there were natural barriers. Jonathan was heir to the throne and had good reason to be jealous of David because of the latter's popularity as a warrior; David had already been acclaimed by the people as one who had killed more Philistines than Saul. David, on the other hand, might well have been envious of Jonathan because he was the son of the king. Yet between the two there was such loyalty and complete understanding that Jonathan saved David's life at the risk of displeasing his father. Each was willing to die for the other.

Jealousy and selfishness are subtle enemies of friendship. The one who would have enduring fellowships must put these enemies out of his heart.

O God, keep me from being envious of those who possess advantages that have been denied to me. May I rejoice in the good fortune of my friends while I seek better opportunities for myself. May no tinge of jealousy mar the beauty of my friendships. Amen.

WEDNESDAY—Week 39

ANGER IS RUINOUS TO FRIENDSHIP Read I Sam. 18:5-16

Alexander the Great regarded Clitus as his dearest friend. Clitus was the son of the king's nurse; from childhood they had played and studied together. More than that, they had fought side by side in many battles, and on one occasion Alexander's life had been saved by the heroism of his friend.

At a banquet given by the king, when both had been drinking too heavily, Clitus was foolish enough to compare Alexander unfavorably with his father, Philip. The king, angrily seizing a javelin, hurled it at his friend and killed him instantly. He was smitten with remorse but was powerless to bring back the life of his friend.

Alexander had conquered the world but could not conquer himself. He could command an army but never learned to discipline his own temper.

No bond of affection is strong enough to hold people together in spite of outbursts of anger and moods of sulkiness. Emotional control is an essential of lasting friendship.

Heavenly Father, keep me from putting any unnecessary strain on my friendships. Grant that I may not have a disposition like weather when sunshine is quickly succeeded by storm. May I grow more like thee, with whom there is "no variableness, neither shadow of turning." Amen.

THURSDAY—Week 39

SHARING OUR BEST WITH OUR FRIENDS
Read Matt. 17:1-23

Jesus had no money to share with his friends, but he gave them something better. He tried to impart to them his three great possessions—peace, love, and joy. We can perform no higher service for our friends than to reveal to them the secret sources of our inner satisfactions. Many friendships are shallow because the friends do not fully open their lives and share their best with each other.

The most enriching friendships are those which are formed on the basis of a common desire to discover life's highest values. Said Addison in the play *Cato*:

> The friendships of the world are oft
> Confederacies in vice or leagues of pleasure;
> Ours has severest virtue for its basis,
> And such a friendship ends not but with life.

O God, make me willing to give my friends the gift they most crave—myself at my best. Break down the barrier of reserve which so often keeps me from talking with others about Christ and help me to share with them my Christian faith. Amen.

FRIDAY—Week 39

PRAYING FOR OUR FRIENDS
Read Luke 22:31-40

The highest service we can render our friends is to pray for them. "I have prayed for thee," said Jesus to Peter. Can you truthfully say that you are remembering your friends in the same way? Are you seeking to make them strong and true and pure by the prayers which you offer in their behalf?

More things are wrought by prayer
Than this world dreams of. Wherefore, let thy voice
Rise like a fountain for me night and day.
For what are men better than sheep or goats
That nourish a blind life within the brain,
If, knowing God, they lift not hands of prayer
Both for themselves and those who call them friend?
For so the whole round earth is every way
Bound by gold chains about the feet of God.

O Thou who hearest prayer, teach me how to pray for my friends, not casually, but earnestly and often. So may I become a true friend who can meet the deepest needs of those whom he loves. Amen.

SATURDAY—Week 39

A PICTURE OF JESUS' LOVE   Read I Cor. 13

Many students of the New Testament believe that Paul was thinking about Jesus when he wrote his famous chapter on love. Whether Paul had Jesus in mind, we cannot be sure, but we do know that the words in the scripture lesson for today are a beautiful picture of Jesus' loving and friendly spirit.

Read over sentence by sentence the phrases which describe the meaning of love. Then ask yourself whether you are expressing these attitudes toward your own friends. "Love suffereth long, and is kind; love envieth not; . . . seeketh not its own, is not provoked, taketh not account of evil."

If your life becomes an expression of this kind of love, your friendship for others will have a Christ-like quality. You need not worry lest your friends forget you; they will be tied to you with bonds of steel.

Heavenly Father, help me to love as Jesus loved. Cleanse my heart of selfishness and give me a Christ-like spirit. Keep me from thinking about what my friends ought to do for me, but make me concerned to learn how I can be a better friend. Amen.

THE FRUITS OF FRIENDSHIP

SUNDAY—Week 40

NO ONE IS SELF-MADE   Read Rom. 1:1-16

Do you recall the opening words in Dickens' story of David Copperfield? "Whether I shall turn out to be the hero of my own life, or whether that station will be held by anybody else, these pages must show." The book is based on what happened to Dickens during his early life, and the author seems to imply that he was the main factor in shaping his own career. The story shows, however, that his life would not have been the same had it not been for the help he received from his aunt and many others.

Neither Dickens nor anyone can rightly pride himself on being self-made. It would be far more accurate to say with Tennyson's Ulysses, "I am a part of all that I have met." Our lives are so intertwined with countless others that what we are and what we achieve bear a direct relationship to what we have received from those who bless us with their friendship.

Make me humble in thy sight and in the presence of my friends, O Lord my Creator. Help me to understand how deeply I am indebted to those who have given me their help. May I not think of myself more highly than I ought to think. Amen.

MONDAY—Week 40

THE STIMULUS OF FRIENDSHIP   Read Matt. 4:17-25

It was said of Disraeli that he was not only brilliant himself, but that he made others brilliant. When we meet a new friend, his influence may be the beginning of a new era in our lives. Says the author of Proverbs: "Iron sharpeneth iron; so a man sharpeneth the countenance of his friend."

What an inspiration Robert Browning and Elizabeth Barrett were to each other! Both wrote better poetry than either could have produced without the stimulus of the other. Their mutual love brought their genius to full flower. Schiller and Goethe were kindred spirits who helped to awaken each other's talents. The disciples were ordinary men, but under the warmth of Jesus' friendship they became leaders who could change the world.

169

Something far-reaching and creative can happen in your life as the result of friendship.

Heavenly Father, as the disciples were transformed and strengthened by their association with Jesus, so may my friends be for me a stimulus to holy living and noble action. Grant that I may be a blessing to those who love me and a worthy follower of thy Son. Amen.

TUESDAY—Week 40

A SAFEGUARD FROM TEMPTATION   Read John 17:11-1

There is no greater safeguard in the hour of temptation than the knowledge that others are expecting us to be worthy of their love and to be true to the high standards which they hold for us. So an unknown author has written:

> Because of your firm faith, I kept the track
> Whose sharp-set stones my strength had almost spent—
> I could not meet your eyes, if I turned back,
>   So on I went.

> Because of your strong love, I held my path
> When battered, worn, and bleeding in the fight—
> How could I meet your true eyes, blazing wrath?
>   So I kept right.

Gracious God, I am ever grateful for those who trust me, and who by their steadfast faith challenge me to new heights of achievement. Keep me from disappointing them. For their sakes may I sanctify myself. Amen.

WEDNESDAY—Week 40

THE VALUE OF FRIENDLY CRITICISM
Read Matt. 17:13-2

One of the great gains of tried and tested friendship should be the opportunity to get honest advice, and, on occasion, helpful criticism. A true friend will never needlessly hurt his comrades but will not hesitate to speak the truth in love when his counsel is asked. "Faithful are the wounds of a friend," says the Book of Proverbs, but even among friends criticism must be tenderly given. People talk about the necessity of being brutally frank, but all too often critics are frankly brutal.

Let it also be remembered that only the one who gives just praise where praise is due has earned the right to point out another's mistakes. Peter was willing to have the Master rebuke him when he was wrong because Jesus had previously commended his spiritual insight in recognizing him as the Messiah.

Keep me from being sensitive and irritable, O God. Make me ever willing to accept the honest criticism of my friends. Help me not to shut my mind to any truth that is unpleasant, for I ask in the name of him whose truth can make me free. Amen.

THURSDAY—Week 40

SHARING OUR FRIENDSHIP Read Luke 5:18-32

A jeweler who was visited by a distinguished friend showed him his precious gems. The most valuable one was an opal, but the visitor considered it dull and lacking in beauty. "Hold it in your hand for a few minutes," he was told. The visitor did so, and the gem began to glow with all the colors of the rainbow. The warmth of the human hand was needed to bring out its beauty. So there are many lives which at first seem dull and colorless but will shine with radiance when they feel the stimulating clasp of a friendly hand.

Do your most cherished comradeships make you more willing to be friendly with the lonely and loveless? If our friendships make us snobbish and selfish, they hinder rather than help our efforts to attain to the fullness of the Christian life.

> I thank Thee, Lord, for lavish love
>   On me bestowed,
> Enough to share with loveless folk
>   To ease their load;
> Thy love to me I ill could spare,
> Yet dearer is the love I share. Amen.

FRIDAY—Week 40

EVEN THE PLANETS INFLUENCE EACH OTHER
Read Matt. 3

Back of the discovery of the planet Neptune is an interesting story. For a long time astronomers had been able to account for the motion of all the planets except Uranus by the attraction of the sun and by the attraction of the planets for each other. Uranus kept deviating from the path that scientists thought it should follow. An astronomer by the name of Bouvard finally expressed his belief that Uranus was being influenced by some unknown body. Careful calculations were made. A telescope was turned to the part of the heavens where it was thought the disturbing planet might be located, and lo! Neptune came into view.

Like the planets in the heavens, the lives of young people exercise their influence upon each other. You should be friendly toward everybody but you should not allow yourself to be swerved from your proper orbit of conduct by those who have lower standards.

Thou Sun of my soul, grant that my life may revolve around thee as its center. Give me the wisdom to admit to my heart only those influences which will keep me on my true course and not cause me to deviate from the path of thy righteousness. Amen.

SATURDAY—Week 40

THE ROOTS OF FRIENDSHIP DETERMINE THE FRUITS
Read Ps. 55:12-23

In *Timon of Athens* Shakespeare has given us a picture of a man who made his friendships on a superficial basis. Timon was wealthy and generous. He gave lavish parties and enjoyed having people look upon him as their benefactor. His home was thronged with those who pretended to be his friends although they were interested only in what they could gain for themselves. The time came when Timon's money was gone. He refused to worry because he was sure he could rely upon those who had previously been the recipients of his favors. To his amazement, those who had once praised his generosity now criticized him for not having been more careful with his money. In the end, Timon, cynical and disillusioned, betook himself to the forest to live on roots and berries.

Friendship, instead of having joy and inspiration as its fruit, may end in bitterness and disappointment. Everything depends upon its motive. Only Christian friendships can be counted upon for lasting satisfaction.

My Father, I pray that my friendships may rest on something deeper than a desire for a good time. Grant that my associations with others may be ennobled by a devotion to the work of thy kingdom. May all our friendships be enriched by our common love for thee. Amen.

CHOOSING A LIFE PARTNER

SUNDAY—Week 41

WILL YOU BE WORTHY OF THE ONE YOU MARRY?

Read John 2:1-11

Somewhere is the person you hope someday to marry. Will you be worthy of your life partner? To be able to give to the other person the best you have, that the best may come back to you and both may find enduring happiness, is one of the finest and holiest desires of youth. Says Tennyson in "Guinevere":

> For indeed I know
> Of no more subtle master under heaven
> Than is the maiden passion for a maid,
> Not only to keep down the base in man
> But teach high thought, and amiable words
> And courtliness, and the desire of fame,
> And love of truth, and all that makes a man.

Thou Christ, who didst bless the wedding at Cana with thy presence and first miracle, grant that I may look forward with reverence to the possibility of my marriage. For the sake of the person who may become my life partner, may I keep myself strong and pure. Amen.

MONDAY—Week 41

MAKE HASTE SLOWLY

Read Prov. 4:1-13

The writer was once performing a wedding ceremony in the home of the bride when the groom, asked the usual question about taking the woman to be his wife, made no answer. The question was repeated a bit sternly, as though to reprove him for his inattention. He then said hesitantly, "I've been thinking it all over and I don't know as I will."

The girl fainted and fell to the floor. After she regained consciousness, she retired to the dining room with the young man; prolonged discussion followed, and they decided to go ahead with the service. Evidently they had rushed into the arrangement for marriage without fully discussing all the issues involved.

An act of such far-reaching consequences as marriage should be entered into thoughtfully, prayerfully, and only after a long

173

period of acquaintance. It takes only a few minutes to get married, but the happiness or unhappiness of a lifetime is at stake.

Guide me, my Father, that I may make the great choices of life thoughtfully and wisely. Make me willing to listen to the advice of my parents and friends. Thus may I be spared the vain regrets that often follow hasty decisions. Amen.

TUESDAY—Week 41

BIBLE ROMANCES

Read Gen. 24

Contrast the scriptural story of the marriage of Isaac and Rebekah with that of Jacob and Rachel. Isaac's wife was chosen for him by his father's oldest servant, who jumped to the quick conclusion that a good-looking and hard-working girl who would draw water for his camels ought to make a good wife. He knew nothing of her character. Little wonder that the home which was established was marred by misunderstanding and deceit! Rebekah became a party to the shabby trick by which the blind Isaac was deceived into giving Jacob the birthright.

Jacob, fleeing from Esau's wrath, became a changed man through his experience with God at Bethel. Going to the home of Laban, he served fourteen years to win Rachel as his wife. His love for her was so great that he could work and wait. No other girl could possibly take her place. A marriage like that of Isaac and Rebekah is on a shaky foundation; one like that of Jacob and Rachel can be counted on for lasting happiness.

Dear Father, I thank thee for my present home and pray for thy guidance when the time comes to establish a home of my own. Help me to develop now the disposition and virtues that will enable me to do my part in making marriage a success. Amen.

WEDNESDAY—Week 41

MORE THAN AN EXPERIMENT

Read Eph. 3:14-21

A college professor of English literature asked a class this question in an examination, "What did Shakespeare do in his experimental period?" As an answer he expected the students to give the titles of some of Shakespeare's early plays; but one of the girls, who had observed married life more keenly than she had studied Elizabethan literature, gave the reply, "Shakespeare married Anne Hathaway."

Marriage is often looked upon as something to be tried out, with the reservation that any difficulties can finally be settled in the divorce court if necessary. Young people should realize, however, that one does not regain the lost happiness simply by being released from the partnership. No one can go through the experience of an unsuccessful marriage and be quite the same afterward. Failure in anything so vital as marriage tends to warp the personality and leave one's life impoverished.

Keep me, O God, from being a failure in anything which I undertake. Develop within me the spirit of patience and of perseverance. Whatever I do, may I give to it the best endeavor of which I am capable. Amen.

THURSDAY—Week 41

THE QUESTION OF RELIGIOUS DIFFERENCES
Read Eph. 4:1-7

Daniel Defoe, author of *Robinson Crusoe*, also wrote a novel based on the difficulties involved in mixed marriages. He makes a young Protestant widow say, after the death of her Catholic husband: "The condition can never be happy, God faithfully served, children rightly educated, or the duty of the relationship faithfully performed, where the opinions of religion differ."

The comment most readily made on Defoe's statement is that conditions are different today, as people have become more understanding and broadminded. The chief difference is that the rules of the Catholic Church now require the Protestant to sign a written promise that children of the union will be brought up in the Catholic faith. Protestant young people should not allow themselves to fall in love with a person of a different faith without considering that religious differences add to the difficulties of having a happy married life.

Keep me from being narrow or intolerant, my Father, but give me the wisdom to face all the facts involved in the choice of a life partner, that I may not endanger my own happiness or that of another. Amen.

FRIDAY—Week 41

THE HAPPINESS OF THE BROWNINGS
Read Rom. 12:9-18

One of the happiest marriages of all history was that of Robert Browning and Elizabeth Barrett. It is pictured on the screen as a beautiful romance, as indeed it was. But it was something more. It was a companionship based on a common interest in literature and other pursuits. It was the marriage of two people each of whom had achieved a high state of moral self-discipline and a spiritual outlook upon life. They were bound together, moreover, by ties of Christian devotion. Put these elements together and you have an adequate background for enduring love which can triumph over all difficulties and hardships.

"Love never faileth," said the Apostle Paul. It will not fail in marriage if people enter into it intelligently, reverently, and unselfishly.

Praise be to thee, O God, for those men and women of lovely lives who have shown what marriage can be when two people truly love each other. May their example give me the faith that my own dreams can be made to come true. Amen.

SATURDAY—Week 41

WILL YOUR LOVE STAND THE TEST? Read Eph. 5:25-33

A story tells of a wealthy man in the Orient who wanted a rug of special design with many threads of different colors. He hired the best weaver in the land, who spent nearly a lifetime upon the rug, finally completing it and delivering it to the one who gave the order. The rich man commended the weaver on his artistic work but said he must submit the strands to various chemical solutions to see if the colors would retain their hue. The threads met every test, and the rug was accepted and paid for.

Young people looking forward to marriage must ask themselves if their love will stand all the different tests to which marriage is submitted in the strain of modern life. Will their love keep its beauty forever? Can it endure the possible tests of sickness, misunderstanding, poverty, and all the varied experiences the years will bring? The answer depends on the inner integrity of those who plight their troth to each other.

Grant, O God, that I may learn how to live with myself and so be able to live happily with others. Teach me to control my temper. Help me to discipline my desires and see all life in the light of thy goodness and truth. Amen.

DECIDING ON A VOCATION

SUNDAY—Week 42

ANY USEFUL WORK CAN BE MADE CHRISTIAN
Read I Cor. 3:1-13

Any form of work in which you can be true to your inner convictions, earn a living for yourself and those dependent upon you, and perform a needed service for your fellowmen is a Christian vocation. Many people talk as though ministers and missionaries were engaged in "sacred" work and speak of ordinary forms of labor as "secular." Whether or not one is in a Christian occupation depends upon the motive behind one's work.

A well-known story tells how Sir Christopher Wren passed unknown among the men working on St. Paul's Cathedral in London. Three persons were engaged in the same identical task, and he asked them what they were doing. "Shaping a stone," said the first. "Earning my wages," said the second. "Building a cathedral in which men can worship God," replied the third. Whatever our work, we should look upon it as one of the ways in which we cooperate with God in the service of mankind.

Thou Christ, who on earth didst labor as a carpenter, help me to make my work an expression of my love for thee. Keep me from slighting my task. Grant that I may be a workman who needeth not be ashamed. Amen.

MONDAY—Week 42

THE DIGNITY OF MANUAL TOIL
Read Luke 2:42-52

At twelve years of age Jesus decided that his life purpose must be to do the will of God. "Wist ye not that I must be about my Father's business?" he said to his parents in the temple at Jerusalem. But for eighteen years afterward he stayed in Nazareth and worked at the carpenter shop. Joseph had probably died, and, as the eldest son, Jesus assumed responsibility for supporting his mother and the younger members of the family. If we are ever tempted to look down upon manual labor and to think there is greater dignity in working with a pen or typewriter than a hammer and saw, we need to recall the example of our Savior.

Browning makes Pippa, the factory worker, say, "All service ranks the same with God." In the sight of God the faithful service

177

of the ditchdigger may be more important than the work of the business executive.

I thank thee, O God, for the patience and loyalty of thy Son during the years at Nazareth. May all who labor with their hands have a sense of fellowship with him. Help me to see that no work is menial and to have respect for all who toil. Amen.

TUESDAY—Week 42

DO NOT GIVE UP YOUR PLAN
Read Luke 3:1-22

Jesus was not free to begin his public ministry until he was thirty years of age, but the years in the carpenter shop had by no means been wasted. His own experience as a worker gave him a sympathetic knowledge of people and their problems. He knew what was in man, says the Gospel. One reason why the common people heard him so gladly was that he understood their needs.

Do not abandon your cherished plans because you are not immediately able to secure the education you need to carry them out. Follow Jesus' example of doing the best thing you can within the limitations of your situation. Meanwhile work and pray for the time when you can go forward in your preferred vocation. You may at last perform a finer service because of the patience and perseverance that have been developed.

I remember before thee, Father, those who must postpone their dearly cherished plans. Strengthen them, that without complaining they may cheerfully do their present duty. Grant to them and to me the peace and joy which come to those who earnestly seek to do thy will. Amen.

WEDNESDAY—Week 42

WHAT IS A CALL FROM GOD?
Read Isa. 6

George Washington Carver had artistic ability and in his youth wanted to be a painter. One of his teachers convinced him that the greatest need of the South was for someone to develop its agricultural possibilities. So he kept his art as a hobby and became head of the science department at Tuskegee Institute, Alabama, where he made wonderful discoveries about what could be done with peanuts and sweet potatoes. Thomas A. Edison offered him a handsome salary to join his research staff, but Carver stayed in Alabama because he felt that was where he was most needed.

Does not this suggest one of the guiding questions by which one should decide one's lifework: "What is the most important service that I can perform in this needy world?" The other question that must be considered is: "What am I naturally best fitted to do?"

The need of the world, plus my ability to meet it, constitutes my call from God.

Give me wide-open eyes, dear Lord, that I may look out and behold the needs of the world in which I live. Help me to appraise rightly my own abilities. Make me ready to use them in any field to which I hear thy voice calling me. Amen.

THURSDAY—Week 42

PIONEERS ARE STILL NEEDED   Read Heb. 11:1-27

Everyone loves the stories about the early pioneers of America. We admire the colonial settlers who first came to an unknown country and the people who later trekked across the prairie to make their homes in the West. We wish there were a chance for us to be pioneers today. There is! Frontiers still exist. Great moral and spiritual areas of life have not yet been explored. Pioneering needs to be done in the realm of human relationships and in the relations of men to God. Only as people come to understand and obey the laws of God will they be able to build the kind of civilization for which they long.

Charles P. Steinmetz, shortly before his death, said the world must wait for its greatest advance until there are people who can make needed spiritual discoveries. Ministers and missionaries and religious leaders dedicate their lives to leadership in this type of pioneering. Have you ever thought of entering the full-time service of the church? Why not talk to your pastor about it?

Praise be unto thee, Almighty God, for the far vision of those who have been willing to forsake ease and comfort and follow the gleam which led them into an adventure for thee. Give me the courage to be a pioneer of a new world of brotherhood and peace. Amen.

FRIDAY—Week 42

A BLESSING IN DISGUISE   Read Luke 14:25-35

When Henry Fawcett was a young man of twenty-five, he lost his eyesight in a hunting accident. He had recently graduated from Cambridge University and was looking forward to a useful career in public service. Instead of deciding that a blind man had no chance, he made up his mind he would show that, without eyes, he could still do a man's work in the world.

He became a professor at Cambridge University. Later he was elected to Parliament, and appointed Postmaster General of England, a position which he filled with high honor. His blindness, which had seemed to be such a handicap, stirred him to greater effort than he would normally have put forth and became a blessing in disguise.

Does there seem to be some great obstacle which interferes with the carrying out of your plans? Refuse to be a quitter. God will still use you if you have the faith and grit to go forward.

Upon all who are disheartened by hardship or handicap, I pray for thy blessing, thou God of love. Renew their faith in themselves and their hope in thee. Help them to learn that weakness can be turned into strength and that difficulty may become a spur to high achievement. Amen.

SATURDAY—Week 42

CHOOSE YOUR CENTRAL LOYALTY   Read Rom. 12:1-9

Dwight L. Moody heard someone say that the world had not yet seen what could be accomplished by a person who completely dedicated his life to the will of God. He decided that he would be the man. Although a youth with limited education, he became one of the greatest evangelists the world has ever known and is still a power for Christian education through the schools which he founded at Northfield and Mount Hermon.

Even though you may not yet be able to choose your vocation, you can make the decision to dedicate your life to the service of Christ. The weakness of most lives is in their lack of a central loyalty. They have no controlling purpose. "He was nothing wholly. Pleasure in one form or another was his only aim," said Thomas Carlyle of Robert Burns. "Nothing wholly"! That is the reason so few persons lead lives of noble achievement. Why not decide now to be wholly Christ's?

Father, help me to say with Paul, "One thing I do." May I press toward the mark of a life fully committed to thy keeping and thy service. Reveal to me thy plan for my life and give me the grace to say, "Lo, I come to do thy will, . . . O God." Amen.

TURNING DEFEAT INTO VICTORY

SUNDAY—Week 43

GREAT RESULTS FROM MISCARRIED PLANS
Read Acts 16:6-15

When Paul started on a missionary journey through the cities of Asia Minor, he apparently had no intention of crossing over into Europe. He expected to go to Bithynia, but the Book of Acts says that the Spirit prevented him. Some unexpected situation blocked what he wanted to do. Then during the night he had a vision of a man saying, "Come over into Macedonia, and help us." Paul accepted it as the guidance of God and set sail the next day. When the Apostle carried Christianity into Europe, it was one of the great events in the history of civilization. He did it because, when not successful in what he started to do, he was ready to go to anyone who wanted help.

Paul spent no time lamenting his miscarried plans, but started at once to do the next best thing for Christ. No one ever knows when some disappointment, rightly accepted under God's guidance, will open the door of opportunity.

Dear Father, when I cannot do what I would like to do, help me cheerfully to enter whatever door thou dost open for me. May I shrink from no work because it is hard and despise no task because it is small if I believe it is assigned to me by thee. Amen.

MONDAY—Week 43

FAILURE MAY BE YOUR FRIEND
Read Luke 5:1-11

When Phillips Brooks graduated from Harvard, he started out to be a teacher. Before the first year was over it was evident that he was a wretched failure. Disliked by his pupils, he was asked to resign. He was so chagrined that for a time he kept in seclusion and would not even talk to his friends. "Phillips will not see anyone now," said his father to a visitor, "but after the feeling of mortification is over, he will come and see you."

What was the net result of his failure? One of the most successful careers in the ministry that America has ever known. He attended theological seminary; became rector of a Philadelphia church, where he had crowded congregations; and after a few years accepted a call to Trinity Church, in Boston, where the influence of his ministry still remains. Don't be discouraged if you fail in some undertaking. Failure may be your best friend if it leads you to study your capacities more closely and guides you into a career for which you are better fitted.

O Lord, forgive me for the times when I am tempted to rebel against thee and to cry out that life is being unfair and unkind. May I have the faith to believe that what appears to me like a road through the desert may lead to more fertile fields than any I have yet seen. Amen.

TUESDAY—Week 43

BEING A GOOD LOSER
Read Acts 1:15-26

After Judas committed suicide, the disciples decided someone should be elected as his successor. Two candidates were nominated, Justus and Matthias; and Matthias was chosen. Surely Justus was disappointed not to be elected to the apostolic band. It is never easy to accept defeat and to see other people in the positions we have cherished for ourselves. But Justus was not one to stand back and sulk because he was not made an officer of the church. He continued to give it his loyal support. His other name was Barsabas, and he is mentioned again later in the Book of Acts as one of those sent from Jerusalem to assist the church at Antioch. Strangely enough, Matthias is not referred to again in the New Testament; evidently he did not make a strong leader.

The first step toward transforming defeat into victory is to be a good loser, to avoid bitterness, and to keep free from jealousy of those who seem more successful.

Heavenly Father, help me to accept without complaining the facts which I cannot change. Grant that I may endure hardness as a good soldier of Jesus Christ and fight more valiantly when the number of my enemies is increased. Amen.

WEDNESDAY—Week 43

A CHANCE FOR SELF-KNOWLEDGE
Read Acts 26:1-19

Every failure ought to be looked upon as an opportunity for self-discovery. If you will analyze your situation correctly and discover the reason for your lack of success, you will have usable new knowledge about yourself. Too many people are satisfied to remain in ignorance of their weaknesses. Consider this statement from Charles Darwin in which he speaks of what he learned as a scientist:

"I have also during many years followed a golden rule—whenever a published fact, a new observation, or a thought which is opposed to my general results comes to me, to make a memorandum of it without fail. I have found by experience that such facts and thoughts are far more apt to escape my memory than favorable ones."

Have you failed in any undertaking? One question that must always be asked is "What can I learn from my failure?"

Give me an open mind, dear Lord. May I have the courage to face my mistakes and failures without being discouraged. Reveal to me some way in which they can be made the steppingstones by which I may rise to higher things. Amen.

THURSDAY—Week 43

WEAKNESS CAN BE TURNED INTO STRENGTH
Read Neh. 4:13-23

When Nehemiah was leading the Israelites in rebuilding the walls of Jerusalem, he had a trumpeter ready to sound the alarm should any enemies attack them. The workmen kept their spears by their sides and were instructed to rush at once to the part of the wall which was threatened, that it might be turned into the spot of greatest strength.

You can strengthen your character or increase your ability by the same method. That was what Theodore Roosevelt did with his body; a sickly and tubercular boy, he built himself into a giant of physical endurance. Similar was Demosthenes' attitude toward his failure over his first appearance as a public speaker. He had a rasping voice and an impediment in his speech; with pebbles in his mouth he declaimed to the waves and, by relentless practice, became the greatest orator of the ancient world.

What is your weakness? Sound the trumpet! Rally all the resources of mind and body! Out of weakness you can be made strong.

O God, by myself I am weak; but I can become strong through thee. Help me to realize that divine resources are always available to me if I can learn how to lay hold on them. Teach me how to ask and seek and knock, that the doors of truth may be opened to me. Amen.

FRIDAY—Week 43

HELPING OTHERS RETRIEVE THEIR FAILURES
Read Acts 9:10-22

Nathaniel Hawthorne had an ambition to become a writer; he had succeeded in publishing a book and some magazine articles, but it seemed impossible to make a living for his family by relying on his pen. Through the influence of his friend George Bancroft he secured a position as weigher in the Boston customhouse. After two years he lost his job. He went home to his wife a failure—a college graduate thirty-seven years old who had lost a job paying only a hundred dollars a month and had no prospects at all for the future.

Mrs. Hawthorne greeted his dismal announcement with the words, "Now you are free to write your book." Under the stimulus of her faith he wrote one of the greatest of all American novels, *The Scarlet Letter*.

Many a person is not strong enough to turn defeat into victory unless he receives encouragement from others. One of the finest services you can render your friends is to inspire them to new effort and to keep them from losing faith in themselves.

O God, help me to look with sympathy upon all the thwarted souls of men. Make me swift to speak the cheering word and to hold out the strengthening hand. Teach me how to love others as thou hast loved me. Amen.

SATURDAY—Week 43

HOW PAUL WON HIS GREATEST VICTORY
Read Rom. 8:28-39

"All things work together for good to them that love God," wrote the Apostle Paul to the Christians in Rome. He did not mean that sickness, hardship, and the failure of one's plans are good things in themselves, but that they can be turned into good if one has in one's heart enough of the love of God.

Could we want better proof of the truth of his words than in Paul's later experiences? He told in the epistle of his desire to visit Rome and preach the gospel there at the very heart of the empire. The time came when he reached Rome, but not as he planned. He was a prisoner in chains, awaiting trial and death. So what? He spent his time writing letters to his fellow Christians in other cities; and ever since, people have turned to the Bible and found comfort and strength in his messages of faith. He showed that no experience is a calamity in itself. The spirit in which it is met determines the result.

God of love, help me to win the victory which comes from surrender to thy will. Make me willing to follow thy guidance, knowing that what seems to me a failure may be turned into a glorious achievement by thee. Amen.

FINDING LIFE BY LOSING IT

SUNDAY—Week 44

A TEACHING WHICH IMPRESSED JESUS' FOLLOWERS
Read Matt. 10:34-42

"Safety first" is a good rule for pedestrians on a traffic-crowded street or for motorists at a railroad crossing. We must look out for ourselves, or we run the risk of being injured or killed. Yet the motto is more pagan than Christian if we try to make it a general rule of life. Jesus said that dangerous and sacrificial living is the only path to self-realization. "He that findeth his life shall lose it: and he that loseth his life for my sake shall find it."

Jesus emphasized this idea so much that every one of his four biographers remembered it. The verse about finding one's life by losing it occurs in Matthew, Mark, Luke, and John; it appears in two different places in Matthew and Luke. Evidently this was no casual remark but something deep and fundamental, vitally related to his philosophy of life.

O God, impart to me the spirit of thy son, who died that others might live. Lead me into an understanding of the mystery of the cross. Reveal to me the truth which will liberate me from selfishness and littleness and bring me the fullness of life. Amen.

MONDAY—Week 44

THREE IDEAS OF LIFE
Read Luke 5:27-32

In Shakespeare's *Merchant of Venice* the men who sought to marry Portia were confronted with three caskets made respectively of gold, silver, and lead. Portia's picture was in the leaden casket, and the one who chose it was the winner of the quest.

Each casket had an inscription. "Who chooseth me shall gain what many men desire," was on the gold one. The silver casket had the words, "Who chooseth me shall get as much as he deserves." On the leaden chest was the motto, "Who chooseth me must give and hazard all he hath."

The inscriptions suggest three philosophies of life. The first leads to a search for money and what it can buy; the second implies that life owes us something and ought to confer all sorts of favors upon us; the noblest philosophy is the third one, which

makes life a sacrificial adventure and demands that one hazard al
he has. To give your life away and spend it lavishly for others—thi
is what wins love and honor.

Lead me forth with thee, O Christ, in a glad adventure of love. May I fea
no loneliness or hardship, knowing I am with thee. Grant that I may we
come each new day with joy and zest because it brings me new opportun
ties of serving with thee. Amen.

TUESDAY—Week 44

MAGNIFICENT OBSESSION
Read Matt. 6:1-

Lloyd Douglas' book *Magnificent Obsession* tells the story of a
doctor who had been sick and discouraged. He found the key t
health and happiness by helping others so secretly that he neve
received any public recognition for what he did. He said that i
others found out about his kindness he would not receive any per
sonal benefit from it in his life. It might still do good to the on
who was helped, but it would no longer be a source of enrichmen
to himself.

The novel was a bestseller and was made into a popular movie
What was the reason for its wide appeal? Not so much its literar
merit as the fact that the author struck a responsive chord in th
human heart. Thousands of people instinctively felt that the bool
was true to life in its basic idea—that one finds the abundant lif
when he loses himself in the service of others.

Forgive me, O Father, that so often my good deeds are done that I ma
have the approval of my neighbors. Help me to give gladly and generously
with no thought of reward except the secret joy of serving others and enjoy
ing a richer fellowship with thee. Amen.

WEDNESDAY—Week 44

HALFHEARTED GIVING OF SELF NOT ENOUGH
Read Luke 9:57-6

A man read *Magnificent Obsession* and afterward said to hi
minister: "The idea of finding your happiness by helping other
sounds good, but it doesn't work with me. I gave a man ten dollars; and instead of being grateful, he was like the dog which bites
the hand that feeds it." The trouble was that the man merely gave
his money; he did not share his own life with the person in need
and so he found no happiness in his act.

"I taught a Sunday School class for several years and never go
any reward for the sacrifice of my time except frazzled nerves and
a tired body," said a woman. She missed the joy of service because

she did not really *lose herself* in the lives of the boys and girls; she was merely going through the motions of teaching a class. She was hoarding herself and her time, giving as little of herself as possible; and so she missed the heart of the Master's teaching.

Set me free, O God, from my dread of self-denial and my indifference to human need. Help me to find the larger life which comes to those who lose themselves in thee and in the work of thy kingdom. Amen.

THURSDAY—Week 44

A MAN WHO MISSED THE LARGER LIFE
Read Luke 18:18-30

If you have a copy of Hofmann's painting of the rich young ruler, study it closely to get the message which the artist seeks to convey. The young ruler has just asked the Master how to find eternal life. Jesus is pointing to a ragged old man, so infirm that he can walk only with the aid of a cross-handled stick, and to a woman dressed in black, whom one may assume to be the old man's widowed daughter.

Jesus seems to be saying: "If you would find life, you must help people such as these. You must tear yourself lose from your easygoing life and take an active part in relieving the world's distress."

The young man knows that Jesus is speaking the truth, but he is too self-centered to do what Jesus demands. He goes away sorrowful, for no one finds the larger life when he remains wrapped up in the small bundle of his selfishness.

We thank thee, Lord, thy paths of service lead
To blazoned heights and down the slopes of need;
They reach thy throne, encompass land and sea,
And he who journeys in them walks with thee. Amen.

FRIDAY—Week 44

FORGETTING HERSELF INTO FAME
Read Ruth 1

Kate Douglas Wiggin wanted to be an author. She succeeded in getting a story published in a magazine for young people but lacked ideas for further writing. Because of her interest in poor children she started a kindergarten in San Francisco. Wealthy people maintained the school, but she continually needed extra money for toys and equipment.

After thinking over several schemes for making money, she wrote a story called *The Birds' Christmas Carol*, which illustrated the courage of the boys and girls she was trying to help. She had it printed as cheaply as possible and urged her friends to buy it. She

had no idea of doing anything more than raising a little money fo
her school. Soon it became evident that many people were buying
the book simply because they enjoyed reading it. Then it was pub
lished by Houghton Mifflin Company and won immediate liter
ary recognition. Kate Douglas Wiggin forgot herself into fame. By
trying to help others she became a popular author.

Let others have fame and fortune and jewels and palaces, if I may bu
have the kindly spirit! Give greatness and power to those that want them
but give me Brotherly Kindness. Make somebody else to be comely of visage
if only I may wear a kindly countenance.—George A. Miller.

SATURDAY—Week 44

PALESTINE'S TWO SEAS

Read Matt. 20:20-29

In Palestine there are two lakes, each of which is formed by the
widening of the Jordan River. One is the Sea of Galilee. Flowers
bloom on its shores and vineyards flourish on its hillsides. Fish
swim in its sparkling waters. Four of Jesus' disciples made their
living as fishermen there, and people today still earn their liveli
hood the same way. The lake is always clean and wholesome, because it gets its water only to give it away and let it flow onward
through the country to the south.

The other lake is the Dead Sea. Its water is so salty that no fish
can live in it. No trees or flowers grow on its brackish banks. It has
no outlet, but keeps its water to itself; for this reason it is stagnant
and dead. The two lakes in the land where Jesus lived are a permanent illustration of his teaching that overflowing generosity is the
source of life and that selfishness ends in useless stagnation.

Thou loving and giving Christ, keep me from being a hoarder. May I
never try to keep my life or my possessions to myself. Let my love flow out
like a steady and refreshing stream into the lives of thy needy ones. Amen.

CARRYING A CROSS

SUNDAY—Week 45

THE COST OF DISCIPLESHIP   Read Luke 9:18-27

What did the cross mean to Jesus? There is a mystery about it we cannot fully fathom, but there is no question about one thing it must mean to his followers. Jesus said plainly: "If any man will come after me, let him deny himself, and take up his cross daily, and follow me."

Quintin Hogg, the Christian philanthropist who founded the Polytechnic Institute in London as a place where poor boys could get an education, was one of those who knew what Jesus meant. When asked what it cost to build up such an institution, he answered, "Not very much, only one man's lifeblood." That is always the cost of following Jesus in any triumphant work for mankind.

People will go varying distances in the service of Christ. Some will speak for him; others will give their money. Only those who give themselves are meeting the deeper demands of discipleship.

Heavenly Father, make me willing to serve thee without counting the cost, that I may be thy son and not thy slave. May I bring to thy work the full dedication of all my resources and powers, withholding nothing for myself. Amen.

MONDAY—Week 45

TREATING THE CROSS TOO LIGHTLY
                                    Read Mark 10:35-45

The stirring hymn "Onward Christian Soldiers" was written by the English rector Sabine Baring-Gould for a children's processional. One of the boys carried a cross while the rest followed, singing:

> Onward, Christian soldiers!
>   Marching as to war,
> With the cross of Jesus
>   Going on before.

The minister was criticized for having the procession led by a cross; some people thought it looked too much as though they

189

were imitating the Roman Catholics. Baring-Gould is said to have remarked that he might have to change the words to the song to make it read:

> With the cross of Jesus
> Left behind the door.

Too often the cross becomes nothing but an ornament which might as well be left behind the door. It is placed on the altar or worn as a piece of jewelry instead of being the symbol of those who are marching forward to conquer the world for Christ. The place where the cross ought to be worn is in the heart.

Dear Father, though the way be steep over which thou leadest me, and I must follow with weary body and bleeding feet, still may I go joyously forward in the companionship of thy Son. May I never shrink from any service because it is hard, but pray for added strength to perform it. Amen.

TUESDAY—Week 45

SALVATION BY COSMETICS Read II Cor. 11:18-33

A well-known religious leader was asked to speak at a gathering of ministers on the subject of salvation. He wished to have his address written out but was away from home and had no chance to type it. So he dictated it to a public stenographer of the fluffy type, who might be best described by the words "all vogue without and all vague within." In the course of the talk the clergyman used the phrase, "For these people salvation is a cosmic process." When he received his typewritten manuscript, he was surprised to find the words, "For these people salvation is a cosmetic process."

Is it not the desire of many people to have a superficial religion, which will make their outer life attractive without involving any painful inner transformation? There is no easy way in which we can find salvation for ourselves or take it to others. Salvation involves God's suffering love and our own willingness to make sacrifices.

O God, make me tolerant of others, but intolerant of the sinful tendencies in my own heart. Help me to know that only by self-denying devotion can I fit myself for large usefulness in thy service. Amen.

WEDNESDAY—Week 45

PRAYING FOR A CROSS Read Mark 14:32-42

During the first World War a widely told story may or may not have been actual fact, but was true to the spirit of many men in the army. An officers' training camp was asked to send a certain number of men to France. The colonel knew all the men were eager for overseas duty and hesitated to give the privilege to some and deny it to others. So he prepared as many slips of paper as there were men and marked part of them with a cross. A hat was passed down the line of soldiers; each took a slip, and if it bore a cross the coveted chance was his. That night one of the men wrote to his family: "If ever I prayed in my life, I prayed that I might draw a cross."

What do you ask for when you pray? That God will shield you from hardship and give you an easy life, or that he will count you worthy to have a sacrificial part in his enterprise of building a Christian world?

I would not pray to escape the cross, O God, knowing thou hast made it the symbol of those who truly follow thy Son. Rather, I pray that I may have the courage to assume a part of its burden. Amen.

THURSDAY—Week 45

A VOLUNTARY LOAD Read Mark 15:15-25

When Jesus collapsed beneath the weight of the cross on the way to Calvary, Simon of Cyrene was forced to carry it. He is described as a man from the country; he probably had never seen Jesus until the Roman soldiers picked him out of the crowd. Though at first Simon shouldered the cross because he was compelled to do so, he seems afterward to have borne it gladly as an opportunity to ease the suffering of Christ. Evidently it was the beginning of a new spiritual experience for him and his family, for the Gospel of Mark refers to Simon's sons as though they were well-known men in the early Christian church.

According to the Christian interpretation of the phrase, we are carrying a cross, not when we are enduring a hardship we cannot escape, but when we willingly assume some heavy load to help a person in need or to assist some worthy cause.

O my God, let thy unwearied and tender love to me make my love unwearied and tender to my neighbor, and zealous to procure, promote, and preserve his health, and safety, and happiness, and life, that he may be the better able to serve and to love thee. Amen.—Bishop Ken.

FRIDAY—Week 45

GOD'S ETERNAL PLUS SIGN Read I Cor. 1:18-31

A man took his little boy to visit a great cathedral. As they were walking up the long central aisle, the boy pointed to the cross on the altar and inquired of his father, "What is that big plus sign?"

If we have thought of the cross as something that subtracts from life and robs it of its finest satisfactions, we have been mistaken. It adds new and enriching elements—sympathy, unselfishness, patience, courage. When a person begins to carry a cross, that person is more alive than he or she was before; for that person is becoming like Christ.

The cross is God's eternal plus sign! Recall the names of those who are remembered as the benefactors and saviors of mankind. Do they impress you as little people? Their willing sacrifices made them into spiritual giants who tower above the mediocrities of their generation.

Lift up my heart, O God, to understand the true nature of the Christian cross. Help me to see that the one who carries it does not end his journey in a dark valley but on a hill of triumph, that he does not travel the path of despair but the highway of joy. Amen.

SATURDAY—Week 45

THE JOY OF THE CROSS   Read II Cor. 4

There is danger that we miss the note of joy which runs through the lives of all great Christians who have really entered into the deeper meaning of the cross. They think in terms, not of what they have given up for Christ and humanity, but of the fun which they have had in their adventures of self-giving. So Mary Slessor, a timid and bashful girl, became a missionary to the cannibals of Calabar and looked back on her work with so much satisfaction that she said, "I am the happiest and most grateful woman in the world."

Livingstone had the same attitude when he said: "People talk of the sacrifice I have made in spending so much of my life in Africa. It is emphatically no sacrifice. Say rather it is a privilege."

Such people, who have a cause worth living and dying for, know the experience of Jesus, of whom it was said that he endured the cross because of the "joy that was set before him."

O Lord, renew our spirits and draw our hearts unto thyself that our work may not be a burden to us, but a delight. Oh, let us not serve thee with the spirit of bondage as slaves, but with the cheerfulness and gladness of children, delighting ourselves in thee and rejoicing in thy work. Amen.—Benjamin Jenks.

THE POWER OF INFLUENCE

SUNDAY—Week 46

THE ENDLESS INFLUENCE OF A GOOD LIFE
Read Prov. 4:18-27

Go out at night and look up at the stars that shine down upon you. What you actually see is a light that has taken years to reach the earth. In far-off stellar spaces the light started on its way before you were born, but it is still a source of beauty and illumination to people today. Similar is a person's never-ending influence. Longfellow's words about Charles Sumner are true of everyone who has lived a good life.

> Were a star quenched on high,
> For ages would its light,
> Still travelling downward from the sky,
> Shine on our mortal sight.
>
> So when a great man dies,
> For years beyond our ken,
> The light he leaves behind him lies
> Upon the paths of men.

Dear Father, give me the faith that in thy universe no good deed is ever lost. Help me to scatter sunshine and to make my hours bright with helpfulness, knowing that through the endless chain of influence countless lives will be cheered and blessed. Amen.

MONDAY—Week 46

CONTAGIOUS COURAGE
Read John 20:1-10

After the resurrection of Jesus, when Mary Magdalene had reported to the disciples that the tomb was empty, Peter and John started running to the sepulcher. John was fleeter of foot and arrived first but was too timid to enter. Impetuous Peter, arriving a few moments later, did not stop to consult with John but stepped boldly inside. The Gospel says, "Then went in also that other disciple." John hesitated to go in alone but was ready to follow since Peter had led the way.

Example is more powerful than argument. The man who goes bravely forward in the right direction will be followed by a host of souls too timid to advance alone. Columbus was ridiculed for sailing west over an unknown sea, but those who laughed at his logic soon headed their ships toward the land he discovered. What we need most is not arguments in favor of Christian living but living exponents of Christian truth.

Forgive me, O God, that so often the moral courage of others has been weakened by my cowardice. Help me to go forward each day in the path of duty without faltering, knowing that my own faithfulness will make it easier for others to be true to their tasks. Amen.

TUESDAY—Week 46

THE INFLUENCE OF A NEGRO SERVANT
Read Judg. 16:7-16

One Sunday in Plymouth Church, Brooklyn, before a great congregation, Henry Ward Beecher paid tribute to Charles Smith as a major influence in his boyhood life. Who was this man who helped to determine the future of one of the greatest preachers America has ever known? Was he a college professor, a church leader, or some well-known personality of his day? Not at all. Charles Smith was a Negro who for a time worked as a hired man on a farm which belonged to Beecher's father. This is what Beecher said about him:

"He did not try to influence me, he did not know that he did it, I did not know it until a long time afterward. He used to lie on his humble bed and read the New Testament, unconscious that I was in the room. He would talk about it and chuckle over it. I had never heard the Bible really read before. It was a revelation and an impulse to me."

A Negro servant read the Bible, and a boy became a better man!

Dear Lord, I never know when my actions are exerting their strongest influence over others. Therefore, keep me ever true to the best that I know. May there be something about me which makes it evident that I believe in thee. Amen.

WEDNESDAY—Week 46

GREAT CONSEQUENCES FROM SLIGHT CONTACTS
Read Jas. 3

In the Canadian Rockies a stream known as Kicking Horse Creek is on the continental divide. Part of its water flows into the Atlantic, and part into the Pacific. Concrete runways have been built to channel the water permanently in both directions. The slightest influence—a ripple caused by a passing breeze—may determine whether water flows east or west. There are times when lives are so delicately balanced that a chance remark will turn them to the right or left, cause them to sink in despair or lift up their heads with hope. The peace and poise of your own life may determine an other's destiny.

> May every soul that touches mine,
> Be it the slightest contact, get therefrom some good,
> Some little grace, one kindly thought,
> To make this life worth while
> And heaven a surer heritage.

Eternal God, make me mindful of the many people in thy world who have confused minds and aching hearts. They are on every street corner and often in my home. Help me to renew their drooping spirits by the faith and gladness in my own soul. Amen.

THURSDAY—Week 46

PETER'S HEALING SHADOW   Read Acts 5:12-16

The influence of Peter's shadow is one of the most striking incidents recorded in the Book of Acts. The Apostle had performed several miracles of healing, which made such an impression upon the people of Jerusalem that they had faith in the power of his shadow. Sick people were brought from their homes and laid on couches in the street where Peter was expected to pass by, so that his shadow might fall upon them and exercise its healing effect. Simply by walking down the street Peter was spreading health and happiness.

Everyone has an unconscious influence similar to that of Peter. Wherever our shadow falls, it has its effect: if the light of goodness shines within us, other lives will be made brighter; if darkness reigns within, a cloud will be cast over those around us. Said Emerson, "Men imagine that they communicate their virtue or vice only by overt actions, and do not see that virtue and vice emit a breath every moment."

Gracious God, I thank thee that goodness is so contagious it spreads not only by direct contact but even by the shadow which one life casts upon another. Grant that the influence of my own shadow may have a healing power on some soul today. Amen.

FRIDAY—Week 46

OUR LENGTHENED SHADOWS   Read John 15:1-16

There are special reasons which give the fact of unconscious influence an added meaning for our own day. We are bombarded with so much advertising and propaganda that we harden our minds against the deliberate efforts of people to control our thinking. We will not allow ourselves to become the victims of high-pressure arguments. Even the truth now has difficulty in making its way into men's hearts by direct approach.

On the other hand, it was never so easy to reach people by indirect influence. We are so closely tied up into a single bundle of life that all sorts of people whose names we do not even know are casting their shadows upon us. Modern means of communication and transportation have thrown us so closely together that we cannot help being influenced by each other. Let a man have a personality that is truly Christian and his influence can cast a far-reaching shadow.

Forgive, we beseech thee, our unkindness one to another. Forgive us that in honor we have sought our own selves first, and not others; that we have not borne one another's burdens, and fulfilled the law of God. Amen.— Henry Ward Beecher.

SATURDAY—Week 46

STANDING IN THE LIGHT   Read John 12:35-50

How can we be sure that our unconscious influence will be a constant source of healing to others? Only by making our own lives so Christ-like that we constantly reflect the Master's spirit.

Peter's shadow did not always exert a healing power. His profane outbursts, hot temper, and moral cowardice served to undermine faith rather than to stimulate it. But by the power of Christ he became a "rock," so that not only his deliberate acts but his unplanned influences were all serving the purposes of Christ.

What is it that determines our physical shadows? It is our positions in relation to the sun. There must be no barrier that shuts off the source of light. So the shadow of our unconscious influence is controlled by our relationship to him who has rightly been called the Light of the world. When that Light shines upon us with undimmed brightness, our lives will radiate a healing power.

Thou Sun of Righteousness, shine upon my heart and drive away its gloom and darkness. May every person whom I meet have a happier face and a braver heart because of the radiant quality of my own life. Amen.

OUR CHRISTIAN FAITH IN THE FUTURE LIFE

SUNDAY—Week 47

IS IMMORTALITY TOO GOOD TO BE TRUE?
Read John 20:11-31

Do we have an honest right to believe in the future life? This question has recently assumed a new importance. We have usually thought of the grave as junk heap for old worn-out human machines, but during a time of war the adventure of death is made by thousands of young men who are in the prime of physical vigor.

Some people seem to think that immortality is too good to be true. They would like to believe in it but are afraid that science has made such a faith unreasonable. Let it be emphasized that no one can possibly prove that the soul is not immortal! The subject is outside the field of science. The soul cannot be put into a test tube and analyzed, nor can the most powerful telescope see into the realm of spiritual value. Not the slightest evidence has been produced to disprove the future life. On the other hand, there are strong arguments to justify our ancient Christian faith.

Dear Father, give me the faith to believe that nothing is too good to be true in a universe which is controlled by thy love. Keep me from living under the shadow of darkness and doubt. Make my life bright with the hope which comes from comradeship with thee. Amen.

MONDAY—Week 47

A PARABLE OF THE FUTURE LIFE   Read I Cor. 15:42-58

In the bottom of an old pond lived some grubs who could not understand why none of their group ever came back after crawling up the lily stems to the top of the water. They promised each other that the next one who was called to make the upward climb would return and tell what had happened to him. Soon one of them felt an urgent impulse to seek the surface; he rested himself on the top of a lily pad and went through a glorious transformation which made him a dragonfly with beautiful wings. In vain he tried to keep his promise. Flying back and forth over the pond, he peered down at his friends below. Then he realized that even if they could see him they would not recognize such a radiant creature as one of their number.

The fact that our friends cannot see us or talk with us after the transformation which we call death is no proof that we cease to exist.

Father, give me the vision to see that this life is but the first stage in our existence. Help me to start now toward the goal of achieving a Christ-like personality, confident that it can be carried to completion in the life to come. Amen.

TUESDAY—Week 47

IS GOD A FAKIR?   Read Ps. 8

People who have traveled in India tell how the native magician sits by a pond with piles of colored dust. With skillful ingenuity he drops a handful of it upon the water and makes a portrait of some distinguished person. A handful of dust, and lo! a Lincoln. Another handful, and behold! the features of Jesus of Galilee. Then the wind sweeps over the pool, and the faces are gone. Is God such an Indian fakir? Does he put us here simply to exist for a few decades and then to be blown away by the breeze which we call death? If that is the situation, then God is careless of his choicest possession; for man is the climax of all creation. It was because he believed in a resonable universe that Tennyson could say:

> Thou wilt not leave us in the dust:
> Thou madest man, he knows not why,
> He thinks he was not made to die;
> And thou hast made him: thou art just.

O God, help me to trust in thy eternal goodness and to believe that thy love and care are not only for the brief space of an earthly existence but for all eternity. Make me fit for companionship with thyself. Amen.

WEDNESDAY—Week 47

THE MIND SURVIVES THE BODY'S CHANGES
Read Luke 24:1-35

Does it seem unreasonable to believe that the human personality can continue to exist after the death of the body? Then remember that the mind is continually surviving all sorts of bodily changes.

Each person gets a completely new body every seven years. You are not now the same physical person you used to be. Seven years from now you will be a completely different man. If you live to be seventy years old, you will have had ten different bodies; yet you may have vivid memories of events that occurred in your childhood. If your mind can survive all these changes of the physical organism, is there not good reason to believe that it may withstand the final change which we call death?

Matter may change its form, but it is never destroyed. It may be reduced to its elements, but it continues to exist. Why should we think that mind, which can control matter, is some day to be blotted out forever?

Eternal God, help me to make my mind the master of my body. Amid the changes of life sustain me by an unchanging faith in thee. Grant that with resolute will I may fight the good fight and lay hold on the crown of eternal life. Amen.

THURSDAY—Week 47

THE PROOF OF CHRIST'S RESURRECTION
Read Acts 2:22-39

For the Christian the final proof of immortality is in the resurrection of Christ. What is the evidence that he rose again? We have the testimony of all the New Testament writers, but the church itself is the weightiest argument for faith in a living Lord. When Jesus was crucified, the disciples fled in dismay. Only when they became convinced that he was still alive did they become bold witnesses of his gospel, then they went out to conquer the Roman Empire and turn the world upside down.

Could an institution like the church be founded on an illusion and win such widespread victories for nineteen hundred years? Did the martyrs of the faith throughout the centuries die for a falsehood? To ask such questions is to answer them, for there is only one adequate explanation. It is that of Peter at Pentecost when he said, "Whom God hath raised up, having loosed the pains of death: because it was not possible that he should be holden of it."

Grant, O Christ, that thy triumph over death may take away my fear of the grave. Help me not only to believe in thee but to live in thee and to seek earnestly the things which are above. Then may I have the joy of thy presence in this life and evermore. Amen.

FRIDAY—Week 47

MANY MANSIONS
Read John 14:1-14

What did Jesus mean when he told his disciples, "In my Father's house are many mansions"? The word "mansion" means a large place in which one may live. So Jesus was saying that in God's universe, or home, there are many dwelling places. What we call the present world is one room in the Father's house; what we describe as heaven, or the future life, is but another room in the same spacious home. Death is not an enemy, but a friend who opens the door that we may pass from one room into another which is more beautiful.

We go to a place prepared for us. The new room will be furnished to meet our special capacities and needs. And when we change our abode, we will not feel like a stranger, for we will still be in the Father's house; the Savior will make us feel at home. Could we want a more satisfying picture of the future life? Jesus assures us that personality and individuality will always have a properly prepared home with God.

Heavenly Father, give me the grace to look toward the unknown future with hope and not with fear, knowing that neither life nor death nor any other power can separate me from thee. May I commit myself to thy care, knowing thou carest for me. Amen.

SATURDAY—Week 47

PREPARING FOR THE FUTURE LIFE   Read John 21:15-25

How can we prepare for a happy entrance into the future life? There is but one way; it is to do each day the will of God as he has revealed it to us in the life and teachings of Christ and to be faithful in the performance of our present duty.

Back in Colonial times there occurred the famous dark day in Connecticut when people were terrified and thought that the end of the world had come. The legislature was in session in Hartford but the house of representatives decided to adjourn. Members of the council were about to follow suit when Colonel Davenport objected. He arose and said: "Gentlemen, it may be that the day of judgment is upon us; yet it may not be. If this is not the end of the world, there is no reason for us to adjourn. If it is, let the Lord, when he comes, find us doing our duty. I urge that candles be brought and we continue our business." The council went ahead with its meeting.

Thou Lord of all life, help me to live now as one who lives with thee, overcoming all temptations, rising above all difficulties, faithfully doing my work, seeking and serving thy holy will, and so finding the sources of eternal joy. Amen.

UNIFYING LIFE BY DEVOTION TO CHRIST

SUNDAY—Week 48

A MAN OR A MOB   Read Mark 5:1-20

When Jesus was in the country of the Gadarenes, he healed a
man who was possessed by several demons. Jesus asked the man
his name and he replied, "Legion." The Bible explains the meaning of the word by saying that many devils had entered into him.
He was like the character in one of H. G. Wells's novels who said,
"I am not a man but a mob."

People who are still in their right minds know the experience of
being several persons in one and of being torn by conflicting desires. A person may be a member of a family, a church, a school, a
fraternity, an athletic team, a Y.M.C.A., and several other organizations. All make demands upon his time and interest. Trying to
be fair to them all creates the confusion of trying to satisfy diverse
allegiances. How can a person cease to be several different people
and become a unified personality? If you have this problem the
best way for you to solve it is to center your life around Christ and
put all other relationships in their relative importance in a program of Christian living.

O God, help me to learn that I am fully myself only when I completely
lose myself in thee. May I yield myself to thy guidance and in all things seek
to do thy will. Lead me out of the confusion of my conflicting desires into
the simplicity of thy service. Amen.

MONDAY—Week 48

BRUSH HEAP OR TREE?   Read Ps. 1

Life can be like a brush heap or like a tree. In a brush heap, the
branches, which have been broken or sawed off, have no living
connection with each other. But in a tree all the branches are in a
vital relationship and make their contribution to the beauty of the
whole.

Too many people are heaping up brush. They engage in a
scramble for money, popularity, social prestige, and all sorts of
honors; they throw their achievements together in an imposing
pile and say, "See what a success I am." Yet in their hearts is no

happiness or lasting satisfaction. Life for them is a hodgepodge of activities that have no spiritual meaning.

The Psalmist says the righteous man—which to the Hebrew meant the religious man—is like a tree. His life is integrated by his faith in God and his desire to make his life acceptable to his Creator. This central unity gives his life a dignifying purpose and makes him "blessed," or happy.

Dear Father, forgive me for spending so much energy in piling up the little successes which have brought no enduring joy. Take away my fear of following thy Son and give me the liberty of those who have unified their lives by devotion to his purposes. Amen.

TUESDAY—Week 48

LOOKING AT THE PATTERN
Read Ps. 95

The famous tapestry weavers of France do their work without being able to see the beauty of the patterns which they are creating. They spend their time pulling threads and tying knots behind a frame. The same thing is done over and over again. The work is slow and monotonous, but occasionally the weavers leave their places; going out to look at the design, they find inspiration in the beauty which is to be the final result of their efforts. If it were not for the design which they are faithfully trying to reproduce, the work would be almost killing in its drudgery.

Does not this suggest the high purpose which is served by engaging in the worship of God? When we bow in prayer we see life from the standpoint of its larger meaning. We look at the pattern which God has set for us in Christ and feel the glory of trying to reproduce the beauty of his character in our own lives.

O God, grant that I may keep Jesus before me as my example and ever seek to reproduce the beauty of his character in my own life. Keep me from careless workmanship as I weave the threads of my destiny; help me to attain to the fullness of his likeness. Amen.

WEDNESDAY—Week 48

IS YOUR THINKING UNIFIED?
Read Ps. 63

A man sat before the fireplace in his club, seemingly wrapped in thought. Two friends were looking at him, and one said, "Jones is thinking very deeply tonight." The other man, who knew Jones more intimately, replied, "Jones thinks he is thinking, but he is merely rearranging his prejudices." Is it not too true that the thinking of most people is a jumble of prejudices and unrelated ideas? If we are to have unified lives we must organize our thinking around some guiding principle.

We need a philosophy of life which is like a solar system, revolving around the fire of a central idea. What is this great idea which can light our lives and unify our mental outlook? It is the conviction that God is the Creator of all life, that human existence finds its meaning in him, and that the chief duty of any society is to help people live together in obedience to God's will for all mankind.

> Take thou ourselves, O Lord, heart, mind, and will;
> Through our surrendered souls thy plans fulfill.
> We yield ourselves to thee—time, talents, all;
> We hear, and henceforth heed, thy sovereign call. Amen.

THURSDAY—Week 48

A UNITED CHURCH   Read John 17:20-26

A woman in Labrador had tuberculosis of the ankle, and Dr. Wilfred Grenfell amputated her leg. On his next visit to the United States, when speaking in a Congregational church, he asked if anyone knew of a person who could donate an artificial limb to the needy woman. After the address a Methodist woman went up to him and said that her husband, a Presbyterian, had died and left behind him a good wooden leg. Said Grenfell: "When I, an Episcopalian, took that Presbyterian leg, given to me by a Methodist in a Congregational church, back to Labrador, it fitted my Roman Catholic friend and she could walk."

The cooperation of many persons of different churches gave a woman the help she needed. Young people need to work for a united Christian church which can perform larger miracles of healing and helpfulness than can be accomplished by separate churches or denominations.

Heavenly Father, break down the barriers that divide thy churches; make us willing to answer the prayer of thy Son that his followers may all become one. Draw thy children together into a closer unity, that they may more truly love thee and more worthily serve thee. Amen.

FRIDAY—Week 48

INTERNATIONAL UNITY   Read Isa. 9:1-7

After the American Revolution, the colonies faced the question whether they would remain as separate states with conflicting governments or unite as one nation. For some time it looked as though the Constitutional Convention would be unable to frame a form of government acceptable to all the colonies. Compromises were finally made, and our present constitution adopted. As the convention broke up, Franklin pointed to the back of the chair in which Washington had been sitting as the presiding officer. Emblazoned on its back was a gilded half sun with streaming rays, and Franklin said: "For six weeks I have been wondering whether that was a rising or a setting sun. Now I am sure that the sun is rising and that this is the dawn of a new day."

Is the sun of civilization now setting, or just beginning to rise? The answer depends largely on the willingness of the nations, after the war, to unite in a new and effective international organization.

Lord of all nations, stir our souls with a vision of a better world. Make us ashamed to be content with bitterness and lasting divisions. May we be satisfied with nothing less than a world in which all men live together in a true brotherhood. Amen.

SATURDAY—Week 48

CHRISTIANS HOLD THE WORLD TOGETHER
Read Eph. 2:13-22

The world cannot be held together in unity simply by the power of an international organization. It needs the binding force of religious faith. There is a message for today in a letter called *The Epistle to Diognetus*, written by an unknown Christian in the second century, when the Roman Empire showed signs of breaking up:

"What the soul is in the body, Christians are in the world. The soul is spread through all the members of the body; so are Christians through all the cities of the world. The soul dwells in the body, and yet is not of the body; so Christians dwell in the world, and yet they are not of the world. . . . The soul is enclosed within the body and itself holds the body together; so too the Christians are held fast in the world as in a prison, and yet it is they who hold the world together."

Christians, hold the world together! Unless you succeed in doing so, the world will fall apart.

Eternal Father of all souls, grant that I may feel myself bound to my Christian brothers everywhere by ties of spiritual kinship that overleap all racial and national barriers. Make me a strong link in the chain of Christian fellowship that stretches around the world. Amen.

DOING THE BEST THINGS IN THE WORST TIMES

SUNDAY—Week 49

LIGHTING A CANDLE IN THE DARK Read Luke 11:33-36

In an English church in Leicestershire is a memorial tablet with this inscription: "In the year 1653, when all sacred things throughout the nation were either demolished or profaned, Sir Robert Shirley, Baronet, founded this church, whose singular praise it is to have done the best things in the worst times and hoped them in the most calamitous."

A hasty reading of English history will show how turbulent the times were. The king had just been executed in a civil war; the country was torn by strife and dissension; the atmosphere was tense with hate; and the outlook for a united nation was dark indeed. At that time Sir Robert Shirley decided to do something constructive. He built a church.

The worst times demand the best deeds. If we are disturbed—as we ought to be—over the conditions in our own day, we need to throw our influence on the side of the forces working for righteousness and moral stability. It is always better to light a candle than to curse the darkness.

Dear Father, increase my strength and my courage for thy work. When others are forsaking thee, then may I be most loyal. When the night grows dark around me, then may the light of my life shine more brightly. Amen.

MONDAY—Week 49

BAD TIMES CAN BE MADE GOOD TIMES
Read II Tim. 1:6-14

If you could not belong to the present generation and were free to choose any period of the past in which to live, what time would you select? Many people would take the first century in Palestine, because they would have a chance to show themselves worthy followers of Jesus. Others might prefer the early sixteenth century, when Martin Luther and the reformers were laying the foundations of the Protestant church. Americans might choose the seventeenth century, when the Pilgrims were crossing the Atlantic to make their home in a new world, or the eighteenth century, when George Washington and his associates were organizing our republic.

All these glorious eras of the past have one thing in common: they were troubled periods, yet they were days when great events were stirring and brave men were blazing new trails for the feet of mankind. The worst times are the best times to develop Christian manhood and to strike telling blows for the great causes of God.

I thank thee, O God, for all those who have endured hardship as good soldiers of Jesus Christ. Give me the grace to join their ranks. May I have a stout heart to bear my own burdens and be willing to help bear the burdens of those weaker than I. Amen.

TUESDAY—Week 49

SAINTS IN CAESAR'S HOUSEHOLD   Read Phil. 4:19-23

Paul closes the letter written to the Philippians from Rome by saying, "All the saints salute you, chiefly they that are of Caesar's household." Saints in the royal palace! How could one be a Christian if one were a servant of the debased Nero, who was a party to the death of both his mother and wife because they interfered with his personal plans? The sensuality of our day cannot compare with that which characterized life at the royal court in the time of Paul. The early Christians won their moral victories in the face of an environment that was unbelievably difficult. If there could be saints in Rome, we can be Christian today in spite of all the forces that are arrayed for our undoing.

One of the best services any person can render to his fellowmen is to develop the inner strength which enables him to be in the world but not of it. That is what Jesus did. He never held himself aloof from any group, but wherever he went he was like a current of fresh air cleansing the atmosphere of its impurities.

Thou Lord of all those who have lived in an evil world and have kept themselves unspotted, keep me from blaming my environment for my moral failures. Teach me how to win the victory through the power of thy Spirit within me. Amen.

WEDNESDAY—Week 49

"WE CAN DO IT IF WE WILL"   Read Mark 9:14-29

In the year 1806 a group of five students at Williams College went out to a grove a little distance from the college grounds to hold a prayer meeting. They were interrupted by a thunderstorm and took refuge behind a nearby haystack, where they continued their meeting. They had been praying and talking about the need of sending the gospel of Christ to lands where it was unknown.

"We can do it if we will!" said Samuel J. Mills, the leader of the group. And then and there the young men dedicated their lives to the foreign mission enterprise. On the spot where the haystack once stood is now a monument which has on it the inscription "The Birthplace of American Foreign Missions."

Those who attempt great things for God and allow God to work through them can accomplish amazing results. "We can do it if we will!" That is the spirit in which young people can carry forward the work of Christ today.

Father, I pray that my heart may be cleansed of all selfish ambitions. May I be willing to give thee the right of way in my life. Help me to become one of the doorways through which thy love enters into the world with its healing ministry. Amen.

THURSDAY—Week 49

NOW IS THE TIME TO BEGIN   Read Luke 8:1-15

André Maurois, a French writer, has told how Marshal Lylutey, who conquered Morocco, was riding through the forests of the country when he came to a place where many giant cedars had been destroyed by a terrific storm. The marshal turned to his assistant and said, "You will have to place new cedars here." The man laughed and said that it took two thousand years to grow cedars like those that had been uprooted. "Two thousand years?" said the marshal. "Then we must begin at once."

The storm which is sweeping over the world today has left widespread destruction in its wake. A civilization which has been thousands of years in the building has been well-nigh destroyed, and the task of reconstruction will not be easy. If a new world order is ever to be erected above the ruins, then we must begin at once. The place to take hold is where you are. The time to start is now.

Dear Lord, help me to remember that the kingdom of God is like a seed planted in the ground. Keep me from delay in beginning the good I hope to accomplish. May I start at once, knowing that the night will soon come and my labors be over. Amen.

FRIDAY—Week 49

"BUT IF NOT . . ."   Read Dan. 3

Except for Jesus on Calvary, nothing is more thrilling than the spirit in which Shadrach, Meshach, and Abednego faced the fiery furnace. They had been ordered to worship a golden image, but to have done so would have violated the innermost sanctity of their souls. Haled before King Nebuchadnezzar and threatened with a cruel death unless they obeyed the decree, they replied: "If it be so, our God whom we serve is able to deliver us from the burning fiery furnace; and he will deliver us out of thine hand, O King. But even if our God does not save us, be it known unto thee, O king, that we will not serve thy gods, nor worship the golden image." Even if God did not come to their rescue they preferred to die like heroes rather than live like cowards.

"But if not"! What if God does not save you from your difficulty? What if he leads you through a dark valley instead of through green pastures? Can you still go forward in the path of duty and trust yourself to God? To be true to the best in spite of the worst is the final test of a noble life.

Heavenly Father, I am grateful for all the brave souls who have been afraid of nothing except betraying their own honor and being disloyal to thee. Help me to follow in their train, choosing to be a hero rather than a coward, whatever the consequences. Amen.

SATURDAY—Week 49

BUILDING A WALL OF CHARACTER   Read Neh. 4

After Galveston was overwhelmed by a terrible flood in 1900, the city leaders came together while the water was still in the streets and began to plan for the future protection of their people. A famous engineer was hired to build a protecting sea wall around the city. Later, when he was in a construction camp in the Northwest, a telegram came saying that the wall had been swept away by a tidal wave. The engineer smiled and said: "This message is a mistake. I built that wall to stand." It turned out that he was right. Another fierce storm had come, but the wall stood secure.

A tidal wave of irreligion has swept over much of the world. Religious persecutions have been common in Europe; in our own land there is widespread spiritual indifference. In the midst of this situation, without waiting for a more favorable time, let us begin to erect around ourselves and our country a wall of Christian faith and character. We must build the wall so that it will stand.

Be thou a protecting wall around me, O God. Keep me from being overcome by temptation when the forces of evil threaten my soul. May my character be secure because I have steadfastly committed myself to the doing of thy will. Amen.

SHARING OUR RELIGION

SUNDAY—Week 50

KINDERGARTEN CHRISTIANS Read Acts 3

Everyone has heard of the old man who made the prayer:

> Lord, bless me and my wife,
> My son John and his wife,
> Us four and no more.

Farther down the same street was a childless couple who prayed:

> Lord, bless us two,
> And that will do.

Around the corner lived an old bachelor whose prayer was:

> Lord, bless only me,
> That's as far as I can see.

People with such attitudes toward life actually exist, and many of them are members of the church, although they have never graduated from the kindergarten department. The first lesson to be learned in Christianity is that God is the Father of all and expects us to share our blessings, including our religious faith.

Dear Father, save me from allowing my life to be hemmed in by the narrow boundaries of my own selfishness. Help me to realize my brotherhood with all mankind and to reach out to the uttermost parts of the earth with a desire to share my Christian faith. Amen.

MONDAY—Week 50

CHRISTIANS MUST NOT BE DUMB Read John 1:35-42

"I am no longer dumb." This was the first full sentence uttered by Helen Keller after she had begun to speak in a hesitant and stammering manner. The same words will express the feeling of one who has become a true follower of Christ. He will be glad to tell about his experience, even though it be in a halting way. If his religion is the most important thing in his life, he will not be tongue-tied about it; he will be like Andrew after Jesus had been pointed out to him by John the Baptist.

Andrew went to Jesus' dwelling place and spent a never-to-be-forgotten day. He remained in Jesus' presence long enough to become intimately acquainted. Then he hurried to find his brother, Simon Peter, and exclaimed, "We have found the Messiah." Telling what had happened, he took Simon Peter at once to meet the Master. Andrew was not satisfied to keep his new-found happiness to himself. It was worth talking about, and he was not dumb. He wanted to share the good news with the one who was dearest to him.

Forgive me, O God, for being so timid about speaking a good word for thee. I gladly tell my friends about the things in which I have found special pleasure. May I not be bashful in opening my heart to them about the joy of my friendship with thee. Amen.

TUESDAY—Week 50

HOW CHRISTIANITY CONQUERED THE ROMAN EMPIRE
Read Acts 17:1-15

Nothing will do more to strengthen our faith in the power of the gospel to win its way amid the difficult conditions of today than to recall its amazing triumph in the early centuries in spite of a hostile environment. The historian Gibbon, in accounting for the rapid spread of Christianity through the Roman Empire, says the chief cause was the enthusiasm of the Christians in telling their friends and neighbors about Christ. Celsus, a second-century philosopher, complained that "fullers and weavers and teachers are constantly talking about Jesus." Pliny said: "The infection has spread through cities, villages, and country districts." The good news was contagious. It spread by personal contact, and nothing could stop it.

Christianity routed the forces of paganism, not simply because of great leaders like Peter and Paul, but through what was done by ordinary people, working at regular occupations but losing no chance to say a good word for their religion.

Heavenly Father, give me the enthusiasm of the early Christians. Teach me how to talk about Christ simply and naturally so that my religion may become a normal part of my conversation. Above all, make my life so sincere that my actions will speak louder than my words. Amen.

WEDNESDAY—Week 50

A CHURCH WHICH GAVE ITS BEST   Read Acts 11:19-30

The church at Antioch holds a unique position in the history of Christianity. Its members were the first people to be called Christians. Probably the name was given in ridicule. They were always talking about Christ and what he wanted to do, so some wit made fun of them by saying they were "Christ's men." Whether the name was used in irony or praise makes little difference. The important thing is what happened in the church whose people were so sincere that they became known as "Christ's men."

This church at Antioch sent out the first apostles to the Gentiles. It started the missionary movement when Barnabas and Saul were commissioned as ambassadors for Christ. Note that the church sent out its ablest men. What vision! What an example for us today! "Christ's men" do not give the world-wide work of the church the leftovers after meeting their local needs. They make the missionary cause their first responsibility.

Dear God, in Jesus Christ we have the best gift which it is possible for thee to bestow upon mankind. In gratitude may we give our best to thy kingdom. If we ourselves cannot go out as Christian missionaries, grant that we may ever be missionary Christians. Amen.

THURSDAY—Week 50

THE CALL OF THE AFRICAN DRUM   Read Matt. 22:1-14

One of the rules of the Christian churches in West Africa is that no one can become a full member until he has introduced another person to Christ and helped him to find the joy and power of the Christian faith. The black people take their religion seriously. No one is considered to have given convincing evidence of his own knowledge of Christ until he has shown his concern for the spiritual welfare of his friends and neighbors.

Dr. Phillips Elliott, of Brooklyn, when in Africa on a tour of the mission fields, went with a drummer who beat out the call to church on a drum made from a hollowed-out section of a tree. The words which the man sounded, and which could be heard for miles around, were these: "Stop what you are doing, and come at once to hear the word of God." The people obeyed. They came to worship God and then went out to give his message to others.

Our Father, the loyalty of the faithful followers of thy Son in other lands often puts us to shame here in America. Baptize us anew with thy spirit. Make us more eager to learn thy truth, more ready to share it, more willing to follow wherever it may lead. Amen.

FRIDAY—Week 50

PERSISTENCE WINS RESULTS   Read Acts 14:19-28

One passage in Hitler's *Mein Kampf* is worth careful reading by those who wish to get others to accept their ideas. It describes the initial efforts of Hitler to spread his gospel of national socialism. When he started holding public meetings, invitations were type-written and distributed among acquaintances and friends. Time after time meetings were held with only seven in attendance. On one occasion Hitler personally delivered eighty invitations. Again the same seven were present, and no more.

Many groups of Christian young people would give up in de-spair if they were continually reduced to an attendance of seven. But Hitler kept on and worked harder. Finally eleven were pres-ent, then fifteen, and at last thirty-four. From such beginnings Hitler rose to power. One secret of success in Christian work, as in any other enterprise, is to keep on keeping on. Nothing takes the place of undiscouraged persistence.

Teach me thy patience, O God. Make me steadfast, unmoveable, always abounding in thy work, knowing that no labor for thee is ever in vain. For-give me that I often become discouraged so easily and am not more persis-tent in my Christian endeavor. Amen.

SATURDAY—Week 50

JESUS IS COUNTING ON US   Read Mark 16:14-20

An imaginary conversation between Jesus and the angel Gabriel, after the ascension, describes Gabriel as asking the Master what plan he had made for completing his work of telling every-one about God's love. Jesus answered: "I asked Peter and James and John, and some more of them on earth, to make it the business of their life to tell others. And the others are to tell others, and the others still others, until every man has heard the message and had his life transformed by it."

Gabriel stood in meditation as though he saw a flaw in the Mas-ter's plan. He said, "Yes, but Master, suppose after a while Peter forgets and John loses his enthusiasm. And what if their succes-sors, down in the twentieth century, get so busy or so timid that they do not have the time or the courage to tell the others. What will you do then?"

The voice of Jesus answered quietly and confidently: "I haven't made any other plans. I am counting on them."

O Lord Jesus Christ, who hast placed upon us the responsibility for carry-ing forward thy mission, make us faithful that we may not disappoint thy hopes. Keep us from becoming so occupied with other things that we forget our chief occupation to live as thy followers. Amen.

THE HOLY SPIRIT

SUNDAY—Week 51

CHRIST IS ALIVE!   Read Matt. 28:1-10

Dr. Robert Dale, a famous English minister, who was formerly pastor of Carr's Lane Church in Birmingham, was in his study on the day before Easter preparing his sermon on the resurrection of Jesus. The message he had written seemed inadequate to the occasion. As he meditated prayerfully on the meaning of Easter, he took a blank sheet of paper and wrote on it in big letters, "Jesus Christ is alive!"

Suddenly he had a vivid sense of Christ's presence. He went into his pulpit the next day and preached to his people with compelling conviction about a living Christ. From that day new power came into his ministry. Always afterwards, as part of the worship program in every Sunday service, he used some hymn that had in it the message of a Christ who is alive.

To believe that Christ is alive today in your world and your own life is to be filled with the Holy Spirit. This was the experience that came to the disciples on the Day of Pentecost and changed them from cowards to heroes.

Thou living Christ, come into my heart with thy joy and thy strength. Help me to become so conscious of thy presence that evil no longer attracts me and that my constant purpose is the desire to have my life approved by thee. Amen.

MONDAY—Week 51

THE TRINITY   Read John 14:25-29

An amazing transformation came over the first disciples on the Day of Pentecost. They had been frightened and discouraged when Jesus was crucified. A little later we find these same men as bold as lions. They became convinced that Christ was still active in the world and that his spirit could work through them.

They had known God as the Creator, or Father, and had seen him in the earthly life of Jesus Christ, the Son. Then they had a continuing experience with Christ as a powerful invisible Personality calling them to new life and greater achievements. This unseen Presence was called the Holy Spirit, or Holy Ghost.

213

The Trinity is a word used to describe the doctrine that God makes himself known to us in these three different ways as Father, Son, and Holy Spirit. St. Patrick explained it to the Irish by pointing to the shamrock, or clover, which has three heart-shaped parts in the same leaf. It looks like three different hearts but is actually one leaf reaching out in three directions.

Our Father God, thou hast revealed thy greatness in the works of creation and thy love in the life of Jesus Christ, thy Son. Help me now to know thee as the One who dwells in my own heart, and in whom I live and move and have my being. Amen.

TUESDAY—Week 51

THE DAILY COMPANION   Read John 21:1-14

Many people see Jesus in history but are not acquainted with Christ as their daily Companion. They read the Gospels and think what an inspiring experience to walk beside Jesus on the road to Jerusalem, to row with him across the Sea of Galilee, or to sit at his feet during the Sermon on the Mount. They know the Jesus of Palestine but not the Christ of today.

Others turn from the past toward the future. While filled with joy at the hope of Christ's second coming or at the thought of being with him in heaven, they are blind to the meaning which Christ should have for their lives today.

> But warm, sweet, tender, even yet
>   A present help is he;
> And faith has still its Olivet,
>   And love its Galilee.

Grant, O God, that every road may be a highway to Emmaus on which I walk beside my Master. May my heart burn within me for joy while I talk with him each day. Make the invisible Companion as real to me as he was to the first disciples. Amen.

WEDNESDAY—Week 51

A SPIRIT-FILLED MAN   Read Acts 6

What kind of a person will one be if the Holy Spirit comes into one's life? Turn to the Book of Acts and read the story of Stephen. He was one of seven deacons appointed in the Jerusalem church to have charge of the distribution of food after there had been a complaint that the Grecian widows who were Christians were not getting their share. The deacons were said to be "men of honest report, full of the Holy Ghost and wisdom." So honesty and sympathy with the poor were among the qualities of the Spirit-filled man.

If you read on, you will find that Stephen was also a man of courage. He did not hesitate to talk publicly about his faith in Christ, even though it caused his death. Because of his boldness, he was singled out by the authorities and made the first martyr. As he died, he prayed that God would forgive those who stoned him.

Do you wish to become brave, kindhearted, forgiving, free from hate? Pray that God's Spirit may come into your heart.

Dear God, I need thy Spirit that it may change me from the person I am into the person I would like to be. Help me to yield myself to thee. May thy Spirit be in all my life and not merely in some small part of it. Amen.

THURSDAY—Week 51

CHRIST IN ME   Read Gal. 2:16-20

A group of theological students in New York City were returning to their dormitory late at night when they came upon a drunkard lying in the gutter. Most of the young men would have passed him by in disgust; but one student, who had worked in a rescue mission and had more sympathy for those who had become moral failures, stooped over and put his arm under the shoulder of the drunken man. He said, "Tell me where you live and I will call a taxi and take you home." The man looked into the face of the one who had made the offer and mumbled, "If Jesus Christ ever lived on earth, he must have been like you."

The only Christ some persons will recognize is the one whose Spirit lives in men. Every Christian ought to pray daily that he may have the experience of Martin Luther when he said: "If somebody should knock at the door of my heart and ask who lives here, I must not say 'Martin Luther' but 'Jesus Christ.' "

O God, if thy Spirit lives within me my heart will be filled with thy love. Help me to make my life a reflection of thy compassion. Give me sympathy for all who are in need of a friend, and grant that others may see Christ in me. Amen.

FRIDAY—Week 51

ONE WHO KEEPS US AT OUR BEST   Read Eph. 3:14-21

A conversation in Lloyd Douglas' book *The Robe* describes the influence which the Spirit of Christ can have upon our daily lives. A disciple of Jesus by the name of Justus is talking to Marcellus, the Roman tribune who had been in charge of the crucifixion. Justus is telling about his faith in a living Christ. He says: "I only know that he is alive—and I am always expecting to see him. Sometimes I feel aware of him, as if he were close by.' Justus smiled faintly, his eyes wet with tears. 'It keeps you honest,' he went on. 'You have no temptation to cheat anyone, or lie to anyone, or hurt anyone—when, for all you know, Jesus is standing beside you.'

" 'I'm afraid I should feel very uncomfortable,' remarked Marcellus, 'being perpetually watched by some invisible presence.'

" 'Not if that presence helped you defend yourself against yourself, Marcellus. It is a great satisfaction to have someone standing by—to keep you at your best.' "

Teach us, by the Spirit of Christ, the sacredness of common duties, the holiness of ties that bind us to our kind, the divinity of the still, small voice within that doth ever urge us in the way of righteousness. So shall our hearts be renewed by faith. So shall we ever live in God. Amen.—John Hunter.

SATURDAY—Week 51

LINKING YOUR LIFE TO UNIVERSAL POWER
Read Acts 4:23-37

A bridge was to be built over a river not far from where it flowed into the ocean, and the first step in the project was to remove an old hulk that had been imbedded in the river's bottom. Divers placed chains about it, and an attempt was made to pull it out by tugs. The efforts were in vain. One of the young engineers suggested a different plan. He fastened the chains to some scows when the tide was low. Soon the ocean came flowing in with its mighty power. The hulk was lifted and towed away. Success came easily and quickly when universal power was harnessed to the task.

When the Spirit of God comes into a person's life, it brings a power for moral victory and personal achievement. Habitual sins, deeply imbedded in one's character, are uprooted and cast out. Tasks that formerly seemed too difficult can now be accomplished. Christ becomes more than our example; he is a source of dynamic energy which enables us to say, "I can do all things through Christ which strengtheneth me."

> Holy Spirit, Power divine,
> Fill and nerve this will of mine;
> By thee may I strongly live,
> Bravely bear, and nobly strive. Amen.

FOLLOWING JESUS TODAY

SUNDAY—Week 52

TAKING JESUS SERIOUSLY   Read Rom. 10:1-17

If you intend to take the Christian life seriously, you must become a serious student of the life and teachings of Jesus. You must search the facts about the Master as a man of history, sitting down before him, meditating on his words, considering his works, and listening to his prayers. This means that you must know the Bible, for it is the only original source for a knowledge of the historical Jesus.

One reason why Jesus means so little to modern men is that they know so little about him. Even among church members there is an appalling ignorance. Ask the average professing Christian to outline the main events during the years of Jesus' public ministry, and he will stammer in confusion. Ask him to give the basic ideas of Jesus, and he will be compelled to admit that he does not know.

No one has the foundation on which to build an intelligent Christian life until he is familiar with the basic facts about the Master.

Heavenly Father, I thank thee for the Bible, through which I gain my knowledge of Jesus Christ. Grant that as I read it I may come to know him more fully and love him more deeply. Then may I follow him with faithful obedience. Amen.

MONDAY—Week 52

FACE TO FACE WITH CHRIST   Read Matt. 27:19-26

During the French Revolution, a lawless and vengeful mob broke into the palace of the king. Bent on loot and destruction, they rushed down a long corridor and into the room beyond it. Hanging on the opposite wall was a painting of Jesus on the cross. Suddenly the marauders were brought face to face with the suffering Savior. The spirit of the mob was broken. Everyone became silent. Some of those in front knelt in prayer. Many reverently removed their hats. Some near the door turned and quietly left the room. Then one of the leaders went forward, turned the picture of Christ toward the wall, and yelled to the mob to continue its plundering.

What happens to us today if we come face to face with "that strange Man on the cross"? He makes us ashamed of our sinfulness, our selfishness, and our vindictiveness. Either we must cease to look at him or yield to his influence upon us. We must flee from his presence, or we will at last be captured by his spirit.

Dear God, help me to keep unclouded the vision of my Savior. May the sight of him purge my life of its evil. Grant that as I remain in his presence and gaze upon his face, my own life may be transformed into his likeness. Amen.

TUESDAY—Week 52

THE NIGHT AND THE DAWN
Read John 13:18-30

"He . . . went immediately out: and it was night." When Judas left the presence of Jesus in the upper room and stumbled out into the darkness, the night of the outside world was symbolic of the blacker night in his own heart, and of the inky darkness which enshrouds a civilization that forsakes the Savior's standards. Is there any more accurate analysis of the present world situation than to say we have gone out from Christ and it is night?

When the League of Nations was being debated in Congress after the first World War, Senator Henry Cabot Lodge declared that if Jesus Christ should come to the Senate chamber in person and ask the United States to join the League, he would still vote against it. Christian international ideals were openly repudiated, and the night of a second World War was the result.

"I am the light of the world," said Jesus. "He that followeth me shall not walk in darkness." A new day will dawn in the relationships of nations when they accept Jesus' idea that all men are brothers and must learn how to live together as one family of God.

Thou Sun of Righteousness, shine upon our hearts and dispel the darkness of sin and ignorance. Grant that thy glorious light may be spread abroad over the world until all men come to an understanding of thy truth. Amen.

WEDNESDAY—Week 52

THE KEY TO WORLD RECONSTRUCTION
Read Gal. 6:1-10

A man prepared to spend the evening reading a long magazine article dealing with the postwar world. He was frequently interrupted by a noisy young son. Tearing off the back cover of the magazine on which was a map of the world, the father cut it into bits and made a jigsaw puzzle. "Here is a puzzle for you," he said. "Put the map of the world together." The man returned to his reading, but in a short time he heard the boy say, "Here it is, Dad; I have it finished."

"How did you do it so quickly?" asked the father. The boy answered: "On the other side was the picture of a man. I put the man together and then found the world in perfect order." The key to the whole task of permanent reconstruction is to "put the man together." So long as man himself is disordered, the world will be in chaos. When more men unify their lives around obedience to Christ, we will begin to have an adequate basis for an enduring fellowship of nations.

O Christ, whatever the problem, thou are the only solution. Help me to untangle my own life and to find my peace and happiness in thee. Then may I be able to reveal thee as the one hope for a stricken world. Amen.

THURSDAY—Week 52
THE END AND THE BEGINNING OF AN ERA
Read Rev. 21:1-7

A book called The Nuremburg Chronicle was issued July 12, 1493, by a group of German scholars. Its contents were described by the following words: "The events most worthy of notice from the beginning of the world to the calamity of our time." At the end of the book six pages were left blank so that the reader might use them to record any further important events that might occur before the day of judgment!

The writers of the Chronicle had not yet heard that Columbus had discovered a new world. Just as they thought the story of mankind almost completed, one of the most momentous events of history had taken place.

The pessimist is always wrong. New worlds are ever waiting for discovery, and the end of one era means the beginning of another. If the powers released by modern science can be brought under control by the spirit of Christ and dedicated to the welfare instead of the destruction of mankind, we will move toward a civilization better than our fondest hopes.

Eternal Father, as John on the island of Patmos had a vision in which old things passed away and all things became new, so give us now the eyes of faith to behold the new earth that is waiting for us when we yield ourselves to the doing of thy will. Amen.

FRIDAY—Week 52
WHOLEHEARTED LOYALTY
Read Luke 20:20-26

Not long ago the newspapers told of an American citizen of Italian birth who owns a gas station in New Jersey. Each morning when he goes to work, he follows a regular routine. He runs up the American flag over his place of business and salutes it; then he deposits a nickel in a tin can. At the end of the year he empties the can and sends $18.25 to the treasurer of the United States as an expression of his gratitude for the privilege of living and working under the American flag.

All honor to the man who starts the day by saluting the nation's flag and making a gift to his country! But let us remember that as followers of Christ we have a higher loyalty than that which we give to our nation. We will start the day by committing ourselves anew to the cause of our Savior. And we will do more than drop a nickel in a can. We will offer ourselves—time, talents, all—to the service of Christ's kingdom.

Be thou the Lord of my life, O sovereign Christ! Grant that I may never be ashamed to float the banner of my loyalty to thee. May my allegiance be full and complete, so that I serve thee without compromise or fear. Amen.

SATURDAY—Week 52

TRUST THE VOICE OF GOD   Read Acts 22:1-15

After Joan of Arc had succeeded in winning repeated victories for France and in having the king crowned in the cathedral of Rheims, she was betrayed into the hands of her enemies and tried as a witch. The prosecutor tried to make her say that she had been mistaken in the source of her guidance and that her voices might have come from the devil instead of from God. Over and over again she said, "My voices were from God, they did not deceive me." She went to her death in the flames with these words upon her lips.

The one who seeks to follow the voice of God may be told by others that he is suffering from an illusion and is being led astray by some will-o'-the-wisp which cannot be trusted for guidance in the practical affairs of life. Cling to the conviction that your moments of religious insight are your truest moments. Dare to believe that the voice which calls you forward in obedience to Christ is none other than the voice of God.

Dear God, keep me from forsaking my ideals. Make me steadfastly true to the best that I know. Grant that I may be able to say with the Apostle Paul, "I was not disobedient unto the heavenly vision." Amen.

OUR SOURCE OF STRENGTH

SUNDAY—Week 53

THE WATER OF LIFE   Read John 4:1-15

The Nile River runs through a hot and sandy plain for much of its course, yet it has never been known to fail. For centuries people wondered what might be the source of such a constant supply of refreshing water that flowed through the arid desert and made the riverbanks blossom like a flower bed. Explorers at last discovered why the water never wasted away in even the driest season. It had its source high in the mountains and was fed by eternal snows. Its secret was in the heights which men had never seen.

No less do our souls need some high and secret source of strength. The place where we have quiet fellowship with the eternal Father of our spirits will send forth a refreshing stream to keep our lives hopeful and fruitful. Whatever experiences may lie ahead of us, we can keep our lives sweet and strong, and fit for useful living.

I thank thee, O Christ, that thou art the water of life, a never-failing source of refreshment to my soul. Teach me to say, as did the woman by the well of Samaria, "Give me this water that I thirst not." Amen.

REFERENCES AND ACKNOWLEDGMENTS

ACKNOWLEDGMENT IS GRATEFULLY EXPRESSED TO THE PERSONS and organizations, indicated by asterisks (*), who have given permission to quote selections or to adapt illustrative stories.

WEEK

1-Tu: Rufus Jones, *The Testimony of the Soul*, The Macmillan Co.,* 1936.

3-M: Edward Bok, *The Americanization of Edward Bok*, Charles Scribner's Sons,* 1923.

4-Su: Mary S. Edgar,* "God, Who Touchest Earth With Beauty."

4-M: Stuart Nye Hutchison, *The Voice Within Us*, Fleming H. Revell Co.,* 1932.

6-F: Harry Emerson Fosdick,* sermon "Belief in the Cross."

7-M: *Cincinnati Times-Star.**

9-Th: Bruce Barton, *The Book Nobody Knows*, The Bobbs-Merrill Co,* 1926.

12-Th: James Myers,* *Prayers for Self and Society*, Association Press, 1934.

13-Su: William H. Foulkes, "Take Thou Our Minds, Dear Lord." Copyright, 1918, by Calvin W. Laufer. Board of Christian Education of the Presbyterian Church, U. S. A.*

13-Tu: *Ibid.*

15-Tu: Harry Emerson Fosdick,* "O God, I Offer Thee My Heart," in *Sermons I Have Preached to Young People*, edited by S. A. Weston, Pilgrim Press, 1931.

18-M: George Herbert Palmer, *The Life of Alice Freeman Palmer*, Houghton Mifflin Co.,* 1908.

18-F: Joseph Fort Newton, *Living Every Day*, Harper & Bros.,* 1937.

19-F: William H. Foulkes, "Take Thou Our Minds, Dear Lord." Copyright, 1918, by Calvin W. Laufer. Board of Christian Education of the Presbyterian Church, U. S. A.*

25-Su: Henry Hitt Crane,* a sermon.

29-Th: Margaret Slattery,* *Paul the Victorious*, Pilgrim Press,* 1941.

32-Th: Hamlin Garland, "Let the Sunshine In," *The Rotarian*,* October, 1939.

35-Tu· Glenn Cunningham, "Speed and Endurance," *Christian Herald,** March, 1943.

35-F: Gene Tunney, "Nicotine Knockout," *The Reader's Digest,** December, 1941.

36-Sa: Phillips H. Lord,* "Your Church and Mine," *Seth Parker Hymnal,* Carl Fischer, Inc., 1930.

37-Tu: Erdman Harris, *Twenty-one,* Harper & Bros.,* 1931.

40-Th: Robert Davis, "I Thank Thee, Lord, for Strength of Arm," from *Social Hymns of Brotherhood and Aspiration.* Copyright, 1914, by A. S. Barnes & Co. and The Survey Associates. Copyright assigned to A. S. Barnes & Co.;* 1941.

41-Sa: E. T. Dahlberg, *Youth and the Homes of Tomorrow,* Judson Press, 1934.

44-Th: Calvin W. Laufer, "We Thank Thee, Lord, Thy Paths of Service Lead." Copyright, 1919, by Calvin W. Laufer. Board of Christian Education of the Presbyterian Church, U. S. A.*

44-F: Kate Douglas Wiggin, *My Garden of Memory,* Houghton Mifflin Co.,* 1923.

45-F: Oscar F. Blackwelder,* a sermon.

47-M: Albert W. Palmer, *The New Christian Epic,* Pilgrim Press,* 1928.

47-Tu: Harry Emerson Fosdick, *Successful Christian Living,* Harper & Bros.,* 1937.

48-M: Henry Nelson Wieman, *Methods of Private Religious Living,* The Macmillan Co.,* 1929.

48-W: William H. Foulkes, "Take Thou Our Minds, Dear Lord." Copyright, 1918, by Calvin W. Laufer. Board of Christian Education of the Presbyterian Church, U. S. A.*

48-Th: Joseph Fort Newton, *Living Every Day,* Harper & Bros.,* 1937.

49-Sa: Walter Dudley Cavert, *Story Sermons from Literature and Art,* Harper & Bros.,* 1939.

50-Su: Lewis H. Chrisman, *Ten-Minute Sermons,* Willett, Clark & Co.,* 1935.

50-Th: Phillips P. Elliott, *The Christian Facing Today's World,* Westminster Press,* 1943.

51-F: Lloyd C. Douglas, *The Robe,* Houghton Mifflin Co.,* 1943.